Bug Swamp's Gold

BILLIE H. WILSON

WestBow Press
A DIVISION OF THOMAS NELSON
& ZONDERVAN

Copyright © 2014 Billie H. Wilson.

All rights reserved. No part of this book may be used or reproduced by any means, graphic, electronic, or mechanical, including photocopying, recording, taping or by any information storage retrieval system without the written permission of the publisher except in the case of brief quotations embodied in critical articles and reviews.

This edition of the Marked Reference Bible is published by special arrangement with Holt, Rinehart and Winston, Inc. New York 17, N Y., USA

Disclaimer: Every thought in this manuscript is either true to my memory, or it's how I perceive happenings. Certain names are changed to protect the innocent, and the guilty.

Creative nonfiction, written mostly in Bug Swamp's vernacular

WestBow Press books may be ordered through booksellers or by contacting:

WestBow Press
A Division of Thomas Nelson & Zondervan
1663 Liberty Drive
Bloomington, IN 47403
www.westbowpress.com
1 (866) 928-1240

Because of the dynamic nature of the Internet, any web addresses or links contained in this book may have changed since publication and may no longer be valid. The views expressed in this work are solely those of the author and do not necessarily reflect the views of the publisher, and the publisher hereby disclaims any responsibility for them.

Any people depicted in stock imagery provided by Thinkstock are models, and such images are being used for illustrative purposes only.
Certain stock imagery © Thinkstock.

ISBN: 978-1-4908-2478-9 (sc)
ISBN: 978-1-4908-2479-6 (hc)
ISBN: 978-1-4908-2477-2 (e)

Library of Congress Control Number: 2014901837

Printed in the United States of America.

WestBow Press rev. date: 04/18/2014

Contents

Acknowledgements ix
Bug Swamp's Background xi

Chapter 1	Time's Shadows 1
Chapter 2	*What Was:* One Cold Night; Then Happier Times 5
Chapter 3	Before Me, 1931 8
Chapter 4	The Arrival 11
Chapter 5	Biscuits and Possum Gravy 17
Chapter 6	To Smoke or not to Smoke 22
Chapter 7	A Picture Leads to a Barn Raisin' 25
Chapter 8	Billie and the Bear 30
Chapter 9	The Gator 37
Chapter 10	Transplanting, Dancing, Cleaning, and Napping 43
Chapter 11	Another Esau, About 1925 53
Chapter 12	Tobacco Barnin' 57
Chapter 13	Curing Tobacco 63
Chapter 14	Selling Tobacco, Plus a Carnival 68
Chapter 15	My Jimmy 72
Chapter 16	The Birth of a Brother, October 24, 1937 77
Chapter 17	A Five Year Old's World 89
Chapter 18	First Grade, 1939 96
Chapter 19	Santa Clausin', 1939 102
Chapter 20	Aunt Leatha 106
Chapter 21	A Visit, Plus the Woman and the Bear 109
Chapter 22	A Doggie Story 114
Chapter 23	A Mocking Bird Summer 119

Chapter 24	An Eldorado Experience and More	123
Chapter 25	Ruby and Lister	126
Chapter 26	Killing Old Red	132
Chapter 27	Summer into Fall, 1941, a Pore Old Man	142
Chapter 28	"A Day Living in Infamy," Cold Weather, and a New Crop	147
Chapter 29	That Old Time Religion	157
Chapter 30	I'll Have a Bite of That	166
Chapter 31	A Year Later, Our Radio	172
Chapter 32	A Tobacco Barn Birthday Party	177
Chapter 33	Fishing at the Waccamaw	184
Chapter 34	The Day of Liberation	188
Chapter 35	Questions and Answers	199
Chapter 36	Bug Swamp Teeters into Balance	207
Chapter 37	1946, A New Beginning	212

DEDICATION

To:

My grandchildren, with love:

Niki
Jeremy
Tegan
Rachel
Kayla
Jonathan

Acknowledgements

Friends and family have helped me write this book, and I thank you all. Back at Winthrop College, "University" today, in 1954, an English professor I'll leave unnamed, freed herself from teaching our Friday afternoon English classes. On entering her classroom, we took out paper and pencils. Our assignment: develop the single theme topic written on the board. That lent focus to my fancy. While our professor never returned those Friday musings, and it's likely they found their way to trash heaven, I'm grateful that she fanned my writing flames. Sixty years later they burn with barely a lost flicker.

I thank my friend and mentor, Harriette Austin. She and her host of UGA Center readers and writers taught me that nothing is ever indelibly written.

I thank my coffee group. Most of us have lived on our tree-lined Robin Road, or nearby, for years and years. I turn to them for a listening ear. One of these friends, an artist, Connee Flynn designed the cover for this book. Another coffee mate, Genie Bernstein, edited this manuscript, line after line. Diane Rounds, Becky Trotter, Janine Aaronson, Janice Pulliam, they are all good friends and critics. I hasten to add Betty Reuter's name to the list. True friends, we wrote together, painted together, drank coffee on Mondays, and shared family trivia. A unique individual, Betty, UPSTAIRS of late, is probably suggesting a ritzier logo for St. Peter to place atop The Pearly Gates. I spy my husband, Ruel, and Betty's husband, Les. They're waving at Betty to hurry on in. They got there first.

Family: my parents, my brother, grandparents, aunts, uncles, cousins, childhood friends. I've said plenty about you throughout this manuscript. Thank you, Brice Hardwick, Cousin Frances Marion's widowed spouse.

You've advised me on tobacco growing and curing particulars. I'm grateful to my three children, their spouses, my six grandchildren. Mona is a treasured listener, and my granddaughters, Rachel, Tegan and Tegan's boyfriend, Jon, help me with technicalities. Tim, Bryan, Kayla, Jimmy, Susan, Niki, Chad, Jeremy, Jonathan and my sister-in-law, Ramona, are great cheer-leaders. While many family members have left our midst, recently, Brother Jack and his wife, Marcia, paid me a visit. We perused "our" memoir. For two days Marcie read aloud to Jack and me. Minus their interest, love, and on-the-spot questioning, I could never have put finishing touches to this book.

Thanks to my pastor, Dr. Ed Bolen, to my deacon, Dr. Chester Sosebe, to Peggy Neal, to Joan Humphreys and our Bible study group, to my entire Athens, Georgia, Milledge Avenue Baptist Church family. I'm grateful for your support and interest.

Needless to say, I thank my Maker. Grandma Nettie would never forgive me if I failed to acknowledge Him. Thank you, everyone.

Bug Swamp's Background

Located in what is now Horry County, South Carolina, from the Atlantic Ocean coastline to thirty miles inland, a sandy plain splays out flat and swampy. This plain sweeps through marshes, creeks, forests; it banks fast-paced rivers. High rains escalate floods, especially after arriving settlers clear new ground for houses and villages.

Called South Carolina's tidewater, these islands of sand, woods, and swamp harbor deer, bears, raccoon, alligators, possums, "cooters," "painter cats," wild cats, bobcats, not to mention snakes. Home to these varmints, beauty abounds: oak trees trail Spanish moss, cypresses loom tall above knees birthed in black water; morning glories and wisteria, like raccoons and possums, climb any obliging tree; honeysuckle, laurel, camellias, rainbow the eye while bay trees smell like after-shave. Similarly, magnolia's saucer blooms delight the eye while perfuming the nose. Dependable pines afford an economy in tar and turpentine as well as logs and planks for colonists' and their home building.

Despite the areas' beauty and usefulness, when Grandma Nettie thinks Billie's playmate, the rare Venus Fly Trap, grows too close to a swamp, she admonishes her granddaughter, "Don't let them feet of yours take a step inside that swamp to where the ground turns spongy, for it's not just varmints you have to fear. A honey-pot slough can up and swallow you whole!" Her honey-pot sloughs? Quick sand pits. Today, nestled beneath trees and covered over with leaves, their ground appears solid, unless a poor soul, man or beast, makes a misstep.

Long before Billie Hamilton's family eke out their livelihood from Bug Swamp's sandy fields, Waccamaw Indians call this, their land. Billie's fishing and baptizing river takes its name from that Waccamaw Tribe. Not far away the Pee Dee Indians lend theirs to the Pee Dee River, and from the Lumbee comes the Lumber River. Lesser tribes living in, hunting, and fishing the thirty-mile radius to the sea are the Socastee, the Wachesaw, the Hobcaw, and the Wampee Indians. In their day even nomadic Siouans vacation at what we now call The Grand Strand. In pre-colony days, to reach this beach, feet shod in moccasins pace the same trail tramped upon in 1791, by George Washington's horses, pulling our first president in his "coach 'n four." In 2013, vacationers speed in cars along that same route. They call their paved pathway, Highway Seventeen, or Kings' Highway. And today, students in Coastal Carolina University labs study fossil remains of oyster, crab, clam, and other seafood feasts enjoyed by vacationing Siouans long before Europeans walk, fill, or till the tidewater's sandy soil.

In 1526, about 500 colonists sailed from Hispaniola to found a new settlement near today's Georgetown, South Carolina. Storm-swept, they end up at the mouth of present-day, Cape Fear River. One ship sinks. Its women and children board another. With no space left aboard ship, men resort to horseback. Following the coastline, ships and men head back toward the spot they plan to colonize. These Spaniards, leading and riding horses from Cape Fear to Winyah Bay, are the first Europeans ever to tread Horry's Tidewater sand, to this writer's knowledge.

While the Spaniards' sixteenth century colony fails, over a century later Charles II names eight Lord Proprietors who entice to the area settlers from the West Indies, New England, and Europe. Some of these colonists fight their way through tidewater forests, creeks, and swamps to settle Bug Swamp's country side. Billie Hamilton's ancestors stem from just such adventurers.

Blanche W. Floyd's

Tales along the Grand Strand of S. C.

A wealth of information concerning South
Carolina's tidewater region and its history

Chapter 1
Time's Shadows

Over sixty years have passed since I raced up back steps to Grandma Nettie's Bug Swamp kitchen porch. Closing my eyes I almost see my hundred and eleven-pound grandma, hands palm deep in teacake batter, the oven of her massive iron stove heated, ready, and waiting. So many memories take me back to our low country home: shady oaks trailing mossy beards, Grandma's porch vines, her blue hydrangeas, sandy yards, tobacco patches, mocking bird songs. Grandma's five children were born here. So were my brother and I. With sedge brooms fashioned by my dad and me, I swept our sandy floors, including the front porch, our "pizer," according to Grandma Nettie.

On warm evenings, rare ones when next day required little work, we especially enjoyed our "pizer." So did neighbors. World War II was going "great guns" overseas. Like a combat soldier, Daddy grabbed his weapon. "Take that, Hitler," he'd swat down a mosquito hawk diving after its prey, maybe a yellow fly set to pitch and bite. "You too, Mussolini!" Daddy apologized when he smacked Miz Edna Bullock's arm instead of the yellow fly.

Even Daddy was lulled by our surrounding cricket and tree-frog symphony. Tuned in purely to nature, for a while we'd sit in silence. Then, somebody, probably our neighbor, Mr. Albert Johnson, would perk up. "Did I ever tell you about the time I...?"

In another life Mr. Albert had been a deputy sheriff. One night he and his old coon dog, Ralph, chased an escaped prisoner all over Moonshine Bay. Caught him too. Mr. Albert told stories galore.

I'd turn to my story-teller. "Grandma, tell us about Uncle Bob McNabb, how he wanted to be a witch."

"Child, I can't share that story before I say he never was one." Then, Grandma would spend an excitable fifteen minutes revealing how the best Christian man in Scotland battled "evil powers that be," before he learned God's plans for his life.

Others told tales they'd heard. Some they made up on the spot. Never one to be left out, my young brother announced to any and all, "I'll never walk outside barefoot again, without a light."

I asked, "Why not?"

Jack said, "'cause last night that's how I squished an old toad-frog."

Mother scooped him up. "I saw that yawn, Jackie-Boy. Say 'Goodnight, all.'"

I could have listened to story-telling forever and a day.

In his book, *Look Homeward Angel*, Thomas Wolfe declared, "You can't go home again." That was his opinion. I plan to do just that. Simply put, I'll begin with this eighty-year-old, Bug Swamp child-at-heart.

What is: mirrors must lie. Are those wrinkles etching trails around my mouth? And my eyes, they don't twinkle; they crinkle! Not that long ago Grandma Nettie would touch my face. She'd say, "Little Bushy, yours is a peaches and cream complexion." Then she'd smile, and the scar at the corner of her mouth would tighten, almost disappear.

Lately my vision has gone blurry, like I'm gazing through a translucent curtain. That's what's wrong! It's not my face; it's the curtain that's wrinkled.

Who's fooled? I have a visitor, and I hope Time, my friend, sticks around for years to come. Meanwhile I walk in his shadows. They dart in and out, around about; they cast darkness here, let light in there.

Ambling toward the mailbox the other day, I spy a multitude of quarter-inch long, gold threads. They dance, they shimmer in brightness. Probably those cataracts Dr. Philip says should go. I grab my mail from the box I need to replace, for its lid's loose, and on rainy days my letters get soaked. In the shade of a Crape Myrtle, I tear into a Medicare envelope. Great! They paid Dr. Philip every cent he charged for that last eye exam.

Glancing toward my Robin Road house of forty-one years, these days banked by an arbor and twin Bradley pear trees, I blink. Twice.

What in the world? Is that…? That can't be Grandma Nettie's house! And there's Grandma. Sitting on her "pizer." She's rocking and dipping her Sweet Society Snuff, spit can at her finger-tips.

I blink again. Where are my parents?

I see 'em. Hot, tired, ready to eat, here come Mother and Daddy, traipsing home from the tobacco patch. Grandma has dinner on the table, everything but ice tea. She'll wait to pour that so the ice won't melt.

I step into sunlight. What happened? Where did Grandma go? There sits my same old Robin Road House. Wonder if this new allergy medicine brings on hallucinations? I mosey over to the arbor, plop into the swing, and open remaining mail. Mostly junk.

Back in Bug Swamp I'd scoot down the sandy lane to get our mail. Grandma's box was nailed onto a long plank between two pines. I'd wait for Mr. Proctor to drive up to our box, sort out letters, and hand me ours, lots of times a letter from Uncle Charles, far away in Georgia.

On days like today with warm sun rays glinting on leaves and grass blades, I forget Bug Swamp's icy winters. Shivery nights, sitting around the hearth, Daddy would stare into embers, pondering. I liked hearing him talk about his courtin' days; how in pitch-black darkness going through swamps, he'd brave slick foot-logs to see some pretty girl. One girl's daddy prayed every night Daddy visited. His prayer, "Dear Lord, make this young man's feet stick safely to them foot-logs tonight. He has to cross some ornery swamps, goin' home."

When Mother put a sock in that subject, Daddy could get strung out on another I liked even more. He'd talk about gold around and about Bug Swamp. I knew that eons ago sneaky pirates prowled. Sometimes they sailed inland, and buried trunks filled with treasure. Talk was, some might be close by, if a body knew where to dig. I had to ask Daddy. "What do you know about any gold buried around here? Real gold."

Daddy said, "Bars? Or the round kind you count and hold in your hand? That gold's not so easy to come by; but, Bug Swamp surrounds us with treasures more precious."

I'd already guessed. Daddy's gold? His tobacco, growing green and lush, sparking thoughts of pockets jingling, come market time. Grandma

Billie H. Wilson •

loved her gray cypress house Grandpa Hamp built back in 'ninety-six. Mother sought elusive peace of mind and treasured her family. My brother? He liked flying live mosquito hawk kites tethered to tobacco twine, but he loved Sooner, his part Black Lab doggie.

My gold? Memory, and right now I hope to air out everything and everyone in second millennium sunshine. I'm time-traveling back to Bug Swamp, and I can't wait to get there.

CHAPTER 2
What Was: One Cold Night; Then Happier Times

What can I say about that icy night in 1936, the night I learned life wasn't always sugar-sweet? Mother paced around and around our parlor. She shouted. At Daddy. I clung to Grandma. In my ear her heart beat fast.

Memory tells an eighty year-old girl a lot. At just three I sensed Mother's fear, Daddy's resignation, Grandma's acceptance. Of what, I didn't know. A mite older, I learned what had riled my mom. For years afterwards she bandied around "mortgage, foreclosure, loss," as often as "get up; go to bed; let's eat." Her reason? Daddy had mortgaged our farm without a speck of input from her. Not only did she fear for our livelihood, she felt left out of family decision-making.

The first Christmas I remember, 1936, came and went in a magic haze of red and green, thanks to Mother and her sister, Leatha, who, even then said, "Don't call me Aunt!" Both made me feel special. On Christmas day standing before the tree, Leatha said, "Look, everybody! This girl helped decorate our tree. Billie Faye hung all the lower ornaments."

I hid behind Mother's skirt so they wouldn't see me smile.

A trip to my grandparents' home for Sunday dinner could take from twenty minutes to twice that, according to the whims of Daddy's old Model-A Ford. This last Sunday in December, Daddy couldn't crank "Tin Lizzie." Instead, he hitched Old Pet, our mule, to the wagon. We climbed aboard, Mother and Daddy seated up front. Three and a half years old, I liked sitting in back and swinging my feet. Nearing a watery swamp, and afraid I'd fall off the back, Mother dragged me up front with her. Ahead loomed a grove of over-hanging trees. Mother pointed. "Look!"

Above us snakes dangled. A greenish one dropped at my feet. I cried, "Daddy!" He grabbed its slithery tail and tossed it into the water, saying, "Nothin' to be scared of. Just an old water snake." Where the water was deep, Old Pet had to swim. I liked swaying in the wagon.

By wagon or car, Mother insisted on having most Sunday dinners with her parents, which was fine with Daddy. His mom took those opportunities to visit her daughters, Aunt Sally, Aunt Molly, or Aunt Laura. She couldn't visit Uncle Charles. Since 1934, after graduating from Clemson College, he'd taught agriculture in Waresboro, Georgia, much too far for Tin Lizzie or Old Pet to travel.

On this last Sunday in December, Christmas was but a memory. Papa and Mama, Leatha, Mace, Mother, Daddy, and Billie Faye, yours truly, gathered around Mama Todd's dining table. Certainly I don't recall their exact conversation. Papa and Daddy liked talking shop, in this case, their livelihoods. Papa asked Daddy something like, "When will you and Dottie sow tobacco beds?"

Chicken drumstick in one hand and glass of ice tea in the other, Daddy beamed. "Thanks to Burroughs's Loan Company, as soon as I can." About then Daddy would have speared a bite of sweet potato. "I've already dug up tobacco beds and thrown in a little fertilizer. Seeds need sowing by mid-to-late-February. Most likely the ground won't freeze over after that."

Papa said, "Son, I'm sorry you had to go and borrow money, but you know, sometimes it takes a risk to make a profit."

That's when my ears perked up. Even I knew "money" was our family's sore subject.

Darting eyes toward Mother, Daddy nodded. "That's how I see things."

At four years old I didn't worry about sowing tobacco beds, transplanting, suckering, topping tobacco, and back home across the swamps, if Grandma Nettie Hamilton worried about such, w-o-r-r-y was never a part of her vocabulary, except to disparage it. While Burroughs and Company, according to Mother, all but owned us, according to Grandma, worry equaled fear, the opposite of faith, and Grandma knew all about faith. By 1937, she'd suffered widowhood for seventeen years. After Grandpa Hamp's death, looking after two unwed daughters and two sons necessitated reliance on friends and family, self-trust, but most of all, faith in her maker, God, our Father Almighty.

While I find sharing this memoir impossible without wandering through numerous tobacco patches, right now, so to speak, I've been "puttin' the cart before the horse." There was a time I'd never heard of Bug Swamp, Papa and Mama Todd, Grandma Nettie, or tobacco.

CHAPTER 3
Before Me, 1931

On December 11, 1931, two months before Dottie Lee Todd's nineteenth birthday, she and Rassie Bryan Hamilton slipped away from relatives, and in the Horry County courthouse before Judge Vaught, vowed their love. Twenty-two years into the future, that same Judge Vaught would issue a marriage license to my husband and me.

Possibly Mother caught "the marriage bug" from Zena, for talk in Papa Todd's Adrian community centered on hers and Artie Smith's elopement. At the stove turning eggs over easy, Mama heard their news. She shook her head; pursed her lips. "Mark my words. That girl will rue the day she's marrying so young." Two months separated Mother's and Zena's ages. Papa said, "They might stay hitched a year. Artie's all right, but Zena's a downright flibbety-jibbit."

Already Mother and Daddy had talked marriage, but noting Papa and Mama Todd's reaction to Zena's elopement, Mother couldn't tell them her plans. And why not? Because Dottie Todd was a pure-in-tee coward. She'd lost her nerve.

After a session of self-berating, and before her courage thumbed a ride on the passing freight train, Dottie propped herself in the parlor doorway.

Mama Todd failed to see her daughter. A distant cousin died recently, and Mama was rifling through *The Horry Herald,* looking for obituaries. Papa Todd, quieter, leafed through his bible, *The Almanac.*

Mother's white knuckles gripped the door facing. She cleared her throat. "Mama, Papa, it's time you know. Rass and I are getting married." Mother's lips trembled, but she lifted her chin.

Both parents' eyes darted her way. Three new grooves creased Mama Todd's forehead. "What? You can't mean what I just heard you say."

Papa smiled. "You're teasing us."

"No, Papa. I'm serious. I'm marrying Rassie Hamilton."

"When? Why?" Papa's *Almanac* plopped at his feet.

"Soon," my not-yet Mother said. "Why? 'Cause I love him. And Rass loves me."

Mama Todd sounded lost. "What do you know about love? You're a baby. My baby."

"I'm old enough to know I love Rass, and he's definitely old enough to know he loves me. He's twenty-six years old."

"And you're just eighteen. That's too young."

"Two months short of nineteen, your age when you married Papa."

"Dottie's right, Sis."

Like everyone else, Papa called Mama Todd, "Sis," because she hated "Cleva Felisha," her name.

Papa shook his head. "Sweet girl, think long and hard. Marriage is give; it's take. Are you ready for such?"

Next day Mother's sixteen year-old sister heard the news. Leatha clamped her mouth shut. She knew her time loomed in the offing.

Eight year-old Mace hated the idea of his sister leaving home. Looking right and left, sure no one could overhear, he gripped her hands. Gazing into his sister's eyes, Mace pleaded, "Dottie, if you won't get married, I'll buy you a whole package of talking machine needles." He sometimes earned a pittance by doing odd jobs for his parents.

Mace's offer touched his sister's heart, but so had the offer of that young man, Rassie Bryan Hamilton, son of Hampton Layfayette and Rosahnel Cincinetti.

Seeing their oldest child dead set on leaving home, Mama and Papa Todd dredged up their best advice. "Listen to me, Dottie," Mama warned. "If you're 'die-in-tee' determined to marry a man eight years older, one that missed the boat with a passel of girls 'cause they didn't suit his mama, you'll have to become her daughter, too. If Miz Nettie says 'Jump,' you jump.

You're moving into her house, lock, stock, and barrel. I'm telling you this 'cause I love you. I want you happy."

Papa echoed, "Listen to your mama, Babe. Miz Nettie's a good Christian woman, and if she didn't think a whole lot of you already, Rass would've thought more than once before courtin' you. She's as kind as they come. Just don't think you're gonna walk into her house and take over. I know you well."

"Don't worry so," young Dottie soothed her parents. "I know what I'm doing."

Mother never dreamed that in her married future she'd wear worry like a too-tight hat band, and not always with good reason. However, that day Mother's heart and mind had settled on the young, eight years older-than-she, man, who showed up every Sunday afternoon, swung with her in her porch swing, and whispered wonders into her ear. A friend of hers, Lizzie Thorpe, wrote this poem about Mother and her beau:

> *I know a girl on Adrian sod,*
> *Her name is Miss Dottie Lee Todd.*
> *She has hair of black and a dress of yellow.*
> *She also has a cute little fellow.*
> *At church I saw them as they passed.*
> *I heard someone say his name is Rass.*

That Sunday afternoon in December, 1931, Mother and Daddy returned to Papa's and Mama's "as married as a haint," Papa said. I understand, Grandma Nettie said little. She simply welcomed Mother as graciously as possible for a doting mother of a twenty-six year-old son, who was, always had been, and always would be, her life's focus.

Following Papa Todd's instructions, young Dottie slipped into the Hamilton household like wax into a mold, mostly Grandma's. However, that didn't prevent my future mother from dreaming dreams, for the moment nesting in their chrysalis stage.

Chapter 4
The Arrival

Spring of 1933, Rassie Hamilton's tobacco fields spread out lush and promising, almost touching Bug Swamp's sandy road. Each morning after breakfast, he and his young wife, Dottie, jumped into work clothes. They hoed and suckered tobacco like they were nurturing newborns, at the time, appropriate.

Dottie felt she might just pop from the sheer joy of responsible adulthood. Should she pinch herself? Was this husky man working beside her really her husband? And he loved Dottie. Lots.

No more than she loved him.

At times like these, Rassie, unlike his shy, rather effacing self, discounted every soul in the universe, other than his winsome young bride, her dark hair transformed into ringlets by Bug Swamp's humid air. Dottie bent over to pull up a weed. Rising, her face met Rass's, head-on. He gripped her chin between thumb and forefinger. "Smack!" He kissed her right on the mouth.

"Rassie Hamilton! What'll the neighbors think?"

"What neighbors?" And he kissed her again.

After such intervals, the couple worked even harder.

Dottie loved hoeing and weeding tobacco, but detested sticky, tarry suckering. However, according to Clemson College's smart county agents, pulling new growth from the base of tobacco's main leaves brought about larger leaf growth.

Dottie surprised herself, she felt so ambitious for her new family, destined to become three in some two and a half months. Make that family four, counting Rass's ma.

What had Papa said about Dottie's role in the Hamilton household? That she'd "... walk into Rass's mama's house and take over?" Dottie wouldn't dream of such!

Well, maybe she did have a tendency to lean toward what she wanted. Didn't everybody?

Thursday, their water-bucket sprang a leak. The next two days they "made do" with a couple of pitchers. Then, Saturday morning, Rass, Dottie, and Rass's ma motored to Conway, to Burroughs's hardware store.

Walking through the door, Dottie spied an enamel bucket, rich blue, white-speckled. She would have loved that bucket, even if they'd had indoor plumbing.

Rassie picked up a pail. "This one's a pretty good price. Seventy-five cents. Should I have the salesman wrap it up?"

Rass's ma nodded. "Just like our old one. It served us for twelve years."

Dottie had to ask. "How much for the blue speckled pail?"

"That one?" Rassie scoffed. "A dollar and a quarter. This one'll do just fine. Think so, Ma?"

Dottie shrugged. Truthfully, Dottie loved her new mother-in-law. Who wouldn't love a woman who thought good things about every living soul? Dead ones too. No doubt about it. Nettie Hamilton was a sweet, Christian woman.

So, was it wrong to need some feeling of ownership? Every place Dottie and her family had lived, their yard crawled with meandering tree roots, they'd found little space for flowers, and Dottie loved colorful blooms. *Wait till I get married*, she'd soothed herself. *I'll fill my yard with flowers, every color on earth.*

Today, here sat Dot, old, married, still with no place for blooms. Of course this yard wasn't Dottie's. It belonged to Rassie's ma. Papa said so.

That wasn't the problem. Rassie's ma loved flowers. She'd be happy with a yard full of petunias, daisies, gladiolas, roses, anything bright and blooming. So, what was wrong? All that shade from all those trees. And Nettie Hamilton would die before she'd part with a single, mossy oak.

Of course Miz Hamilton, Ma, Rass's ma, whoever, (Dottie hadn't yet found a name for her mother-in-law.) she doted on a long row of blue hydrangeas hugging the east side of her home. And she babied a bed or two of some kind of verbena, growing in a patch of sun near two china berry trees. A whole acre of yellow flowers danced across the lot next to the house, bigger than Rass's ma's house and yard. She called them "Julie flowers." Her friend, Julie Thompkins, gave Miz Hamilton enough seed, those daisies covered the field all the way down the lane.

So, why was Dottie complaining? She wanted her own flowers.

"No," she told her hubby after they'd eaten breakfast. "I won't go with you to Adrian. I'll stay here and top tobacco." He said they needed more fertilizer.

Breaking off the prettiest thing about a tobacco plant, its single bloom, multi-flowered steeple pointing skyward, went against the girl's nature; but, Dottie popped it off. Threw it aside. Occasionally she'd flinch, but by noon, she'd topped all plants in the field.

Rass returned from Adrian, and the two of them sat on their front porch steps, gazing at the tobacco patch. Rass said, "You did a fine job, Dot." He gestured widely. "That looks great."

Dottie just sat and looked.

No longer did their fields of pinkish flowers ripple in borrowed sunlight, but that sacrifice, along with suckering, helped tobacco grow more saleable, larger leaves. Like Brook and Rob, Leo, Uncle Boss, Papa, Uncle Bert, every farmer they knew, Dot and Rass would scrounge around any way possible to loosen the grip President Hoover's old Great Depression held on their pocketbook.

Of course, Hoover was no longer president. Recently, people said, "If anyone in this country has the guts and the know-how to fix our economy, it's Franklin Delano Roosevelt. He's our man."

Dottie certainly hoped this new President Roosevelt could fix things. She wanted their sweet baby to enter a world where people focused on living, not on fear for their livelihoods, sometimes their lives. She'd heard of men jumping off of buildings and bridges. Sometimes whole families left homes they'd forfeited, carrying all they owned on their backs. Dottie wouldn't wish that happening to her worst enemy.

On July eighth, nearly sand-lugging time, Mother sprang me onto the scene. Luckily, this date fell on a weekend, or at my birthing, Mother could have been minus a husband.

Not really. Daddy would have climbed Mount Everest to witness his daughter's birth. And climbing at his heels would have been his ma, if her "rheumatiz" cooperated. Any doubt about Dottie's place in the fold faded with the birth of Rass's baby girl.

Here's an account of that event. Forgive me if I'm not one hundred percent accurate:

Saturday at their mid-day dinner, Mother felt too full of me to eat. That's when I commenced knocking on her inner sanctum. "Rassie," she yelled at Daddy, in the kitchen finishing his meal. "I need you. Now!"

Daddy ran from kitchen to bedroom; from bedroom, back to the kitchen. He skidded to a stop. "Ma! The baby's coming."

Grandma's next to youngest brother, Hal Buck Holmes, practiced medicine. "Call Hal. Quick!" Grandma went to boiling water.

The only telephone in the area presided over the parlor of Kelly and Purley Thompkins, father and son proprietors of Adrian's general store. If Tin Lizzie drove properly, Daddy could reach Adrian in about three and a quarter miles. With only Old Pet and the wagon available to ford swamps, the distance shortened to, maybe, two and a half miles, but took longer. Luckily, that day Daddy's Model-A cooperated. Papa and Mama Todd's home sat a few hundred feet up a road to the left, beside railroad tracks passing Adrian.

Daddy telephoned Uncle Hal, then braked at his in-law's front steps. "Ooga! Ooga!" Daddy slapped at Tin Lizzie's horn. "The baby's coming," he yelled at his in-laws through their open window.

A speed maniac, Uncle Hal drove twelve miles, turning his two-seater into our yard shortly after Daddy, Papa, and Mama Todd drove their distance home from Adrian.

For a first baby, I popped out in record time. Mother said she couldn't understand women carrying on so about birth-giving. After I was born on Saturday, if Grandma would have allowed it, Sunday morning Mother could have gone to church. As it was, propped on pillows, all afternoon she delighted in sharing her new baby with family and friends. Able or not, she lay in bed for nine days. A Bug Swamp stipulation.

No woman ever experienced a happier first pregnancy. Mother told it like this: "You know, after a rich dinner complete with all the trimmings, you feel full, but not quite satisfied. Then, the cook brings out a lemon meringue pie, and you say 'Yummy.' That's a fraction of how I felt when Rass's ma put my baby in my arms."

My birthday came in July, certainly a time inconvenient for tobacco growers. As soon as possible, Mother turned over her small bundle, me, to Grandma, and returned to farm chores.

At fifty-three and with little help, Grandma Nettie managed our house and her granddaughter. However, she did fear that Mother didn't eat enough to nurse me. "Dottie," she would say when Mother pushed away from the table, "never in my life have I seen anyone but you who can eat half a biscuit, and say, 'I'm full.'"

Ninety-eight pounds before pregnancy, and little more afterwards, Mother ate nothing of the cow, not a hamburger, a bite of roast, nor steak. Frowning, she refused milk, probably Daddy's favorite beverage. If the family hadn't raised a pen full of pigs, a barnyard of chickens, sweet corn, and a vegetable garden, Mother could have starved to death. No morsel of wild game ever touched her lips; certainly not turtle which locals called cooter, no ring-eyed, ring-tailed raccoon, and no possum, which certain Bug Swampians considered a staple.

As a little girl I heard conversations like: "Dot, there's a big old cooter crawling out the swamp. I'm gonna go tell Jim. He'll eat good tonight."

Daddy would race up to the Snow Hill tenant house and return with Jim Jones, our friend and tenant, in tow and dragging a gunny sack.

"You going with Jim, Rassie? Do be careful. Don't let that old cooter bite you. You know if he does, he won't turn loose till it thunders." That sage advice from Grandma Nettie. If a sprinkle of rain peppered down about then, she'd say, "Son, stay out of the rain or your nose'll stop up." Where Daddy was concerned, Grandma epitomized the family's worry-wart, although seldom did she admit to that heresy.

As soon as I grew old enough to comprehend such, I considered Jim Jones and Daddy two brave men to take on our community's fearsome swamp critter.

Insert: *People consider a turtle, slow. Not a cooter. An old fellow outgrows his shell. His body protrudes from all around it, his neck pokes out a good six*

Billie H. Wilson •

inches, and his legs make good time. If you don't believe me, step up to one and stick your foot toward his tail. Mouth open, he can whirl around on a dime, looking like he's dying to spring.

I don't know how I got off onto cooters. I meant to tell you about the time I ate supper with a family who lived in one of Uncle Bert Holmes' tenant houses.

CHAPTER 5
Biscuits and Possum Gravy

Grandma Nettie's youngest brother, Uncle Bert, owned several farmhouses between our home and Good Hope Church, a more refined name for the original Bug Swamp Baptist. In one of these houses lived a family I'll call the Millers.

Returning home after visiting her sister, Aunt Freddie, Grandma scraped feet on the front mat before bolting into the house. She had something to tell.

"Chillern." Grandma addressed Mother and Daddy, munching on Grandma's tea cakes. She took time to untie her straw hat and wipe forehead sweat with her apron. "You two know Bert's new tenants? The Millers? Well Freddie says they're nasty." Grandma hung her hat on a chair back and plopped into her corner rocker.

Feeling guilty, she stopped her rocking. "Do shut my mouth. I never should have said that." She rubbed her hands together, "Forgive me, Lord." To Mother and Daddy: "Don't you dare tell a livin' soul I called them nasty. You hear?"

At Bug Swamp, the word, "nasty," had nothing to do with personalities or morals. "Nasty" meant a family kept a dirty house.

Mind you, Grandma frowned on gossip. Her favorite advice to me, "Little Bushy, if you have nothing good to say about somebody, say nary a word. Remember, the Good Book says: 'Do unto others as you'd have them do unto you.'" Occasionally that old devil got in too close, and even

Grandma gave in to temptation; but, repeating Aunt Freddie's comment, if just to family, preyed on Grandma's conscience. She sought to live by God's word, and she expected the same from us.

The Miller family consisted of James Miller, his wife, Lucy, his sister, Irene, and his mother, old Mrs. Miller. That old lady had lived so long, she could no longer even tie tobacco. She visited. So, on many days Grandma Nettie held court. Early on I remember spying Mrs. Miller dodder from up the lane, looking like her next step might be her last. Her gray hair tried to be a bun. It stuck out every which-a-way, and on the hottest summer days she wore an ancient, matted shawl atop shoulders bony enough to hang a hat on; but, as Daddy said, that scrawny old woman sure could eat. Somehow she managed to wander in just about the time Mother and Daddy left for the fields, and fried ham and biscuit still sat on the table.

"Care for a cup of coffee, Miz Miller?" Grandma would ask. She'd load a saucer with food and pass it to her guest. "Do me a favor. Eat this bread and meat. You'll keep it from going to waste."

I'd watch Mrs. Miller eat. I guess she half chewed and half gummed her food. Her two long, yellow teeth, both on one side of her mouth, helped little.

After the repast, Mrs. Miller was set to chat. "I've got me one fine boy. I don't know what I'd 'a done if the good Lord hadn't blessed me with that'un. His pore old pa, he's been gone from these parts so long, if I didn't have James, I'd have nobody."

"You'd have Irene. And Lucy."

"You know as well as I do. They're both girls. They caint do nothin' I need done. James shoots our dinner about every night. Them girls couldn't do that. He catches a ride with Leo and brings me my snuff, too, as sure as the day is long." Leo was our next-door neighbor and cousin.

"I see what you mean," said Grandma.

She did, too. She treasured her snuff dipping as much as the next one.

For the time being, Grandma let dirty dishes go. She grabbed her yellow-labeled, silver snuff box with the "Society" lady pictured on it, picked up her spit can, a large tin filled with sand, picked up another like it she kept for company, and headed for her "pizer," Mrs. Miller in tow. There the two sat and palavered.

In spite of her unbalanced mouth, Mrs. Miller beat her hostess in the spitting category. While Grandma picked up her can, and like the lady she was, used her tongue and lips neatly to expel snuffy saliva, Mrs. Miller sat upright, puckered her lips, and unerringly "p'tui-ed" brown streams, smack into her can.

Occasionally, foregoing cans, the ladies held a spitting contest. They'd see which could spit farthest. Usually Mrs. Miller won that endeavor.

Mother, home from whatever job called her that morning, would grab a brush yard broom and sweep sand over spit blemishing the yard. One day, fed up with such, she asked Grandma, "Don't you get tired of that old woman, over here day in and day out?"

"Can't say as I do," Grandma said. "Company's company."

While Mother thought old Mrs. Miller a pain, she liked Lucy. James and Lucy married just before they moved to Bug Swamp. Mother and Daddy sometimes traded tobacco chores with the newly-weds. "I've never seen the girl dressed up," Mother told Daddy. "She'd be pretty, too. You know, I'd like to take her to town and buy her a new dress."

Grandma said, "With what?"

Mother said, "Yeah. They probably have as much money as we do. But we are blessed with enough to eat and wear."

Daddy said, "Don't fret for Lucy. She's got James. As long as they can't take their eyes off each other, they won't notice they're poor."

Not that we weren't, but "There's poor, and then there's pore." Grandma's words.

Irene intrigued me. Thinking back, I suppose she was about thirteen. For sure her hair would be in style today. Its color matched the kernels on an ear of dried corn. Uneven, it fell in interesting lengths. Her blue eyes matched the sky, her freckles matched her hair, and the years spent in our community, she personified my ideal of an older, teen-aged girl to admire.

Usually Irene visited near sunset after she, Lucy, and James finished working the crops. I recall little of the following occurrence, since when this happened, I was barely two. However, Mother's harping on it makes it seem my memory.

One afternoon Irene came for her mother. While the two waited for Grandma to divide and share with them a cooked mess of collard greens, Irene played "pee-pie" with me; then took my hand and walked me around the yard. She engaged me in a game of "patty-cake." When she and her mother started home, Irene said, "Miz Dottie, let me take Billie Faye home with me. I'll bring her right back."

Grandma said. "Let her go, Dottie. You took off work early today."

Mother gazed after Mrs. Miller, Irene, and me all the way down the lane until it curved, laurels hiding her view.

Without her little girl, Mother's imagination took over. She hadn't known the Millers long, and Irene had what she treasured most. Her child.

Finally, Daddy came home. "Where's my 'girurs'?" His pet name for me.

"Never should I have let her go." Mother paced the sandy yard. "I'm going after my baby."

"Wait for me to wash up. I'll go too."

"That'll take too long." Mother streaked down the lane. Approaching the Millers' bungalow, Mother viewed a closed front door, no one in sight. Weird thoughts flitted through her head. Baseless thoughts. These were good people. Her little girl was perfectly safe. Mother should feel foolish.

She stepped up the one tree bole onto their front porch. From inside came the sound of forks on plates. And giggles. Mine.

Mother rapped on the door. "Irene!"

James said, "Miz Hamilton. Come in. Have some supper."

Grandma had been correct in her description of the Millers. Their house smelled like dried cooked beans, stewed collards, and... what was *that* smell? Mother failed to retrieve it from her aroma repertoire.

Before her the tableau was poorly lit. Where was her baby? "Where's my baby?" Her voice came out strained. "Irene... ?"

"Tell your mama, 'Hey.'" At one end of the table Irene jiggled me on her knee.

Mother stretched out arms for her child.

"Wait a minute," Irene said. "I'll wet a rag. Billie Faye wouldn't eat Lucy's possum, but she sure did enjoy sopping possum gravy. Her face is right greasy."

It was good Mother hadn't eaten. She could barely make her way through the dim interior to outside light before gagging.

"Never again will I let Irene take home my baby," Mother announced to any and all, especially to Grandma. "And you're not to either." Mother glared at her mother-in-law, one of the few times on this earth she ever did. "Let me tell you. That is one smelly house. And Irene, she fed this child possum, or possum gravy. My sweet little girl sopped a biscuit in that greasy stuff. And ate it!"

Daddy grinned. "Enjoyed it too."

Mother shot him a look. "How can anybody eat overgrown rat?"

"Hungry people. They eat what they can get." Grandma enjoyed a little repartee. Actually, she never ate possum in her life. Raccoon hash, once in a blue moon.

After that, when Daddy wanted a mess of beef steak, Mother didn't complain. If she but opened her mouth, Daddy said, "Maybe you'd rather I brought home a fat old possum instead of this scrawny piece of steak." That shut her up every time.

Chapter 6
To Smoke or not to Smoke

This morning like many, after their coffee, fried ham, flour bread, and scrambled eggs, Mother and Daddy left for the tobacco beds. Our tobacco fledglings were almost ready to transplant, and today my parents would pull weeds. Mother loved freeing her plants from useless interlopers.

Before leaving, Mother rushed around the kitchen, doing last minute things. I tugged on her shirt tail. "Mommie, I want some water."

Mother picked me up and kissed my cheek, then held a dipper of water to my lips. "Billie, I need to get busy. Find your grandma, Honey. She'll help you get dressed." Mornings Mother had little time for anything except work. Before breakfast she had placed shelled butterbeans, flavored by a ham bone, on low simmer; thus, for our midday meal, all Grandma needed to do was bake biscuits, boil rice, fry salmon patties, and open a jar of peaches.

Our dinner bell hung from a nearby oak tree limb. Near midday Grandma boosted me high enough to pull its rope, "Clang, clang." Then we sat on the porch and watched for my parents. Grandma still had time for her dip of snuff.

Before they were within ear-shot, I saw Mother's mouth, grimacing. Something must have gone wrong with their bed plants. Within hearing range, she said, "Looks like cut worms to me."

"Too early for cut worms."

"Then what's wrong with the plants at the far end?"

"Probably a mole dug around in 'em. Just a half dozen plants. We've enough without that few."

Fingers to her lips, Grandma lifted her spit-can and "p'too-ied." "Why worry so much, Dottie. Learn how to give it to God.'"

I said, "Grandma, that's not what you told Grandpa that time he worried so about his little pigs."

Lower lip poked out, Grandma upped her chin and eyed me. "Smarty-Pants," she swatted my bottom.

Mother said, "What pigs? What was wrong with Rass's daddy's pigs?"

"Let's eat. I'll tell you later about Hampie's pigs."

My grandmother was my pal, my confidante, and my treasure. Today she's my role model, except for her snuff-dipping, and while Grandma dipped snuff, Daddy smoked cigarettes. Mother detested both, although she found many uses for tobacco, like paying for food, for shoes, and fabrics for pretty dresses she doted on sewing.

Those years, our ideas about a tarry plant providing us livelihood differed considerably from ideas harbored by today's citizenry. In the thirties and forties, noteworthy people lit up whenever and wherever they chose. Few considered that large-leafed, sticky growth remotely dangerous. Cousin Worth's dad, in another county, developed cancer. It ate away his upper lip and his nose. Few, if any, connected Mr. A.'s forty-five years of smoking to cancer, and most failed to associate smoking with heart disease or breathing problems.

Still, one day when Grandma heard Daddy coughing and hacking, she said, "Son, maybe you smoke too much." But she never pestered Daddy. For goodness sake, who could ask the man to give up something he so enjoyed?

Really, I think Grandma knew she shouldn't dip snuff, and Daddy shouldn't smoke, for when my younger brother, Jack, popped into our family, like a Bible verse, she quoted him this poem:

Tobacco is a dirty weed.
From the devil sprung the seed.
It dirties your hands,
It soils your clothes.

BILLIE H. WILSON •

*It makes a smokestack
Outta your nose.*

Grandma left me out of those "smoking" conversations, for Bug Swamp women never smoked, unless they left home and went to work at some "Audacious place around Myrtle Beach!" Grandma called those females, "loose women."

Once my four years and three months younger-than-me brother spied Mother light Daddy's cigarette. Jack sobbed. "No, Mama. No! I don't want a loose woman for a mommie!"

Mother picked up her boy and smoothed back his hair. "Son, I'll never smoke if you won't. Promise?"

Jack promised, and I believe both kept their promises.

Most Bug Swamp tobacco farmers smoked. And why not? The more smokers, the more demand for their product. These farmers knew, if they grew tobacco, pampered it like a colicky baby; then, sold it at market, in a good year fall sales could stuff their drawstring money bags to overflowing with Bug Swamp's "Green Gold."

Rare nights of my young years our family watched movies at Conway's Carolina Theater. Sandwiched between Mother and Daddy, Jack and I munched popcorn, while on the screen beautifully remote ladies like Greta Garbo or Marlene Dietrich crossed silken legs and puffed on holder-held cigarettes. How glamorous.

Of course Grandma's Sweet Society snuff box pictured a lady so cultured she'd never have posed before a movie camera. Unlike the textured herb Sir Walter Raleigh introduced to England, this society lady represented tobacco powdered into a wispy cloud. When packed into Grandma Nettie's back jaw and moistened with saliva, my grandma could purse her lips and let-fly Sweet Society's citified brown stream, arrow-straight into her Bug Swamp spit can.

On this day, only months before Jackie Boy joined our family, Mother and Daddy came home from pulling tobacco bed weeds. We finished our salmon patty, butter beans, rice, and peaches. Draining his ice tea glass, Daddy pushed away from the table. "Nap time," he said.

I hated nap time.

Chapter 7
A Picture Leads to a Barn Raisin'

An oval picture hung on our parlor wall. A serious looking man dwelt there. Grandpa Hamp.

His hair, dark, wavy, dipped onto his high forehead, and he gazed into the distance seeing something I didn't. His straight nose looked a little like Daddy's, but his lips weren't as curvy, and while his suit looked nice, his necktie was narrower than Daddy's. Since birth I'd lived with his and other wall pictures.

I tugged on Grandma's apron. I asked, "Grandma were you somebody's wife?"

She laughed. "You know I was, Little Bushy. Your grandpa's. Your daddy's pa." Grandma took my hand and led me to his picture. "Look at him. Your Grandpa Hamp was one good-lookin' man. Too bad he never got to know you."

I was just realizing, people didn't live forever. Recently, Uncle Fernie Harris, Aunt Tennessee's husband, died. I saw him, still and white, lying in his casket.

I pointed to our wall's picture. "Grandpa. When did he die?"

Grandma's face brimmed with sad wrinkles. "Thirteen years before you were born. Your Grandpa Hampie died on the longest day of the year. Never since has my world been the same."

She lowered herself into her peach Damask chair. I climbed into her lap, looking at a face I equated with life on earth.

She pointed out the front window. "See the second field across the road? A ditch separates that field from the first. One day, it was June 21, 1920, your grandpa and I were out workin' in that field. Next to us, your daddy, only fourteen, was just a'shrubbin' the ditch bank.

"For some time Hampie had not been the healthiest in the world. Dr. Joe Dusenbury told him, 'Slow down, man. If you don't, your next step could be your last.' I guess Hampie didn't know how to work less. Anyhow, one minute he was saying, 'Net, just think. Little Nonie's coming tonight.'

"Nonie was his name for our first grandchild, Leoma, the only grandchild Hampie got to know. That little girl was the plumb apple of his eye."

I knew Leoma. Everybody but Grandma called her "Leona." She was in high-school and about ready to graduate. Leona's mother was Aunt Sally, Grandma's oldest.

Grandma said she told Grandpa, "I can't wait to see Nonie either. That baby is the cutest thing. And she loves you smack to death."

"After that, your Grandpa stayed silent so long, I stopped hoeing. I turned around. His face looked as white as a lock o' cotton. He said, 'Catch me, Nettie. I'm fallin'.'

"And he did. Crumpled right down in the dirt.

"I screamed, 'Rassie! Rassie!' Your daddy jumped that ditch. Right kadab over some little peach trees trying to take a'hold. My boy knelt down and grabbed up his daddy. He yelled, 'Pa! Pa!'

"No answer. Your grandpa was already with the Lord.

"Your daddy had to be a man real quick, for this farm called for one. 'Course Bert and Dave rallied around. Goodness knows we needed all the help we could get."

My great-uncles, Uncle Bert and Uncle Dave, both lived nearby.

That's when Grandma and I heard Daddy climbing the front steps. We'd left the parlor door open. Picking up on our conversation, Daddy sighed. He sat down on the wicker couch across from us. "Ma, I was just gonna tell you. Pa's old barn is past fixin'. We won't be able to use it again."

Daddy looked tired. "I sure do hate to borrow money for a new one."

Grandma pursed her lips and punctuated words with her eyes and head. "Then don't. Time was around here, people helped their neighbors."

That night at supper Mother started in lamenting. "Please, Rass. Right now we can't afford a new barn. Don't saddle us with more debt."

"Hmm," Grandma mused. "Your Grandpa Bill Hamilton, when he first came to these parts, he bought some land. This'un and more. His new neighbors got together and raised him a log cabin. He lived in it too, till his farm started to pay off, and he built the house Minnie and her family live in till this day." That declaration turned wheels in Daddy's head.

Grandma needed little incentive to entertain. Friends and family were always dropping by. They'd sample her lightly crusted, left-over biscuits. She'd say, "Y'all need a drink. Go get that block of ice out the fireplace."

Pulling back the ice's protective burlap, she'd take a pick and break off enough shards, rinse them, and fill several glasses, which she'd pour full to brimming with super sweet tea, all the while talking about this person or that: who was sick, who didn't go to church Sunday because they were playing hooky. Maybe Cora Somebody's husband had up and left her at home with two little children to feed. Sometimes she and her company took spit cans onto the front "pizer." There they sat trading stories, just a'dippin' snuff and palaverin.'

Mother, quick to learn, whipped up salads and baked pies. Papa Todd? He could build anything. Uncle Mace, young, healthy, he had little else to do. "Aunt" Leatha's future husband, Jeff, came when needed, as did Daddy's cousins, Brook, Leo, and Rob, as well as Grandma's brother, Uncle Dave. So, who, in the Bug Swamp community, needed to hire a tobacco barn built?

Last year, with an eye toward the future, Daddy and Cousin Leo cut down trees, and using Old Mary, Daddy's work partner and favorite mule, snaked logs out of the Bay Swamp field. Daddy and Leo stripped bark from new logs and stacked long, naked rounds into square cages, allowing the wood time to dry.

Later Old Mary broke out of her stall and tore off through a field of tempting, green wheat, where, sad to say, she foundered herself. Goodbye Old Mary.

A big, orange sun heralded barn-raisin' day. The evening before, Mother prevailed upon Daddy to wring the necks of a couple of hens no longer laying, and because they were tough old birds, all night long they simmered on an eye of Grandma's iron monster, a wood-burning stove hogging a third of our kitchen.

I wasn't allowed near the work site. "Keep this child away from that barn buildin'," Grandma ordered. "If you don't, she could get conked in the noggin by a falling hammer."

I witnessed enough activity in the kitchen. On the counter Mother had lined up six baked pie shells. Three of these she heaped with chocolate pie filling and three with lemon, piling mounds of meringue onto each before browning them in the stove's hungry maw.

Meanwhile, Grandma washed her hands and stirred up batter. Baking and cooling three layers of yellow cake, she iced between and atop each layer with buttery chocolate goodness. Next, she set out sour apple tarts. Before baking, she sprinkled each with sinful heaps of granulated sugar. Then just before dinner, while biscuits baked, Grandma whipped up a batch of fresh cream, donated by Hazel, our Jersey cow.

A couple of months later, a rattle snake bit Hazel. She died, poor thing. However, on this day Hazel's cream rested in splendor atop Grandma's sour apple tarts.

In the Bug Swamp community Grandma Nettie acquired fame for those tarts. Her green apples came from what had been young Grandpa Hamp's family farm. At this time Cousin Bertha Mae's mom, Aunt Minnie, and her family lived there. Each summer she shared with us their green, cooking apples, as well as their orchard's sweet, June apples.

Mama Todd slapped a white apron around her minimal waist and went to work. She deboned the two, now tender hens and loaded Grandma's iron pot with rich chicken broth, rice, and cooked chicken pieces. By now our old country kitchen smelled like heaven must. I couldn't keep my feet on the floor or a smile off my face.

Mere chicken and rice would not suffice volunteer barn-raisers. A huge platter of crunchy fried chicken joined other dishes on the menu. Also potato salad. Mother made hers with hard boiled eggs, mayonnaise, mustard, chopped, home-jarred, sweet cucumber pickles, a dollop of apple cider vinegar, a pinch of sugar, and of course, cooked and diced potatoes. Boiled "egg-flowers" decorated the top of the huge bowl. A glass compote heaped with jarred, home-grown pears glistened amid steaming bowls of chicken, yellow rice, and early garden peas.

Near noon, talking, laughing, and wiping sweat, the men crowded around our back yard pump. They took turns pumping water and washing up. Glad to hand them towels Mother gave me, I climbed up the back steps, following our workers into the kitchen.

Such a sight, and everything smelled as good as it looked. Covered in white Damask, the taller than traditional table, thanks to Grandpa Hamp's carpentry skills, groaned beneath its load of delectable vittles. Those working fellows stuffed themselves with food and swigged down tall glasses of tea.

From that day long ago, I remember gobs about dinner preparation and nothing about barn building. However, Grandma noted that those men did a great job, "eatin' and raisin'."

Daddy now owned a fine, new tobacco barn, which was a good thing, for before curing season, Grandpa's old barn decided it had served its purpose. During an early summer storm the barn gave an aged shudder, and like in a game of "pick-up-sticks," rattled to the ground.

Standing before the debris, Grandma blinked her eyes, relieving an overflow of brightness. Shaking her head, she said, "Chillern, that barn sheltered a passel of memories."

Seventy-six years later, I know what she meant.

Chapter 8
Billie and the Bear

Lucky Daddy. Thanks to friends and family, he owned a brand new barn without a cent of extra credit; but, to use this barn he needed a spiffy, new crop.

Before tobacco could be cultivated, harvested, or cured, it had to be planted. Believe you me and Mother, growing that golden weed required careful preparation.

Earlier that year, hitching Old Pet to a plow, Daddy disked oblong beds of blackish, fertilized, Bay Swamp soil, until Grandma could have made fluffy biscuits with that dirt, had it been flour. Next, both of my parents scattered wee, blackish seeds over the beds and covered the whole with see-through, gauzy material. Tobacco canvas.

"Grab that canvas," Daddy told Mother.

"Pull it tighter." Mother anchored her side of the covering at ends and sides of long plots with lengthy nails, wood stakes, or a combination of both.

At home that night, Daddy said, "Ma, we did it. We seeded our beds today."

"Time to pray about it." Grandma crooked her finger, beckoning us. "This won't take long." She brought fingers of both hands together in a prayer peak, looked heavenward, and closed her eyes. "Lord, thank you for bein' our Savior and for every good thing you bring to our lives. You know, sowing these seeds, that's our part. We're gonna need rain real soon.

Thank you ahead of time for the gracious help you'll give us. We trust in you, our Lord and our Master. Amen."

Several weeks passed. Those tiny tobacco seeds, watered by heaven, in no time flat, sprouted and grew into tender shoots. Now Mother's interest shifted into high gear. Aware of enemy, immigrant weeds bivouacked nearby, seeking to invade and displace our family's very livelihood, Mother declared war on all threatening greenery.

This March day I accompanied Mother on one such foray that could have scared us to death, or outright killed us both, mostly because Mother focused as much attention on our recently sown tobacco beds, as *seven months later*, she lavished on my brand-new, baby brother.

That morning we rose early, saw Daddy off on a farm shopping trip, and ate our usual breakfast: fried ham, eggs, and flour bread. Mother wiped egg goo off my chin. She told Grandma, "When Rass gets back from Adrian, tell him I'll be in the Bay Swamp field, pulling weeds and thinning tobacco plants."

I scrambled out of a chair too tall for my short legs. Tugging at Mother's shirt tail, I begged, "Take me. Let me go."

Grandma said, "I'll be lonesome here without you, Little Bushy." My hair had grown from its soft, curly stage and hadn't learned what to do with itself.

Mother said, "Sure, Baby, come with me if you'll be good. Ma, sit down. Put up your feet. Relax today."

Grandma rolled her eyes. "No rest for the weary. I'll wash dishes. I'll make beds. Then I'll gather eggs and go get the mail." She sniffed. "But don't go frettin' yourself. Dinner'll be ready at straight up and down twelve o'clock." Unless Grandma had access to a clock, she told time by sun shadows.

Mother shook her head and smiled a little, knowing full well that Grandma had equally as much to do at home as Mother did, working the fields.

Slinging me astraddle her left hip and heading down our sandy field road, separating what was traditionally corn, cotton, and bean patches, Mother soon tired and let me walk beside her. We passed land that would later teem with rippling wheat or rye. I forget which. Two fields on our right (Grandpa Hamp drew his last breath in the second patch) would eventually become home to the very tobacco sprouts toward which we were headed.

Past the third ditch and to our left lay open, sandy acreage, future home of Daddy's tempting water melons, some long and green, wearing wavy stripes like unto rattle snakes, the others round, dark green, awaiting butcher knives to plunge into red, juicy hearts. Their fate, come summertime.

To the right of our trail, another led toward two tobacco barns, one just built, and beyond that, our Snow Hill tenant house. Closest lay Br'er Rabbit's briar patch, prickly but berry-less at the moment. On warmer days I'd pick briar berries there, carefully, for not only briars gave us problems. Lurking snakes would like nothing better than to bite us "with their mean old fangs." Grandma's words.

Nearing my favorite place on our farm, a not-so-swampy region separating other acreage from the Bay Swamp Field, I turned loose Mother's hand and ran ahead. To the right, left, and straight before us lived some of the South's rarest, most magical plants. I remember one low, leafy specimen adorned with green, splashed with pink, bean-shaped appendages outlined in fringy growth similar to eye-lashes. Inside, these reddish, pupil-less "eyes" opened wide. I'd squat, pick up a twig, and tickle the line creasing the inner eye. It snapped shut. If my twig had been a nectar-seeking fly, goodbye bug. Later, someone told me my playmate plants were insect-eating, Venus Fly Traps.

Other plants during flowering seasons possessed yellow, trumpet-like flowers. Insects foraged down these sweet petal throats, got stuck, and died there. Mary Cut Your Thumb bushes already stood green and lush, although Jack Frost had paid us visits in the not-so-distant past. Mary must have bled a lot, for each green leaf of her plant glowed with a smear of deep, blood-red. Springy green moss provided a magic carpet, cushioning the whole area.

Beyond this bit of Eden, down a narrow path and through a width of fragrant bay trees and thick laurels opening onto a wide field, our two tobacco beds stretched long and pristine white.

Mother cautioned, "Billie, don't wander around. Stay right where you are."

"I'll be good, Mommie." I squatted at the end of a bed, intent on watching Bug Swamp natives, a slew of red ants, scurrying in and out of their underground home, some carrying loads bigger than themselves.

Mother folded back a portion of tobacco canvas. She squatted gingerly amidst her newest off-spring, commencing her task of freeing baby plants from enemy aggressors.

Meanwhile I discovered a doodle bug's hilly dimple. Many times I came across these wee, soft mounds, but hardly ever an inhabitant. Taking up the chant Grandma taught me, I gently stirred the sandy, depressed entrance. I sang out, "Doodle bug, doodle bug, come get a cup of coffee." When that didn't work, I tried another tact: "Doodle bug, doodle bug, where have you gone? Your house is on fire and your children are home." Mrs. Doodle bug must have cared little, for she never deigned to make an appearance.

Interrupting my play, bushes behind me rustled. A strange voice startled me to my feet, the sound somewhere between a growl and a moan. I rolled my eyes toward Mother.

Again, "Gr-umm," this time longer and louder. A branch crackled.

Mother threw caution to the wind. Stomping treasured baby plants, she flew out of that tobacco bed. Scooping me into safe arms, she raced to the far side of the field where a dirt road exited toward civilization. Still she ran, finally depositing me onto our tenant farmer's porch.

Jim and Izzie Jones had seen us coming. Mother could hardly speak. "Jim," she gasped. "Something's in the woods. Something big. Can you check it out?"

I kept my mouth shut. *Why*, I thought, *did Mother think My Jimmy should go check out something we had run from?*

My Jimmy was my name for our Snow Hill tenant farmer. I loved the wee man. He told me stories about elves and dwarfs and fairies.

Izzie looked doubtful, seeing her husband retrace our flight. However, Jim soon returned.

"I saw signs, Miz Dottie. Something big's wrung off a lot of bushes. By the time I got there, the thing was gone. But I saw its sign. Right near where you were working. That booger stomped down bushes it didn't wring off. Looks like it run away, probably as scared of you as you of it."

Izzie shook her head. "I wouldn't count on that."

Ever practical, Mother said, "What about the canvas? Did you re-place the tobacco canvas?"

"Didn't take that much time, Ma'am. I'll do it later."

"Good." Mother drew a deep breath. "I don't think I'm up for going back there right now."

Home, Mother told Daddy and Grandma we'd narrowly escaped a bear encounter.

"You just heard an old fox or raccoon. We haven't had bears around here since Pa was a boy."

"I've never heard a fox or a coon moan low and scary. Say what you will, Rass," Mother tightened her lips. "We're lucky we got away."

Grandma looked askance, and Daddy snickered.

I said, "Can I have a biscuit, Grandma. I'm hungry."

An afternoon or two later Mother, Daddy, Grandma, and I walked next door to visit Aunt Minnie, Daddy's dead daddy's sister-in-law. We sat on her porch and listened to Grandma and Aunt Minnie palaver. I say "listened," for anyone else had trouble squeezing in a word. I played a bit with Cud'n Bertha Mae, but she was two years older than I and considered me a baby. Leo, Aunt Minnie's only son, stretched out his supple frame on a wooden porch chair, his crossed legs resting on the bannister. He chimed in once in a while, when he heard his mama say something about "them Blackwell girls Leo courts over the swamp."

Practically deaf, Leo was blessed not to hear everything his mama said about him and his girlfriends.

Leo's sisters, Una and Myrty, had just met Randolph and Joe, who later became their husbands. Aunt Minnie liked those fellows. Une and Myrt weren't sons. They could like anyone they chose. Jumping ahead, poor old Leo never married. Who would have taken care of Aunt Minnie's tobacco crop, for pity sake?

After our visit we walked home. I sat astride Daddy's shoulders. To enter the kitchen, he detoured around the back of our house.

A clear field, abutted on one side by Cypress Swamp and on the other by a pine thicket, opened up behind us.

With two hands I gave Daddy's head a shake. "Look, Daddy! There's a bear!"

He paid me no mind.

I turned his head, "Daddy! Look! A bear!"

This time Daddy looked. "Well, I swan," he said.

We watched. Wthin two-hundred feet of us, a rangy, black bear, lumbering out of Cypress Swamp, crossed the field and disappeared into the adjacent pine thicket.

For the next few weeks we heard a lot about that bear, but never saw it. Malcolm Harris, Aunt Tennessee's son, lay dying with what my parents termed consumption. Malcolm's family had brought in a supply of fresh meat, and they decided the bear smelled the meat. Anyway, he kept so close to the house, Janie Sue and Lutie, Malcolm's wife and sister, felt afraid to step outside.

Grandma wouldn't let me play in our yard. "Bears are dangerous, Little Bushy." She ushered me inside. "They can rise up on their hind legs and scare you to death if nothing else."

Secretly, I wished Daddy would bring us home a lot of fresh meat, if that would draw the bear.

Sad to say, I never saw the brash fellow again. As was bound to happen after my bear bounded out of the swamp and developed a hankering for Bug Swamp socializing, at least one somebody developed an itchy trigger finger. To my sorrow, an Adrian resident, Mr. Will S., shot the bear, skinned him, and nailed his hide to the wall of Mr. Bert Anderson's tobacco barn.

Now I could play outdoors whenever I wished. However, with no bear set to assail me at every corner, or peer at me from behind a bush, outside proved little fun. At night I no longer lay in bed and pretended bumps I heard beneath my window were made by a rangy, black bear, searching for a four-year-old girl who played with ants.

Since Papa and Mama Todd lived at Adrian, we passed Mr. Bert's barn often. "Drive slow, Daddy," I'd say, sitting up tall and peering out through the car window, as we neared the only material object left of an exciting episode of my life. Riding past, I gazed at the angular, glossy-haired bear-skin tacked to the barn wall. I wanted to cry.

Meanwhile in their canvas beds, tobacco plants freed by Mother from their enemy weeds extended heads against their canvas ceiling. Thus grew Mother's and Daddy's farm work. Before long, seedlings, for which Mother had cared so tenderly, would be plucked from their tobacco bed bosom

Billie H. Wilson •

and transplanted into open fields. There they'd face whatever heat, rain, wind, or hail came their way.

    Most days after that, when Grandma and I had few sugar sacks to rip or tales to hear, I thought about my scary black bear, and how close Mother and I came to becoming bear bait.

Chapter 9
The Gator

Hazel died. Bit by a rattle snake. Grandma sure doted on her old Jersey helper. For years that cow provided gallons of milk, lots of it churned into butter accounting for the goodness in Grandma's cakes.

Although these days I liked Pepsi Cola better than milk, I got a kick out of going with Grandma to milk the cow. I still remember the smell of damp hay I scuffled around in, trying to stay out of Hazel's way. If I stood behind her, she'd stomp, then swish me with her tail. That stung. If I stood too close, the cow got nervous, then couldn't, or wouldn't, let down her milk.

"Poor Hazel," I told Grandma, standing beside her on our front porch, watching Jim Jones and Daddy load the cow onto a drag, old Pet pulling the drag off to a side field where Ben and Frank, Jim's two sons, and Jim and Daddy dug a big hole and rolled poor Hazel into it. Like so many times I tried not to cry, thinking, *I'll never peer into her big old brown eyes again.* I hoped Daddy or one of the hole diggers would say something nice over her, before dirt hid her forever. I thought about the mule. Old Pet and Hazel spent nights in barn stalls next to each other. Reckon our mule knew, and felt sorry that poor old Hazel up and breathed her last?

Then, one morning Grandma said, "Little Bushy, come meet a new member of our farm family." I grabbed her hand. Skipping down our steps, I practically pulled Grandma over.

Whoa! There she stood, nibbling on dry, peanut hay, earlier forked onto the ground by Daddy. The cow tugged at the pile. Her brown eyes rolled in my direction like she thought I might steal her food.

Enjoying herself, our new Jersey wiggled her jaws up, and down, and sideways. Although a little girl, I already knew a cow's habit of swallowing a mouthful, then later, bringing it up to chew; the cud, Grandma called it.

Suddenly the cow slung its head toward me. She stamped her foot.

That old cow couldn't fool me. Cows didn't hurt little girls. At least Hazel never did. She just swiped her tail in my eyes when I stood where I shouldn't.

I reached for Grandma. "Poor cow. She must be scared to death. We're strangers.

"Look at her color, Grandma. Like pale, chocolate milk. Wouldn't it be great if her milk were chocolate?"

"I do declare, Sugar, you come up with the wildest ideas! I don't know about you, but I wouldn't like all my cakes chocolate, and I certainly wouldn't want chocolate butter meltin' into my hot biscuit."

"Let's milk her right now."

"Kelly Todd milked her before he dropped her off. He traded her for your daddy's old Model-A. Lucky for us that contraption held up long enough to get Kelly out the yard."

"I'd lots rather have this cow."

"We won't be able to go to Conway as often, but that car did jolt my rheumatiz."

"What's the cow's name, Grandma?"

"Bessie's a good name."

"Let's call her Petunia."

Grandma gave my rear end her usual swat. "If you knew what you wanted to name her, why ask me?"

The rails around the pen, originally covered with bark, had worn slick. I anchored my feet on the first rail and held on to the top, doing "jenny-jenny" squats. One, two, three squats. I could feel my blue pinafore, Mother made me last week, wave in my breeze.

Grandma said, "Hmm. "Don't know as we ever had a cow named Petunia."

Grandma moseyed across grassy, hard dirt toward our sandy yard. I followed.

"You always had cows, Grandma?" I thought she probably had, because Hazel sure liked Grandma.

Pushing back stray hair tickling her forehead, Grandma said, "Little Bushy, times have changed since I was young. Me and Hampie had a herd of cows, goats, sheep, all over the place. And hogs. We penned up our hogs. The other animals went and ate where they pleased. We had what was called open pasture, back when your grandpa and I were young."

"What's open pasture?"

"What it says. Nobody fenced in their animals. They roamed wherever they pleased."

"How did you know your animals from other people's?"

"We marked ours. Actually, our cows came up to the barn every day to be milked and fed."

"I bet those animals made a mess of the yard."

"No, Grandpa Hamp built us a picket fence. That's what kept out gators."

"Gators? Gators in our yard?"

"They tried that. Many's the morning we'd get up and see where an old gator, bent on wallowing a hole under the fence, had rolled against it."

"He was still there?"

"No." Grandma laughed. "His trail led there. You could see in the sand where he'd rolled and thrashed about."

That was a thought. "I'm glad we don't have gators anymore."

"We still have a few. Just not as many. They kept us awake some nights, bellowin'."

"Ooh. Scary!"

"Your Grandpa Hamp wasn't scared. Mad's more like it, the time an old bull gator set out to eat all his new pigs."

By now we'd reached the front porch. It was late March, and this day's warm air gave promise of weather to come. Grandma picked up a fan she'd left on the steps. "What does that say?" I pointed to the fan's big lettering.

"It says 'Goldfinch Funeral Home.'" Grandma fanned quick little puffs, occasionally sending some my way.

With Grandma sitting on the porch's edge, I plopped onto a lower step. That way I could look up and not miss an expression on her face, from the twinkle in her eye to the way the tiny scar at the corner of her mouth crinkled when she smiled. She looked at me, but I knew she was really looking at "back when."

"They were the nicest litter of pigs we ever had." Grandma's voice trailed off. "Seven, little round, butter-balls, all white with black spots."

I wished I could see what Grandma saw.

"One morning Hampie went out to the pen with a bucket of slop and found just six baby pigs. He looked everywhere, inside the pen, under the sow, the trough. One little pig had plain disappeared. Your grandpa wondered if our old sow, Mamie, had eaten her baby. He couldn't believe that. You see, Mamie was a good mother. Usually, if sows eat their offspring, it's because they're sickly or runty. These pigs were nice. They were fat."

"Did Grandpa find the little pig?"

"Not then, and a few days later, another turned up missing."

"You reckon the Big Bad Wolf got it, Grandma?"

"Not hardly. We had varmints, but no wolves. By this time your grandpa was worried."

"Were you?"

"Billie, you know very well I don't like that word, *worry*. Still, when you love somebody, their worries are yours. Anyway, another pig went missing, and another, until there was just one little pig left." Grandma shook her head. "Your poor old grandpa was so upset, he couldn't sleep. He told me he'd 'be die' if he didn't find out what happened to them pigs.

"The next night Hampie got up about three in the morning, got dressed, and snuck out to the hog pen. What he saw made him mad enough to chew nails!"

"What did he see?"

"He saw a big ole gator, the grand-daddy of 'em all, his front feet planted wide, and in his jaws, Mamie's last little pig, swung back and forth, back and forth. Your grandpa grabbed a tobacco stick and ran for that gator's snout. He beat that beast. He poked his eyes. Finally, using the stick, Hampie prized out the 'would-be' dinner. Hissing and thrashing its tail, that fat old gator turned and waddled off toward Cypress Pond, as fast as his short, stubby legs'd carry him."

"How was the little pig?"

"Dead, poor thing. I worried about Hampie. I was afraid he'd bust a blood vessel. He said, 'Net, find me some big fish hooks.' I was afraid to ask why, but he told me later, even when I put my hands over my ears to shut out what he said."

"What'd he say, Grandma? Tell me!"

"I might not should." Grandma shook her head.

She couldn't stop now.

"For what I'm about to tell you, Billie, you'll have to know, sometimes good people do bad things, and your grandpa was a good man. And he was a mad man. You also should know that a gator's a cold blooded animal in more ways than one. That beast shouldn't have killed Mamie's little pigs!"

"Grandma. What did Grandpa do?"

"He tied the dead little pig onto three big fish hooks and hung what that gator couldn't get a mess of right kadab over the center of Cypress Pond. Your Grandpa never did have the patience of Job, but this time he waited. And he waited.

"Time inched past. Finally, that pig-eater rose and swam as smooth as you please, over to the pig hanging just above that glassy water.

"Hampie watched, his trigger finger tightening. If the bait didn't work, he'd shoot that reptile's cold, glittering eyes clean out!

"For a minute, the gator lay still, resting beneath the bait like a rough, black log. Then, half his body lunged out the water. His jaws opened wide. He snapped on the pig, waggling it back and forth, back and forth. Finally, the pig slid far enough down his throat, Mr. Gator gulped his last meal.

"Hampie went into action. He'd thrown strong lines over and around the heavy tree limb supportin' the pig. Above the pig a'ways was another rope tied to the first, and your grandpa got hold of that'un. Now that old gator had nowhere left to go but 'the bad place.'

"His nose eased out the water; and he doubled up. Back and forth his tail beat. Hampie said that relative of Beelzebub looked like a giant worm, a'squirmin' on a hook. I'm sorry to say this, Billie, but your grandpa got pure satisfaction out of that thing's misery.

"Finally, after proving to the killer that eatin' his pigs was the foolest thing he'd ever done, Hampie tied the rope around a heavy stake, took dead aim with his rifle, and shot that Son of Satan right through the eye, killin' it as dead as a door nail."

I sat speechless. Didn't my card class teacher, Miss Julie, say "If someone does you wrong, turn the other cheek?" And Grandma. She never believed in harming a horse fly. That may be stretching it.

Maybe the same rules didn't apply to gators, especially one that killed seven of Mamie's little pigs. Something else nagged at me. "Grandma, how did Grandpa know he'd killed the right gator?"

"He knew all right. It was the biggest one ever seen around these parts. That gator had been lordin' it over Cypress Swamp nigh onto seventeen years."

I still had my doubts. I felt sorry for the gator.

"Anyhow, after that, some of Hampie's awful mad eased up. People from all over came to see the monster. He hung from that big limb over yonder." Grandma pointed to the oak tree limb my swing hung from. "He dangled right there until Hampie and your Uncle Boss skinned him and sold his hide. Bought a good boar hog with that money, too, your grandpa did.

"I've talked so much I'm ready for a drink of water. What about you, Little Bushy?"

Grandma and I went out to the back yard and pumped a stream onto the clump of red roses Aunt Minnie gave us to root. When the water turned cold, we each drank a dipper-full, then trudged inside. Comfortable in her easy chair, Grandma nodded off.

I wandered around outside, imagining what it would be like if Grandpa's giant gator crept into my yard. As long as I stayed in the swept portion, I wasn't *that* scared. Then, I ventured out a trifle further, past the pear tree, the out-house, through the corner of the corn patch, all the way to the edge of Cypress Swamp where weeds grew, and water from Cypress Pond turned the ground spongy.

What was that racket? Was that a gator, thrashin' in the bushes?

Spooked, I scooted back to my yard. I didn't want any pig-eating gator after me.

Chapter 10
Transplanting, Dancing, Cleaning, and Napping

Meanwhile, gator or no gator, bear or no bear, anxious to get the year's tobacco crop underway, both Mother and Daddy visited their seed beds. Soon they pulled back canvas to toughen up young sprouts.

Keeping close to my parents, I steered clear of bushes from which the bear's low moans sounded. Yes, I knew my bear was dead, but he could have brothers or sisters. And gators? If there were any, they lived in the opposite direction, behind our house.

Several times I trailed after my parents, checking on their plants' progress. As soon as the tobacco took on the right size and color, Daddy declared, "It's time to transplant."

Since Old Mary had foundered herself, Daddy hitched Old Pet to a plough and tilled the tobacco patch, split the rows, and fertilized, preparing rich soil for his prized new growth.

Papa and Mama Todd drove up in their humped-back Chevy. They'd come to trade work. Later Mother and Daddy would help them in like fashion.

Papa brought his trans-planter. This hip-high metal, funnel-like thing, charmed me. Remembering, I see it as a water-fillable, cylindrical chamber, bottoming into a tapered, fish-like mouth. That day Papa showed me how it opened and closed when he squeezed a lever located inside the thing's handle. I tried squeezing the lever. No fun. My hand was too small.

The planter possessed a second v-shaped opening at its top. I pestered Papa. "What's this?"

"That's where you drop in tobacco plants. Squeeze the lever, and the plant drops into the hole dug by this planter. It also spews out water to moisten the plants."

No one needed me today, but Mother said I could tag along to the fields, if I wanted.

In my young eyes, Papa and Daddy looked strong and manly, wielding their heavy trans-planters. They stood in the middles of adjacent rows and held their awesome machines in right hands. Into the waiting mouths of these shiny contraptions, Mother and Mama Todd "dropped plants," the name for this procedure. The women, arms full of young tobacco, faced and followed their men, who, with each plant dropped, took a back-step. The procedure went thus:

> Plunge pointed instrument into ground.
> Drop in plant.
> Squeeze lever, to plant and water seedlings.
> Pack dirt around plant with foot. The men's job.
> Back step to next hill.

I'd seen people square dance at Adrian on a Saturday night. "Mother," I teased. "You said Papa and Mama Todd wouldn't let you dance!"

"What's that?" Daddy glanced over at his father-in-law. "Maybe we should have Bert and Brook and Rob join us. Bring their guitars and fiddle. They could play 'Turkey in the Straw,' or some such piece. What do you say, Dot?"

"I say you're a big silly."

Mother couldn't fool me. She was having as much fun as the rest of us.

Old Pet hee-hawed and nodded his would-be horse face. He pulled a tobacco drag, (a sled) carrying a drum filled with water, needed to replenish trans-planters. The drag also held young plants.

Planting five or more acres of tobacco could turn into days of labor. If time passed with little rain, and our plants seemed to suffer, we prayed prayers similar to this:

> *Father in heaven, this fine day, in your infinite mercy, look down on these your lowly followers. You see our problem. We've planted these healthy tobacco plants, and we need them to live and mature. We're asking you; we're begging you. Please send us rain. Our crop needs to grow and flourish, not die in our fields. We come to you as humbly as we know how, requesting this in the blessed name of your Son and our Savior, Jesus Christ. Amen*

If, for reasons known only to God, rain was not forthcoming, and Daddy had used up all plants in his canvas-covered seed beds, he would visit Uncle Bert, Brooke Harris, or some other neighbor with young plants still in their beds. They'd share with Daddy enough healthy plants to replace those dead or dying.

You already know Mother's nature was to worry. Grandma would chide, "I'm here to say it again, Dottie, worry is another word for fear, and fear is the direct opposite of faith."

Mother's answer, "You're right, Ma," and she'd worry more.

With tobacco plants in the ground and flourishing, other problems arose. Mother drifted into the parlor, wringing her hands, biscuit dough still clinging to her knuckles.

"Rass, I'm afraid rain won't come soon enough. If it doesn't, we could lose every hill of tobacco we've slaved over. And right now the leaves are so pretty and green."

I thought, *Mother, don't get flour on the floor.* I grabbed my child-sized broom and swept up crumbs.

Sitting in her Damask chair in the jamb of the chimney, Grandma Nettie put forth another two cents worth. "I've told you over and over, Dottie. Trust in the Lord." Grandma rocked back and forth like her peach-colored chair wore rockers. Eyeing Mother over rimless glasses, Grandma shook her finger. "Just because it don't rain for a few days means nary a thing. But if you're that worried, go back to church. Ring the bell. Call our neighbors to pray. You know what happens when two or more gather together."

Mother sighed, probably tired of Grandma's piety. "Let's go, Rass," she urged. "Let's check on the Bay Swamp field. Look for cut worm signs I think I saw yesterday."

"Can't you rest a minute? I'm finishing breakfast." At the table, Daddy swiped a final morsel of biscuit into a mound of sugar, wet brown with coffee. "That tobacco can wait ten more minutes."

None too soon Daddy pushed from the table, shoved the straw-hat Mother placed into his hand onto his high forehead, and followed her out the door. They could be gone for one hour, or for several.

Years later when we were both adults, Mother divulged to me this tidbit. "Billie," she said, "you'll never know how much fun your dad and I shared on our trips to those woods enclosed tobacco fields."

Meanwhile Grandma and I moseyed into the kitchen. She poured boiling water over breakfast dishes stacked in the blue-speckled dishpan Mother bought, washed dirty dishes, rinsed them, and handed me plates, saucers, and cups to towel-dry. I used one of her many white sugar sacks she'd stitched into drying cloths.

Time to make beds. I trailed after Grandma. "Why do you shake sheets every time you make a bed?" I was anxious for her to finish. These were times she'd sit in her Damask chair and tell her tales.

I took along my broom and dust pan, sweeping sand off the floors. Grandma said, "You see now why I shake out sheets, Little Bushy."

"Our floors get sandy?"

"Give that girl five cents. This floor's as sandy as Myrtle Beach's grand strand."

I liked that Grandma mentioned Myrtle Beach. Less than twenty miles from Bug Swamp, the beach drew me like flies to a trumpet flower. I loved standing on the strand, ocean water swishing in and out, tickling my toes. If I stood in one place long enough, the ocean washed away sand from all around my feet, creating my own little island.

Grandma and I had swept floors. We'd made beds. With time to kill I stood on the porch's edge, busy at something Grandma said not to do. I swung my body around and around a front column. "Little Bushy," from inside, Grandma's voice rose and fell. "Can you reach under the bed and get me my easy walkers?"

I ran into our bedroom, and slid far underneath the bed. Like usual my tummy bumped cold on the flat linoleum. "Here, Grandma. You kicked 'em way under."

Sometimes Grandma took such a long time putting on her easy-walkers I did "jinny jinny" squats, waiting.

"Want to go get eggs, Billie?"

"Yes, Ma'am."

I trailed after Grandma Nettie down the back steps, past the pear tree in which sometimes snakes lived, on out to the chicken garden. She opened the gate and I followed, trying to keep out the way of pesky old hens brushing my legs. Grandma left the henhouse with more than enough eggs in her apron for a three layered chocolate cake. Umm. I could already taste that goodness.

Instead of setting out flour, butter, sugar, and eggs, Grandma said, "Let's us set a spell." She sank into her Damask chair.

A few years ago, fresh out of Clemson College and teaching agriculture in Waresboro, Georgia, Uncle Charles gave her that chair. I loved the shiny dark mahogany of its arms and legs as well as its silky covering. Grandma's baby boy gave all of twenty-some dollars for that chair.

I also loved Grandma's "Let's set a spell." I dragged the stool Papa Todd made for me close to Grandma's knees. I said, "Grandma, tell me more about Grandpa Hamp."

Recently I had grown more curious about the nice looking gentleman, especially since I learned he'd battled the gator. From his perch on the wall, he still looked into the distance at something I'd never see.

"What about Grandpa, Little Bushy?"

"The hand. You know, the hand."

"Oh, Billie." Grandma closed her eyes and drew in a deep breath. "Hampie always did say if there was any way people could come back from the dead, he'd do it. He'd prove to me he was living on in a better place. Not that I had any doubts, mind you. Anyhow, he said I should sit right here and look out this window."

Grandma placed her hand on the window pane beside her chair.

"Your grandpa said, if possible, he'd place his hand against mine, but on the other side of the glass. He'd stay outside, I guess, so as not to scare me."

"Did he? Did he, Grandma?"

"Night after night I sat here looking out this window. I never saw your grandpa's hand; but," Grandma added, "I've *felt* his hands."

"You have?"

"When he was alive, he'd tuck covers around me to make sure I was snug and warm. I'll tell you this, Billie. It might be my imagination, but many's the night I've been lyin' in my bed and felt them same dear hands, tuckin' my covers."

I leaned over and placed my cheek on Grandma's apron. Grandma's soft hand stroked my hair. I imagined hands from beyond smoothing covers on my dear grandma. Not in a million years would I like that happening to me; but, if it comforted her… I lifted my head. "Grandma, didn't you ever see Grandpa?"

"Maybe I did, maybe I didn't. One night me and your daddy were walking home from my pa's house. The moon lit up the sky to beat the band. We'd gotten just beyond the curve at the end of the lane, but we couldn't yet see this house. I was walking in one sandy rut and your daddy the other. Right then, we saw a man comin' toward us. From a distance he looked like he wore a suit and tie. He definitely wore a hat. I said, 'Rassie, is that Clyde Stevens, do you think?'

"Your daddy disagreed, 'No, Ma, he's too tall for Clyde. I think that's Fed Jones.'

"I said, 'Uh-uh. Fed's skinnier.'

"Well, we argued back and forth, trying to decide who we were meetin' in the dark, till we'd almost reached the man.

"Just as we were ready to step aside for him to pass, poof!"

"He disappeared? Where'd he go?"

"Seemed like he melted into thin air. Then, your daddy and I got to talking about how much he looked like your grandpa. Same height, same build. Your grandpa even had a suit like that. And the hat? Dented in and floppy just like your Grandpa Hamp's."

Little shivers ran up and down my spine.

"One thing your daddy and I never agreed on. I always said the man was walkin' in my rut, and your daddy said the man walked in his."

"Grandma, couldn't he have just stepped off the road into the bushes?"

"The laurels were mighty thick right there. If he hadda', seems like we would've heard branches rustle."

"You really think that man was Grandpa?"

"Honey, I don't know, but if the Lord ever did let me see him, that's the time."

It was still early morning. We strolled through the yard picking us a bouquet of pink crape myrtle and a handful of sweet smelling gardenias. Daddy had flattened out those gardenia bushes to hold Grandma's feather beds when they needed airing. After putting the flowers in water, we walked up the lane to the mailbox. Sure enough Grandma had another letter from Uncle Charles. She opened the mail, then stuck it into her pocket. "I left my glasses on the table."

While Grandma went inside and read her letter, I sat on the roots of our oak tree and looked toward the east. Grandma said someday, from that direction Jesus would come back to earth. He'd return for His people. He'd appear in the east, surrounded by His heavenly host. I figured I was one of His people, but I wouldn't want to go to heaven or anywhere much without Grandma.

Just as I was about ready to run inside, Grandma joined me. She reached under the porch and picked up a trowel she stored on a cast-off table.

Keeping to myself thoughts of Jesus' return, I followed Grandma to a side-yard flower bed. She said, "Let's us separate this white and red verbena."

The verbena hadn't yet bloomed. "How do you tell white from red?" I asked.

"Look at the stems. If they're green, that's white verbena; if red-stemmed, the flowers'll be red."

At noon Mother and Daddy came home for dinner. Grandma had warmed up a pot of collard greens cooked yesterday. Bringing in a cured shoulder from our smoke house, she hacked off slices and fried that.

I ate cornbread and stewed tomatoes. I hated old collards, and fried ham tasted too salty.

Today, instead of resting after dinner, Mother and Daddy took off for Adrian. Maybe Grandma and I could skip lying down.

"Do I have to take a nap, Grandma?"

"No, but you have to lie down."

"I'll stay in the house. I won't go outside."

"You'll lie right here beside me, Billie Hamilton. I won't have you wandering around while I try to sleep!"

"Oh, all right." I climbed over to the far side of Grandma's feather bed and dived under the covers. I peeked out. "Grandma," I said, trying to put off sleep. "I'm the Big Bad Wolf in Grandma's bed. You'd better run, or I'm gonna eat you up!"

Grandma patted the lump beside her. "Shut your eyes, child, or I'll gobble you!"

I tried not to move. Every time I wiggled, Grandma said, "Little Bushy, lie still!"

At last Grandma snored away. I stretched out long and looked up at the beaded ceiling boards. I counted ten boards, ten more, then ten more, before losing count. I couldn't blame myself too much if I couldn't count all those boards. I was a little girl, for pity's sake.

How could a house be so quiet? As if answering me, it cracked. Loud! Grandma's snores skipped a beat, but they came right back. I could have kept time to 'em.

I lay there until feathers turned into rocks. I felt as stiff as Grandma said she was. Trying not to wake her, I eased out of bed. Tip-toeing into the parlor, I climbed into her Damask chair, too deep for my short self.

The chair and room felt empty with just me there.

Uh-uh. There on the wall hung Grandpa Hamp. Next to him, Great-Grandpa Hezekiah Holmes stood with his hand on Great-Grandma Madora's shoulder. Grandma Nettie's daddy looked stern, but her mama smiled, just like she loved me. Next to them hung a picture of Great-Grandpa Bill Hamilton. His dark beard covered his whole shirt collar.

Grandma told me stories about Grandpa Bill. She said he had been so mighty, he could pick up an ox and set it on the other side of a fence. Why Grandpa was so fierce, one day when the mantel clock struck the noon hour, he shook his fist at the clock. After its eleventh stroke, instead of striking the twelfth, it hiccupped.

Oh-oh. That same clock sat right there on our own mantel, ticking right along.

I told myself, *these wall people are dead. They lie cold and still in the cemetery.* I'd seen their graves. But their eyes looked at *me* sitting in Grandma's chair. They gazed at *me* when I stood before their pictures. They eyed *me* when I put Grandma's big center table between me and them, behind the same table that was home to our heavy family Bible where lived Adam and Eve and that awful old serpent. And David and Goliath. Of course I liked David. He played a harp. But Jonah lived there too, and where Jonah was, there might be that fearsome great fish, and he swallowed people.

I needed to see something "ever-day," like blue skies and clouds and grass. I looked out the window.

The window! This window was the one Grandpa Hamp promised to come back to.

I ran. I threw myself atop Grandma.

She sat up, taking me with her. "Billie," she grunted. "What in Heaven's name?"

"I just love you, Granny."

"Well, turn me loose. We've been lying here awake long enough."

"But Grandma, you went to sleep."

"Did not. I never slept a wink."

Oh well, I was just grateful nap-time was over.

"Grandma."

"What, Little Bushy?"

"I'm scared."

I hadn't meant to say that. "Let's sit on the porch a while. It's a real pretty day!" I reached for Grandma's hand. Like usual she sat on the top riser, and I sat on the step beneath. Birds sang happy songs. In the chicken yard Mother's old biddies squawked at each other over a few pitiful worms. I was beginning to feel more normal, even a tad happy.

"Why were you scared, Honey?" Grandma's blue eyes looked serious.

"I don't know. I felt alone."

"Sometimes we have to remind ourselves we're never alone, even if we're stranded in a deep, dark forest with no member of our family within fifty miles."

"The Good Lord's with us. That's what you mean. Right Grandma?"

"I have one smart granddaughter! Now. About that cake. You feel like helping me bake three yellow layers topped with a pile of buttery fudge?"

I forgot about being scared. I said, "I'll break the eggs."

"Which would you rather do, Little Bushy, break eggs or lick the spoon?"

"Lick the spoon."

"I thought so." Grandma smiled so wide her gold tooth gleamed.

Too soon Mother and Daddy returned. They'd gone to Adrian to get more poison for their tobacco pests while Mr. Purley and Mr. Kelly still had some. That pretty Paris Green and pink Arsenic of Lead could disappear off a shelf before old Pet's tail could swish off a horse fly.

Mother thought they needed more poison. "I told you I saw other signs of cut-worms," she was saying as they walked through the doorway.

I planted myself in front of Daddy. He said, "Hey there, Little Chu."

I said, "Let me feel your pockets."

He grinned and leaned over. I poked inside his shirt pocket and found just what I knew I'd find. A handful of Hershey's Kisses. Yummy.

Chapter 11
Another Esau, About 1925

Grandma Nettie made chocolate cakes that cracked when sliced. My thirties and forties version of Captain Kangaroo, Sesame Street, and Mr. Roger's neighborhood, she kissed away hurts, told stories, and boasted Bug Swamp's softest lap. However, by my era, she had mellowed, I hear.

In 1905, during Grandma's twenty-fifth year, having given birth to three daughters in the prior nine years, her belabored ears heard a newborn's cry, then caught Sara Vaught's words. The midwife cried, "Hampie! Look! Nettie's had you a boy!" No queen mother could have been prouder. Eventually, that boy became my dad.

Growing up, Daddy basked in the adoration of his sisters and his mama, especially his mama. Then came that fateful day during his eighth year. He got out of bed, complaining. "Ma," he moaned, "I'm not going to school."

"You're not what?" said Grandma.

"I'm staying home today. I don't feel good."

"Rassie Bryan! Of course you're going to school."

Daddy screwed up his face. He said, "Ma, if you make me go to school today, I'll cuss!"

As the picket gate swung shut behind the small rebel, he stuck his nose back through white washed palings. "Dog bite ringtail!" He gritted mostly baby teeth. "I told you I'd cuss!"

That afternoon, doubled over in agony, Daddy was brought home by his teacher. Quickly, Grandpa Hamp loaded Daddy into his wagon, drove the wagon to Great-Grandpa Hezekiah's farm a half mile up the road, transferred Daddy to Uncle Bert's buggy, then drove the twelve mile journey from Bug Swamp to Conway. Luckily Dr. Joe Burroughs had just opened Conway's first hospital, for Daddy was sporting a ruptured appendix.

Dr. Joe saved his young patient. Since parents were not allowed to remain with their sick children, Miss Vic Long, a caring young nurse, looked after Grandma's boy. Still, the lad fell off his bed and broke open stitches, further pro-longing his stay. None too soon Daddy grew well enough to leave the hospital. "God spared this boy for a purpose," the doctor told my grandparents, and he presented Daddy with a pocket watch as a "going-home" present.

Forever after, Grandma hovered over Daddy. She coaxed him to eat. She begged him to curtail youthful activity. "Careful, son," she'd plead, when he rough-housed with his sisters, brother, and cousins.

On the morning of June 21, 1920, two months short of Daddy's fifteenth birthday, Grandpa Hamp died. "My love died on the longest day of the year," Grandma would say. Only Sally was married. Henceforth, Grandma dedicated herself to the task of raising her four remaining children alone.

Daddy's first grown-up girlfriend raised Grandma's hackles. I'll call this girl, "Priscilla."

At first, Grandma paid no mind to her dear son sauntering over to "the Smiths" on Sunday afternoons and not returning home till animal "feed-up" time.

Then came the box-supper school-breaking where Daddy, Uncle Bert Holmes, and a young Uncle Charles strummed guitars and sawed on fiddles for a cake walk. Priscilla stopped the music, won the cake, plus, during the auction Daddy bought her box, the patriotic one decorated in red, white, and blue crepe paper ruffles. At a corner desk, eating fried chicken with Priscilla, Daddy felt his heart leap, take off, and clean outrun his mama's apron strings.

One day while plumping her feather bed high, Grandma heard a car horn blow. Clemson (Clem) Proctor, the mail man, drove straight up to the door steps. He passed out a package through the car window, not before shaking the box. "Looks like R.B.'s got himself something here, Net."

"I'll be blessed if he hasn't!" Jam-full of curiosity, Grandma turned the package this way and that. She shook it. Daddy was busy ploughing new ground, opening up what would later become our Bay Swamp field. (The same field where decades later Mother and I heard my bear.) Certainly Grandma wouldn't stoop low enough to open her son's mail.

Finally, Daddy drove old Mary, whinnying, into the yard. Grandma rushed out. "Rassie! You've got this package in the mail. Reckon what it is?"

I know Daddy turned red. "Mama," he shuffled from one foot to the other. "That's my package. I ordered it."

"The address told me that." Grandma put on her sly smile, the one where her gold tooth gleamed. "You ordered something for me? My birthday was back in April."

Daddy squirmed. "No, Mama, it's not yours."

"Then whose is it?" Grandma's sudden anger crackled like a blaze in a tobacco barn. "Priscilla! You've gone and bought something for that girl when we don't have money for cotton seed!"

Fanning flies and her hot face with her apron, Grandma sank onto the front steps. "All my life I've washed. I've cooked. I've cleaned. I've scrubbed my fingers clear to the bone for you. And this is the thanks I get!"

That evening Daddy took Priscilla her pearls. She cried, "R.B.," and swooned in his arms. Priscilla's mother began to treat him like family and her father called him "Son." Matrimony loomed ahead like a red brick wall.

One afternoon in late August, Daddy and Grandma Nettie rode out to the Bay Swamp Field. Picking up loose sticks and roots, they piled debris into the wagon until both felt ready to drop. Daddy said, "I'm through for today. My stomach has done met my backbone." He drove the wagon around to where Grandma sat on a stump, staring down the length of her nose.

Daddy tried again. "Ma, time to go home."

Grandma might as well have grown to that stump.

"Ma!" Daddy said. "Let's go!"

Finally, Grandma spoke. "Boy, when you tell me you're not marrying Priscilla Smith, that's when I get off this stump."

Billie H. Wilson •

Daddy gritted his teeth, stomped around the field, maybe even said, "Dog bite ringtail;" but, he knew when he was whipped. "Come on, Ma," he said. "Cook me some supper. I won't marry Priscilla."

Thus, like Esau did with his birthright, Daddy sold out Priscilla for "a mess of potage;" and I'm glad, for if he hadn't escaped Priscilla, Dottie Lee Todd would never have captured him, and I wouldn't be writing this.

Chapter 12
Tobacco Barnin'

Thursday, July eighth, Grandma cooked me a birthday cake. At noon my family did take time to wish me a happy birthday, but little more. For months now they had devoted every waking minute, thought, and effort into poisoning, hoeing, and suckering this year's tobacco crop, preparing it for harvest. Friday afternoon Daddy stormed into the house. He slammed the screen door behind him. "Boi-oing."

Biting off the end of a thread from her sewing, Grandma asked mildly, "What's the matter, Son? Is that any way to treat your front door?"

Daddy plopped into the nearest chair, the wicker one with the pretty flowers. He bowed his head and ran fingers through his pompadour. He looked up and I saw anguish in his huckleberry blues. "I thought I had my hands all lined up," he shook his head. "Redmon King's boarder told me he could round up everybody I'd need to 'put in' tobacco. I just learned, that scamp caught yesterday's train, headin' straight for Chadbourn. I feel like wringin' his fool neck. He ran away owin' Redman a hundred dollars he borrowed last January.

"Where can I find help? By next week that tobacco'll definitely need sand-luggin'."

Mother came in from feeding the chickens. "Sounded like that door was about to fly off its hinges."

Grandma said, "Rassie's man's let him down."

"What man?"

"You remember Lonzie Gause? Redmon King's handyman?"

"I thought he was their boarder."

"He's nothing now. That man up and left Bug Swamp. And he'd promised to get me all the tobacco hands I'd need."

"Stop fussin', Rassie. You've got Jim and Izzie. Ben should be old enough to crop, and Frank can help at the barn or the field."

Daddy said, "You're right, Ma. I guess I'll go to Conway and drive around The Hill. Maybe I can find somebody not promised out for next week."

That afternoon Daddy chugged back into the yard, smiling like he drove a gold chariot. "I did it. I found plenty of help, two croppers and three barn workers. Since I do the dragging, I don't think we'll need anybody else." Daddy liked to go from field, to barn, to field, to see that things at each place went smoothly. "We'll barn next Tuesday."

Mother stopped short. "How much are we paying?"

"Three dollars a-piece to two croppers and two dollars for each of three barn workers. Jim and Ben can crop. This'll be Ben's first try; so, I've hired two more croppers just to make sure we get everything out the field."

My Jimmy's family were sharecroppers and weren't paid for a day's work. Like us, they received their pay at marketing time.

"Let's see," Mother said. "That's six dollars for cropping. We won't have to hire a stringer, since Izzie and I string. Frank's almost nine. He can hand on one side of Izzie, and hiring three handers'll cost us another six dollars. That comes to twelve dollars for one work day. Uncle Bert paid me seventy-fives cents a day, a couple of years ago."

"Times change," Daddy said.

"You think?" Grandma widened her eyes and made her mouth's sarcastic, upside-down "u."

That night after supper Grandma told me, "Little Bushy, fetch me the Bible."

In the center of our parlor floor sat a square, oak table. Atop the table lay a book so heavy, I had trouble lifting it. Beautiful pictures of angels, lambs, fancy chests, square-topped buildings and such, outlined by curlicue markings of gold, decorated this Good Book's pages. I considered that tome so sacred, Grandma surprised me when she let me touch it. That she'd let me fetch it meant real privilege. Laboring under the book's weight, I placed it on her knees.

Grandma said, "Fetch me my spectacles."

"They're on your forehead, Ma." Sitting in the straight-back chair with the deer-skin bottom Papa Todd made last winter, Daddy pulled in closer.

"Come on, Dottie," Grandma called to Mother. "Leave them supper dishes be till mornin'. This day The Good Lord has blessed us. Let's tell him we're thankful."

"Here, Rass." With effort Grandma placed the Bible into Daddy's hands. "It's too heavy for my bony knees."

Mother dragged over the light wicker chair and faced Daddy and Grandma. I climbed into Mother's lap.

Was it my imagination? Or was my mommies' lap shorter? (This took place four months before my brother was born.)

Daddy read, "Psalm 23: The Lord is my shepherd, I shall not want...."

After Daddy finished reading David's tribute, Grandma said, "You know, Chillern, our Lord sees to our every need. He comforts us when we need it, and he makes sure we have a safe place to have our being. He offers us a time to be quiet and still. He's beside us each step we take, showing us the right way to go and what to do when we get there. Even when things don't go as we've planned, even if it seems to us like we've hit a snag in our road, He's right there beside us. He says, "Keep going. Keep that chin up! You'll make it!"

Grandma took off her rimless glasses and cleaned them with her apron. "And then, if we're faithful in our doin's and give him our hearts, what happens when we're through with this old life?"

"What, Grandma," I said. "What happens?"

"We go and live with Him, Little Bushy. We go where we'll never grow old. Where we see our departed loved ones still living on in the prime of their lives. It's as simple as that. Now. You with good knees, get down on 'em. Thank your Maker that He's helped us through this day. Thank him for finding us help to gather our crops, and for everything else good in our lives. Thank him with all your heart and soul, for in the end, the Lord's all we've got, really. Everything else around us is like leaves, blowin' in the wind."

That last statement bothered me. I didn't like to think that everything but God was "like leaves, blowing ever which a-way."

After praying, we all went to bed. I lay still, thinking. "Grandma, I whispered, "I don't want the wind to blow away everything I like." Sometimes we did have heavy wind storms.

Grandma took my hand in hers, so soft inside it felt like velvet. "Little Bushy, I didn't say that right. What I meant was, no matter what goes wrong or right in our lives, God's always with us, ready to help. Other people might give up on us, might leave us to fend for ourselves. Not God. He wants to be needed. That's what I should'a said. Now, close your eyes and feel perfectly safe, for you've got God and me lookin' after you."

For what more could I ask?

Tuesday, the second week in July, our first barning day was upon us. Daddy got up first. Mother followed. Today we'd take a giant step toward paying off our mortgage, a word, long ago, wedging itself foremost atop Mother's mind.

As soon as I saw her, ready for work, I started pulling on my old red shorts.

"Billie, you stay here today," Mother said. "Help Grandma."

"I want to go with you. I can hand tobacco."

"Let her go." That from Grandma. "She won't get in your way. She can take her dolly. The way that child makes believe, you won't know she's there!"

"Can I bring my tricycle? Can I?"

"If you'll just ride it on the hard ground under the hickory tree."

I could go!

By the time Daddy got back from Conway with two croppers and three handers, Mother and I had hitched up old Pet, and using the drag, hauled my pretty green tricycle all the way to the hickory tree.

Almost twice as old, eight-year-old Frank joined me. He pushed me around and around the tree. I held my legs straight out from the trike's side, saying "Whee!" I liked Frank.

"Not so fast," Mother cautioned.

Approaching the barn, two fellows I'd never seen accompanied Daddy; also three girls, years older even than Cud'n Bertha Mae. I'd hoped Daddy would bring girls my age. My doll, Peggy Jo, fell into the dirt. I picked her up quickly and brushed her sandy face. "I'm sorry, Peggy. We'll have to play, just you and me, unless Frank pushes us some more."

Absentmindedly Frank reached for the doll, clutching it beneath his arm.

The fellows with Daddy looked like they'd come for fun. They were talking, and laughing.

"This here's Dewey Smith." Daddy indicated a tall fellow with a lot of dark hair, so curly, I couldn't see which end grew in his scalp."

Dewey tipped his hat, although he wasn't wearing one. Saying nary a word, he nodded at Mother and Izzie.

Jumping in front before Daddy spoke, a stout young man with a grin wider than his face stuck out his right hand and shook it with his left. "Call me Big Al." Pointing to a shy looking teenager with a lighter, cream-colored complexion, he said, "This here is Caldonia!"

Ben, sitting on the barn bench, said, "Just like the song."

"Yeah." Big Al grinned with all the teeth in his mouth. He threw back his head and sang, "Caldonia, Caldonia, what makes your big head so hard!"

The girl named Caldonia turned her whole body away from Big Al and looked down.

Mother jumped up from the bench and walked over to the girls. "Hello, Caldonia," she said. "Who are your friends?"

With no smile in sight, Caldonia looked up out of the corner of her eye and said, "This here's Dolly." Pointing to the third girl, about as talkative as silent Dewey, she said, "She's Emma. She's my cousin."

Mother said, "Hello, Dolly, Emma. Glad you're helping us today. Meet Izzie. She lives yonder." Mother pointed to our Snow Hill house.

Ben Jones stepped in front of his mother. "I'm Ben." He smiled like he liked what he saw.

"Be ashamed of yourself, Ben Jones, pushing in front of your mama. This boy playing with a doll baby, he's Frank."

Frank thrust Peggy toward me and went to counting sky clouds.

Soon Big Al and Dewey left for the field with Jim Jones and Ben. Daddy climbed into an empty crate and giddy-yapped Old Pet out to the field.

Mother and Izzie divided up the handers. "I'll take Caldonia and Dolly. You take Emma and Frank," Mother told Izzie.

"You sure you don't want Frank?" Izzie raised her eyebrows.

I enjoyed every minute of that Tuesday and was sorry to see it over. By the time the day ended I heard that Caldonia liked Dewey, that Dolly had a boyfriend working off the coast of Wilmington, NC, on a boat named The Gull. And Emma said, "I ain't never gonna marry any stinkin' old man."

A few years later, probably the first summer Grandma and Mother both wore mother-of-pearl pens to church, the pens reading "Remember Pearl Harbor," Caldonia worked for us again. I asked her about Dolly and Emma. She said, "Emma got married the very next summer after we worked here, and she and her husband moved to Detroit. Tommy works in a car factory there and they've got two little girls."

I guess Tommy was not some "stinkin' old man."

Dolly had enrolled at Benedict College in Columbia. She was too busy learning, to work at our tobacco barn. The fellow Caldonia was sweet on, Dewey, he'd joined the army and was fighting Nazis across the briny. Caldonia's eyes lit up when she talked about him. She didn't know or care what had happened to Big Al.

Back to that Tuesday in thirty-seven, before the workers had real ideas about their futures. The croppers had cropped, the stringers had strung, and the handers had handed a barn smack-dab full of tobacco. After that, all that was left to do was cure it, grade and tie it, and sell it; nothing much, you might say. Mother and Daddy would beg to differ.

Chapter 13
Curing Tobacco

In case you have little patience for technicalities, skip this chapter. If you're curious about the lost art of tobacco barn curing, read on:

In the thirties and forties, my dad heated his tobacco barns using long, rounded on top, wood-burning, brick and mortar furnaces. To begin curing his five or so acres of tobacco in July, the prior winter he and a helper would have cut and stacked several cords of wood. Supposedly fuel would last from primary tobacco gathering of sand lugs in early July, until August, when croppers popped off final tips, leaving nothing in fields but bare stalks and a few emerald-colored horn worms, futilely searching.

As soon as our barn was packed with precious, leafy green, Daddy lit a fire inside his furnace. For the next two days he kept close watch, making sure heat traveling inside the barn through big, round, metal flues arranged in concentric squares, never grew too hot to dry out any leaf beyond *the coloring stage*.

Just inside the barn's wide-planked door hung a thermometer. For the first thirty-six or so hours, Daddy expected to see that mercury registering somewhere between ninety and a hundred degrees, no more, no less. To do this he kept a low fire burning, with water nearby to douse the furnace if temperature inside the barn grew too warm. He liked hearing friends say, "That Rassie Hamilton sure can cure some fine tobacco." Really he sought to perfect the processing of each tobacco leaf. At the end of this stage he expected a product the color of a luscious, yellow lemon, showing off leaf ribs and stems still green with moisture.

Slow *coloring* released starches stored in green tobacco as sugar. This accounted for aromas, like those of an iron vat of boiling sugar cane turning into syrup, drifting out and mingling with similar fragrances emitted from barn after barn throughout our whole Bug Swamp countryside.

As long as Daddy used wood fires to cure his tobacco, he kept a bedroll at the barn. However, since at this stage of curing, temperatures remained low, Daddy slept parts of many nights at home. Midnight or so, if Mother thought Daddy needed a trifle more shut-eye, she'd slip out of bed, go to the barn, and make sure all was going well with their future mortgage payment. Many times Daddy awoke and joined her, he said to make sure Mother did his job correctly.

In a nearby room, Grandma and I slept on, she too old and I too young to concern ourselves with such.

After *coloring* his tobacco, Daddy saw to it that his lemony *yellow* color remained *fixed*. He did this by opening small windows near the top of the barn to let escape accumulated moisture. Then, he piled more wood into the furnace, for this next stage called for temperatures to climb from a hundred to one hundred forty degrees at approximately six degrees per hour. This process called, *going up on it,* resulted in leaves about eighty per cent moisture free.

Now, Daddy closed upper barn windows. He popped more logs into his furnace, further raising inside barn temperature at the rate of five degrees per hour, to as much as one hundred eighty degrees. Eight hours later, the barn full of once green, now yellow gold, reached its desired temperature. Daddy deemed this tobacco *cured*.

If all went well: if stems and leaf ribs dried out completely, if no sticks fell on the flues, if Daddy didn't oversleep and miss a vital temperature change, if rain didn't fall and mess up his drying stage, or if the barn failed to catch fire, (a decided risk) Daddy would douse the furnace fire, open vents and door, and leave tobacco in the barn overnight to absorb moisture. This rendered leaves more pliable and easier to grade and tie, the next event in tobacco's seasonal fiesta.

Cured tobacco weighed ten to twenty per cent less than its green weight, with a moisture content after curing of eight to eighteen percent.

I grew up hearing a story about Grandpa Hamp's barn, the one replaced by our "barn raisin'." It could've burned down in its prime.

This Coffee Pot Deserved its Place of Honor

One morning Grandma Nettie picked up the coffee pot from the stove, and coffee spouted amber streams in wild directions. "Rassie," she told my dad, "we need us a new percolator."

I pointed to our kitchen mantel. "There's one, Grandma." This pot looked pretty, blue-speckled, tall.

"I can't use that 'un. It belongs to Hampie."

"But he died, Grandma. He can't use it."

"It's still his. That pot's special. It earned its place right here on our mantel. I'll never perk coffee in it again, and that's the truth."

Daddy said, "There's a story that goes with this pot, Little Chu."

Mother's footsteps on the back porch brought on a crack, sounding like a loose board. *Daddy, when'll you fix that step?* Mother pushed open the door.

"Story?" Mother said. "Who's got time for stories? We've got us a barn of good looking tobacco to unload."

Daddy said, "Dottie, for once, forget tobacco. Sit down and listen. We're talking about why Pa's old coffee pot's special. I think I know, but it's been a long time since I even thought about it. Why, Ma? Why does it sit on the mantel?"

"Son, years and years ago, your pa and I were young people. Believe it or not, just like Dottie and you. And we raised our children by growing tobacco, just like you. Cured tobacco in that same old barn you replaced this spring with your barn raisin'."

"I'm sorry we lost Pa's barn, Ma." Daddy looked almost too comfortable in his maple rocker.

"Yeah," Mother said. "Every time I go to the mailbox I miss seeing it. It was a true landmark."

"Well, let me tell you, Chillern, that barn would'a been gone long ago, if not for this blue-speckled pot." Grandma wiped her hands on her sugar-sack dish towel.

The subject of tobacco "pushed to the back burner," Mother and I sat down. Like her, I rested my elbows on the kitchen table.

Billie H. Wilson •

Grandma nestled her bottom in the cane-backed rocker fronting the back, side-window. She smoothed stray hairs, anchoring them into her meager nape bun with her tortoise-shell hair pin. "Your grandpa was mighty particular about his tobacco curing. Instead of sleeping in his feather bed at night, like you do sometimes, Son," she eyed Daddy sharply, "Hampie took his bedroll and slept on the work bench under the barn shelter, for he had him one awesome furnace. You know that already. His furnace was made up of huge piles of brick, cemented together and mounded up almost like an igloo. It had to be big and long to hold the logs we dragged over and shoved in. And it extended several feet inside the barn where it met that whole network of flues. Why am I tellin' you this? You know how tobacco furnaces work. Anyhow, everybody knows flues are inside the barn so heat can move around even-like.

"But, let me tell you. High heat traveled around inside them flues. Fire, too, drying out and curing tobacco leaves hanging several tiers high, turning first the leaf, then the stem the color of gold; gold money, we liked to think."

Daddy chuckled, "We still think like that, Ma."

Grandma sipped from a glass of water since she had no coffee. Her wide wedding band glistened in the light. "Now, you already know your daddy didn't start out on high heat, curing a barn of sappy tobacco. He started it out low, dried it gentle-like. Then, when leaves commenced yellowing, he raised the temperature a little at a time, and watched for color change. After coloring, he piled on the heat, drying out swollen stems until there was little or no moisture left, just good old tobacco richness in them leathery leaves.

"Listen. Here's the story. Early one morning after Hampie had spent a sleepless night, 'goin' up' on his tobacco, I took him a pot of coffee. It was that very same blue enamel pot, full of coffee so strong it could've walked out there on its own. Hampie drank a cup or two and I set the pot on the furnace to keep warm. He yawned, and stretched, and said seein' how I was there, he'd run up to the house for a little shut eye, that he had the heat where he wanted it, and I should be able to keep it like that for a couple of hours.

"Now you know, folks, once a fire starts, a barn's a tinderbox, and fire was always on my mind. About every ten minutes or so, I'd open the barn door a crack to check the thermometer dangling. That room was so hot, it reminded me of Daniel's fiery furnace. Its blast of air about scorched off my eyebrows. If the temperature registered too high, I doused the fire with water from the nearby bucket. If too cool, I added another log to the furnace.

"This time I opened the planked door and saw what I'd always dreaded, a crack in the flue, and your grandpa at home asleep. Dark red flames licked out through the crack, shooting up toward tobacco leaves just a couple of feet higher. I closed the door. Gently. You know very well, a draft was the last thing them flames needed. Then, I dashed for the water bucket.

"Empty. What to do! The only liquid in my reach was the coffee in that speckled pot. Grabbing it, I whirled around. I opened the door. Flames shot up at the fresh air, but I turned that pot's spout onto the flue and poured me a slow, steady stream of coffee, trickling it out until the fire died down; went clean out. Then, I pulled the logs out the furnace and fetched your pa.

"He knew what to do. He rejoined the flue and finished curing the barn of tobacco, just like it hadn't almost burned to the ground.

"After that, I felt it my place to keep that blue-speckled pot atop the furnace, full of coffee anytime tobacco was a'curin', which I did. For years. Then, Hampie died."

Grandma gazed into that place I couldn't see. She said, "I look at that pot and I see my sweetheart sippin' his mug of black coffee. I look at that pot and I remember how it saved our tobacco barn and all in it. It just seems like that speckled pot stands for everything good in my life. Chillern," Grandma looked at all three of us, her triangular eyes the washed-out color of a faded blue shirt. "Hampie's sittin' right now with the Father Almighty; but as long as I'm sittin' here on this earth, I never intend to wear out his coffee pot."

Nobody spoke. Mother took the pot, washed it, and rinsed off suds. Carefully drying our cherished treasure, she returned the pot to its place of honor, the far left end of our kitchen mantel. Grandma stood beside Mother. Daddy joined the two, and I, never one to be left out, gazed at the pot with new admiration. Mother put her arm around Grandma and I reached for her hand. Grandma said, "It's a nice pot, don't you think?"

"Just another example of Bug Swamp's gold." Daddy turned to Mother. "And before you say a word, I know our Gold Leaf awaits in the tobacco barn. So, get a move on."

They were gone before I could say "Lickety-split."

Chapter 14
Selling Tobacco, Plus a Carnival

Next morning, after the cured tobacco had gathered enough moisture from night air that it felt pliable and ready for handling, Mother, Daddy, Izzie, Jim, Ben, and Frank unloaded the barn, wagon full after wagon full, and deposited Daddy's Gold Leaf in the barn loft behind our home. I wasn't allowed near so many workers. Grandma said I'd get in the way.

Now our family concentrated on once a week cropping for a couple of months until every leaf joined the others in their temporary home, the pack house. For this last phase of tobacco preparation Mother rolled up her sleeves. With sparkling eyes, she called in the troops, usually Papa and Mama Todd. Sometimes Grandma got into the act, but usually, she cooked dinner for everybody. Occasionally, Mother and Daddy graded tobacco and invited friends and neighbors to a tobacco tying. Many times we held those "parties" on our front porch.

I liked having everybody over. Daddy went to Arthur's store, or Adrian's store, or somewhere, bringing back enough Nabs to feed an army, along with Pepsi Colas, Coca Colas, Grape and Orange Nehi sodas, Royal Crown Cola, for those who didn't like the other drinks, plus Ginger Ales for one or two. Grandma parched peanuts. Sometimes she made taffy, although few people wanted to pull that sticky stuff and tie tobacco. Uncle Boss Hamilton's children came. So did Aunt Minnie's Bertha Mae, Leo,

Myrty, and Una. I mostly gazed at Bertha Mae in admiration, since she was older and about ready to start first grade.

Prior to tobacco grading, someone needed to unstring the leaves or "take it off the stick," a much easier job than green tobacco stringing. Gleeful that I was asked to help, too young to do it well, I stumbled around carrying armfuls of the dry stuff to Mother and Papa.

Daddy took pride in his curing and Mother in her grading. She'd make four piles, one for first grade, a pile for second grade, one for trash, and a fourth for green tobacco which nobody was proud of finding. If too many green leaves mingled, that meant curing hadn't gone well.

Papa Todd would watch Mother spread out a leaf, peruse it, and drop it into a selected pile. He might say, "Dottie, I don't think that leaf belongs in first grade. Put it in second."

Mother respected Papa's grading prowess.

When the piles grew large enough, tying began. Gathering a handful of stems about an inch and a fourth in diameter, Daddy or Mama Todd, whoever, would select an especially nice, pliable leaf, fold it in half, then double the half into a tie, wrap together the handful of stems, and fasten the end securely by tucking it inside the stem cluster. This was called a "hand of tobacco."

A fast tier kept a fast grader busy.

While earlier barn workers strung green tobacco onto a square-shaped stick close to four feet or more in length, the width of barn tier poles, peons like me, those too young to do much else, opened up the stem end of each hand of dry tobacco and placed it onto shorter, roundly sanded "grading sticks." This way, farmers more easily loaded tobacco onto their pickup trucks before hauling it to sales warehouses.

Going with Daddy to sell tobacco, a little girl like me had to be careful I wasn't run over, or at least stomped on. Trucks drove onto the wide warehouse floor. People swarmed like bees. And excitement! Tobacco-filled air sparked with it.

Tobacco handlers carried such long, hooked sticks, they could have been herding elephants. The men used their sticks to hook onto square baskets fashioned of thin strips of plywood they filled with circularly arranged tobacco. They shifted, they jockeyed baskets, turning wide warehouse floors into row after long row. At sales time an auctioneer, followed by buyers from various companies, Chesterfield, American, Phillip Morris, maybe Liggett and Myers which made Camel cigarettes, formed a procession down aisles between baskets.

Hearts in their throats, from nearby sidelines tobacco growers watched their financial fates unfold. The auctioneer, eyeing buyers, indicating by individual gestures whether or not either wished to purchase a particular basket of tobacco, jabbered his chant, concluding with, "Sold to American," "Chesterfield," or to whatever company purchased that tobacco pile.

It helped to know warehousemen. Once a friend of Daddy's said, "Today, I'll help you get a good price for your tobacco."

Picking me up, he plopped me onto Daddy's first basket. When the stream of auctioneer and buyers grew near, the warehouseman brought them to a halt. He said, "Listen here, Gents. You have before you six baskets of some fine tobacco. It belongs to this little miss sitting right here, looking at all of you with her big, blue eyes. You don't want to send her home disappointed."

Despite the fact I felt uncomfortable, plopped into the middle of a tobacco pile, as I recall, that day Daddy went home rather pleased with his sale.

If a farmer were displeased with his sales price, he "turned the tag." That meant he denied the sale, then consulted a handler, at this junction called a "hooker." The "hooker" used his hook to drag tobacco baskets to a row sales hadn't reached, and the tobacco resold. Some farmers kept hookers busier than others. A few seemed to feel that the next sale would prove magic, like I felt the day I went with Daddy to Conway's Spivey's Warehouse. The day before we'd ridden past the warehouse and a vacant lot sat beside it. Overnight, as if by magic, a carnival filled that lot.

Music from the carnival drew my mother and me like iron filings to a magnet. We left the warehouse and Daddy followed, stopping at the nearest booth. Tossing balls at stacked bottles, he failed to topple one, which would have given him, or probably me, a huge stuffed bunny.

Mother said, "Rass, I told you not to waste your money. You know as well as I do, these things are rigged. Those bottles wouldn't have tumbled down if you'd hit 'em dead on, which, I believe you did!"

Daddy shrugged.

In another booth a funny looking man with inky pictures all over parts of his visible body looked like he was poking needles into people. I even saw a man pay for that.

I was more interested in the stall that sold ice cream. I'd never before seen cones with tops so big, so round. By the time my hand held two dips of ice-cream atop a huge cone, my eyes popped and my mouth drooled. I was licking my way around it when Colonel Spivey, the warehouse owner, joined us. He said, "I'd planned to buy this girl, (me) an ice cream cone. Let me buy you one," the man with chest length white beard said to Mother.

"Thank you, Sir," said Daddy. "I'll buy my wife an ice cream. I'll buy you one, if you'd like. Chocolate or vanilla?"

Colonel Spivey shook his head. "No thanks."

Mother smiled behind her hand.

About that time the top dip of melting chocolate slid off my chocolate/vanilla cone. Before I had a chance to let out a "Waah," Colonel Spivey ordered me a fresh cone.

"Thank the nice man," Mother prompted.

"Thank you, Sir!" I meant that with all my heart.

Colonel Spivey was Horry County's last, living Civil War veteran.

Chapter 15
My Jimmy

Tobacco season, 1937, neared its end. The evening before our final sale, Daddy and Cousin Rob trucked what was left of our cured, graded, and tied tobacco to a warehouse in Tabor City, North Carolina.

Early next morning Mother, Grandma, My Jimmy, Daddy, and I climbed aboard our Model-A Ford and chugged-chugged up the Loris Highway to Tabor City. Jim's wife, Izzie, could have come with us if we'd had room. Before we drove off, she stuck her head inside Daddy's car window. "Any money you get that's ours, bring straight to me."

My Jimmy said, "I speck you should. I speck you should."

When we passed Loris, and Tabor City loomed ahead, I asked, "Can we go to the carnival at Tabor City?"

Mother gave me a pat. "Not today. They do sell ice cream, though. And peanuts."

Tobacco warehouses in general echoed with excitement, fear, and just plain busyness. Workers unloaded tobacco from trucks into baskets, constantly adding new rows to the many in place, repositioning any wayward baskets, with their long, pronged hookers. A few farmers looked happy. Others wore worry on their foreheads like newly-ploughed tobacco rows. These farmers had slaved away all season to put food on their tables, to pay off mortgages, to bring comfort to their families. Not that I thought of their emotions. Mine centered on two or three teen-age entrepreneurs, dancing up and down aisles and in front of on-lookers sitting in chairs against nearby walls. These young fellows tried to see who could shout loudest, "B'iled peanuts, five cents a pack!"

Beside one of these wall chairs I leaned against Grandma's knee. "Can I have some peanuts, Grandma?"

"You say you want penders, Little Bushy?" Grandma called all peanuts, penders. I don't know why.

"A Coca Cola?"

"Oh, all right."

Grandma snapped shut her pocket book. "What'll you want next?"

A woman sitting nearby on an overturned drink crate offered, "Over yonder they sell hamburgers and hot dogs." She pointed to the opposite warehouse wall.

"Not on your life, Young Lady," Grandma spoke out before I could even want. "It's too near dinner time." Of course our dinner time came mid-day.

About six basket rows separated Grandma and me from Mother, Daddy, and My Jimmy. Picking up tags to see how much tobacco companies were paying today, they walked behind a dozen or so buyers. Jim tugged on Daddy's sleeve, showing him what must have been a good sale. They both grinned.

I was glad to see My Jimmy and Daddy look happy. I'd loved both all my life. Daddy? Because he was Daddy. My Jimmy? Because Jim Jones excited my imagination. He stood about five feet tall, he was so black his eyes and teeth lit his face, and I loved him dearly, and while I called him My Jimmy, no way did Jim Jones belong to me. Nor was he a blood member of my family. I could claim only a spiritual connection.

Jim always found time for me. He called me "Little Miss." We'd sit, leaning against an oak tree, my bottom seated on a massive root. Jim would point to a floating cloud. "Little Miss," he'd say, "See that elephant?"

"Where, where?" Then, I'd see it, as clearly as if blobs of gray mist in the sky stood on hind legs and trumpeted.

"Look over there!" He'd poke a finger toward a toadstool, not there yesterday. He'd stoop and peer beneath the slight fungus. "He must'a left already."

"Who? Who left?" I'd say.

"Why Mr. Elf, the wee one hidin' out under here when it rains."

It had rained last night.

Jim had his faults. Izzie said so. She said Jim drank moonshine. I didn't know how he managed that, but if he *had* found a way to turn moonlight into juice, I wasn't a bit surprised.

In the warehouse Grandma and I still sat on the sidelines. For about an hour we watched people mill about. Then, here came Daddy, grinning and waving a paper.

Grandma said, "Son! Did it sell all right? Did you get as much as you thought you would?"

At Daddy's heels, Mother's bright face spoke before she did. "More! This was a better sale than I expected."

Daddy helped Grandma out of her chair. "Let's go find us a restaurant. Come on, Jim."

"Mr. Rassie," Jim hung back. "You know I can't go to a restaurant with you all."

Daddy and Mother looked at each other like they knew something I didn't. Daddy reached into his pocket and handed Jim a wad of bills.

Grandma, Daddy, and I enjoyed a great midday dinner of stew beef and rice, while Mother ate pork chop. When we returned to our car, My Jimmy was waiting for us. Grinning from ear to ear, he sat on the running board of our old Model A.

Time to go home. We piled into the vehicle, Daddy and Grandma in front, Mother, Jim, and I in the back seat. Jimmy started singing, "Shall we gather at the river…" I chimed in. So did Mother, Grandma, and finally, Daddy, bass voice booming.

At Green Sea General Store we stopped for gas. All of us except Daddy stayed in the car. He'd paid for his purchase and headed toward the car when My Jimmy poked his head out the window, attracting anyone nearby. "Mr. Rassie! Mr. Rassie!" Jim shouted. "Bring me some Devil Red Lye. We're gonna kill the chinches at my house."

Daddy went back inside the store and bought Jim some *Red* Devil Lye.

Finally, Daddy pulled into our own driveway beneath the cedar tree. Chin in the air, Izzie strode around our yard, just a'poppin' her frock tail. Jim struggled out of the car, and for a while Izzie turned her backside to him.

Daddy got out the car. "Izzie," he said, "don't be mad." Here's something for you. He produced what looked like a wad of money, and Izzie grabbed it quicker than Jim ever swatted a mosquito.

"I told you," she squinted at Daddy.

"Told you what? What did Izzie say?" I wanted to know why she looked so mad.

"Old man," I heard her hiss at My Jimmy as they trudged through sand, heading up to Snow Hill.

We were all tired after our day in Tabor City, but Mother wanted to count Daddy's money. They laid out bill after bill after bill! How much money did Daddy have? Mother said, "This looks like a lot, but there's still not enough here to pay off our mortgage. You'd better go see Burroughs tomorrow and work things out. Somehow," she added.

Daddy handed Grandma his treasure. She turned her back, pulled up her skirt tail, and tucked precious bills inside her money bag. Everybody in our family went to our personal banker for money.

At our house we had another money problem. Mother and Daddy knew rules of tithing. *You make money, you give God ten percent. That's his money.* Daddy thought God's ten percent should come off the top of earnings. Mother said God expected his portion to come out of "net" earnings, whatever "net" meant. I never knew how they worked out that problem. Grandma helped, probably.

A day or two after his ma took charge of our wealth, Daddy withdrew it. He whisked almost every penny of it to Conway, to pay Burroughs and Company.

After he left, Mother tried to make Mama Todd an apron, but ended up pacing the length of the house. "I hope that'll be enough money for this year. I hope they won't take our farm. I do hope Rass handles this right."

Shaking her head, Grandma rocked in her kitchen rocker, its squeaks, one long and a short. "Dottie, it won't do you a mite-a-good to worry yourself sick. Don't borrow trouble. You're 'too far along' to walk yourself to death."

I tugged at Grandma's apron. "What do you mean, Grandma? Where is Mother too far along to?"

"She's walked enough she should be in Conway by now, Little Bushy."

Mother came over to where I sat. She pulled up a chair next to me at the table. I was coloring a pretty red hen pecking at a lemon-yellow worm. I said, "See my picture?"

Mother didn't look. She stood up and paced.

Before long Daddy pulled up beneath the cedar tree. I ran to meet him, Mother close behind.

He looked happy, I thought.

Mother pushed around me. "Rass! What did Burroughs say? Did he agree to take what you could give him?"

"Yep. He didn't blink an eye when I told him we couldn't come up with all we owe. He said, 'There's always next year.' And I said, 'Sir, if I pay you this, I'm gonna need more credit the comin' year.'"

"Then what did he say?"

"He said, 'That's what I'm here for. When you aim to pay a debt, I'm ready to help. I don't need or want every farm in Horry County.'"

"See, Dottie?" Grandma said, "I pegged Mr. Burroughs for a reasonable man."

"Hmm." Mother didn't sound convinced.

Chapter 16
The Birth of a Brother, October 24, 1937

That Tabor City sale was not just our last tobacco sale of the year, it was the last important happening before another upheaval burst into my family's sphere. His name was Jack Edsel Hamilton, my baby brother. He dropped in out of nowhere and usurped both of my parents, especially Mother.

At our new family member's arrival, I had lived in this world for four years and three months. Neither Mother, Daddy, nor Grandma Nettie considered it "proper" to tell a child my age her mother was "expecting." Really, that wasn't necessary. Doctors found babies peeking out of hollow logs. They put the babies in their black satchels and took them to their mothers. Izzie said so.

The day before this cataclysmic event, Mother said, "Come on, Sugar, let's go for a walk." Mother felt restless. Older, I learned she thought walking over the farm might help bring on labor.

What a magical October afternoon! Leaves normally green were turning yellow, orange, and red. Skipping along the ends of ploughed rows, I gripped Mother's hand. Yesterday Daddy had seen a wildcat lurking right here at the edge of this swamp.

Passing fields of tobacco stalks I'd watched planted and cropped, we soon reached cleared swampland where our weird plants resided. I fooled a Venus Fly Trap, late in the season, into snapping shut. I trailed bits of straw along its still ticklish, pink inner hinge.

Mother waited while I chased stray butterflies. Recently we'd had rain. I stooped to peek under new toadstools for stray elves. Going home, Mother said, "Billie, when I was in the fourth grade, I wrote a story. Want to hear it?"

"Yes, Mommie."

"My brownie's name was Jo Jo."

"I like that name. What's a brownie?"

"A brownie is a kind of mischievous fairy creature. Irish people tell stories about brownies."

Mommie stopped in her tracks. "Mama Todd's great-grandparents came from Ireland! I bet that's why I wrote about a brownie.

"Anyway, Billie, this is my story, and since it's mine, I'm putting myself, Papa, and Mama into the story. Understand?"

I wasn't sure, but I was eager to hear it. Mother talked as we walked. I held her hand.

"No one in my family knew about Jo Jo. (Remember, Billie. This isn't really true. I wrote this story.) Anyway, Jo Jo hid things. Papa would get up in the morning and say, 'Where's my shirt? I hung it right here last night.' Behind the door, Jo Jo would snicker. Papa thought I laughed, and I let him, for I liked Jo Jo. He was my friend. We played hop scotch. We picked wild flowers. We tickled each other's toes.

"One day Papa said we had to move to another community. He and Mama packed everything we owned into a wagon. Papa hitched up his mule and we climbed aboard. Soon, we reached our new home.

"Papa and Mama unloaded our possessions and placed them into our pretty white house with green shutters." Mother squeezed my hand. "Like you, I wanted a white house with green shutters.

"Inside my bedroom next to Mama and Papa's room, I looked for my dresser. 'Where's my dresser, Mama?'

"She said, 'It was so old I left it behind.'

"I burst into tears.

"Mama tipped up my chin. 'What's wrong, Child?'

"I said, 'Nothing.'

• BUG SWAMP'S GOLD

"Mama and Papa never knew. I couldn't tell anyone I'd hid Jo Jo in my dresser drawer. Grown-ups don't believe in such.

"I missed Jo Jo, but comforted myself by thinking about another little girl finding him and loving him like I had. That's the story."

"You really had a brownie named Jo Jo?"

"No, Honey. I made him up. He's a part of my story. My teacher gave me an A."

I still couldn't believe Jo Jo wasn't real. I told Mommie, "I'd like a brownie named Jo Jo."

She laughed and ruffled my hair.

That night I slept with Mother and Daddy. Before daylight someone disturbed my nesting place. I opened my eyes. There stood Papa Todd, smiling. He said, "Wake up, Sleepy Head. We're going to Papa's house. This is a day you'll long remember."

Light hurt my eyes. I flounced over and burrowed under the sheet.

Mother pulled back the cover. "Wake up, Billie. Papa'll take you to see Cud'n Ted. She has little girls you can play with."

Daddy chimed in. "Come on, Girrurs, let Daddy put on your clothes."

They'd ganged up on me. I hated to leave Mother. When she kissed me goodbye, uneasy feelings stirred my heart. Something not quite right here was happening.

Papa carried me to the door. I turned to wave bye. I couldn't help saying, "Mommie, your face is white." In contrast to her dark curls, Mother's face looked as snowy as the pillow she leaned against.

Stars glittered in the sky as Papa and I climbed into his 'thirty-six Chevrolet. He drove us to Adrian to his house.

He helped me out of the car. I pulled at his shirt. "Papa, why did Mama stay at my house?"

"Big girl, I traded her for you. Want some breakfast?"

I watched while Papa fried ham slices and stirred up flapjacks. He flooded my flapjacks with cane syrup, just like I liked 'em.

After breakfast Papa took me to Adrian general store for a Johnnycake, a saucer-sized sugar cookie with a hole in its middle. I liked Mr. Kelly, the store owner. I liked the way his blue eyes twinkled. I liked his hair as white and light as a baby's. He slid a wide-mouthed jar across the counter and said, "Reach your hand in there and get you a Johnny Cake."

Refusing payment from Papa, Mr. Kelly shook his doddering old head. "No, no! That's my present to Blue Eyes!"

I enjoyed trips to Adrian. Mr. Kelly kept interesting creatures, sometimes in a cage, sometimes wandering around out back. Once he trained a chicken to count. He caged up raccoons and rabbits. He even split a crow's tongue, saying that would help the crow to talk. Today, Mr. Kelly became a statue for a gray squirrel. The furry little fellow ran up Mr. Kelly's pants leg and perched on his shoulder. There it sat, bright eyes staring into mine. Using tiny, hand-like paws, it cracked a peanut in its teeth, ate the meat, and tossed away the shell, immediately reaching for another.

Too quickly, Papa said, "Let's go see Cud'n Ted."

Ted Causey was Mother's first cousin. Ted and her husband, Anson, had two older daughters and a baby girl, Sally Belle.

"This is not good, Papa." I just knew Ted's daughters would boss me around.

Papa simply handed me over to Ted, with or without my consent. He said, "Sugar, I have to go now. I'll be back before long." And he left.

I didn't know the meaning of the word, indignant, but that's what I felt. I'd been jarred awake from a sound sleep, kidnaped from my warm bed. Now, Papa, the culprit, was abandoning me to people I barely knew.

In the middle of that thought my two cousins grabbed my hands and whisked me out the back door into their, their *gourd* patch! Vines grew all the way to their back porch steps.

Gourds. All shapes. All sizes. All colors! I stared at a sight I'd seen never before. Round gourds, long gourds, crooked gourds, yellow, green, orange gourds, all peeped out from amongst lacy, green leaves, like they wanted to play hide and seek. And I'd thought Daddy's water melon patch neat. Papa had left me with Cud'n Ted, and I'd stepped straight into the pages of my Mother Goose book.

And I was wrong about Marie and Loraine. They didn't boss me at all.

Ted brought us three of Sally Belle's blankets. We wrapped them around hard, hollow, rattling shapes, pretending the bundles were real live babies. Small, round gourds we rolled and tossed to each other. That leafy patch seemed a magical kingdom, alive with treasure.

Cud'n Ted knew what was happening at my house. She brought out Sally Belle and very carefully placed her baby into my arms.

For a bit I sat stiffly. My arms felt full; but Sally was a pretty, sweet little thing with big blue eyes and yellow, peach-fuzzy hair. I liked that Cud'n Ted thought I was big enough to hold her baby. Tiny hands reached for my nose, and something stirred in my heart. I looked up at Cud'n Ted. "This baby's sweet. I'm calling her Peggy Jo. After my stand alone doll."

Oddly enough, the name I gave Sally Belle took hold. Thereafter, she became Peggy Jo. Too soon Papa returned. "Let's go home, Sugar Foot."

Regretfully I said goodbye to my cousins and all of our "gourd babies." In the car Papa said, "I know a surprise. Guess what's at home, waiting for you."

I swallowed a yawn. "A new baby doll? A brownie?"

Papa frowned. "A brownie? A lot better than that. You have a darling, little, black-haired baby brother. He's waiting to meet you for the very first time!"

A baby brother? That jarred me. "I don't want a baby brother!"

I'd seen all the time Cud'n Ted spent with Sally Belle, or rather, Peggy Jo. My mommie's time taken up by a squealing little interloper? No-sir-ee bob-tail!

There must be a way out of this. I could think of just one solution. "Papa, we'll feed him to the gators."

Looking at me as much as the road, Papa pushed my hair back. He frowned. "No, Sugar. You wouldn't want to do that to a sweet, helpless, little baby. That would be terrible!"

He was right. We couldn't throw a baby to alligators. I felt helpless. There was absolutely nothing to do but try to make the best of an awful situation. *One thing, though,* I thought, *baby or not, don't think you're stealin' my mommie!*

Back home, relatives flew around just like something important had happened. Mama Todd, arms full of a soft-looking, blue bundle, came toward me.

Scooting past Mama and her bundle, I made a bee-line for Mommie. I scrambled onto the bed where she lay, propped on pillows and looking tired; however, not too tired to return my kisses, several of them.

Mama Todd brought Mother and me her blue bundle. Together, we counted ten pink little toes, and he had the same number of stubby little fingers, which for some reason, curled around mine!

I couldn't believe I'd ever wanted to throw this helpless, sweet little doll to old gators. I felt ashamed of myself.

Every inch the big sister, I said to Mama Todd, "Mama! My baby's hungry. Bring me a bottle and I'll feed the little thing!"

Wonder if, unlike my birth, Mother and Daddy planned Jack's so it wouldn't interfere with tobacco season? October was a month when few of Daddy's chores centered on our prize crop.

Jack entered our household October twenty-fourth. Soon Halloween would roll around. However, on this day Mother felt like celebrating nothing. She had a hot fever.

Daddy sent for Uncle Hal. He drove up in his little two-seater, hopped out, and took our steps two at a time. I felt awe for this boisterous great-uncle. He seemed to fill whatever room he entered. He looked at you, yet beyond you, like he had things other than you on his mind.

Uncle Hal taught Daddy fourth grade. Apparently this doctor/teacher had been a strict task master, for in his presence, Daddy always seemed on edge.

Actually, when Uncle Hal took Daddy's blood pressure, it shot up. Uncle Hal thought his nephew had a heart condition. After all, didn't weak hearts run in the Hamilton family? "Hamilton's fall dead," was what I heard from older uncles, aunts, and cousins. I prayed that didn't apply to my daddy.

By this first week in November, I was used to visitors popping in, oohing, and aahing over my new family member. Most of the time I could have been a fly on the wall. I'd be mighty glad when my mother felt better.

I heard Uncle Hal tell Grandma, "Net, I'm beginning to think there's something inside Dot that didn't come out with the after-birth."

After-birth? What was that?

Uncle Hal said, "I have an idea. The next time Dottie starts to cramp, fill a slop jar with boiling water and have her sit on it."

Years later I learned that after sitting on the slop jar, something fell out of Mother, into the pot. Daddy said it looked like a piece of liver. Grandma said it was part of the after-birth, whatever that was, but as soon as Mother passed the infectious thing, her fever ebbed and she perked up. Still, her recovery took longer than we liked.

Grandma showed Uncle Hal her knee. She pulled down her stocking. "What do I do with this, Hal? It stings and burns something awful. It even hurts to bear weight on my foot."

Uncle Hal gave his sister an "Unction" of something or other to apply twice a day, and told her when pain became severe, to apply hot poultices to her knee. Daddy found a substantial tree branch and whittled Grandma a cane. Using this, she hobbled around, cooking and helping with the baby.

Of course I was always underfoot. It was, "Bring me a diaper, Little Bushy. Hand me that talc. Call your daddy. We need a bucket of water."

One day Daddy came in from feeding Old Pet. Daddy shoved a kitchen chair so hard it almost fell over. He spit out his words. "Ma, I'm so mad I could chew nails."

This wasn't like Daddy. "Why? What's the matter?"

"Hogs. That's what's wrong. Gimp's hogs. He won't keep 'em penned up. They got out and dug up our turnips. Ate a bunch of 'em. I went over and told that man to come get his hogs. He said he would, but no, they're still out. They'll dig up our whole garden. I'll give Gimp one more chance. Then, if he won't come after his pigs, I'll pen 'em up myself."

Hearing the commotion, Mother came in from the parlor. "I wish I could help, but I don't work with hogs. Now that Jim moved, you've got nobody."

According to Izzie, a man over toward Shell offered them a better living than we could. To our sorrow, the Jones family moved away just before my brother was born.

"I'll go get Leo." Daddy was out the door.

Next day, after Gimp said he still couldn't round up his hogs, Daddy and Leo penned up all six: one boar, two sows, and three "shoats."

Baby Jack was three weeks old when the following transpired. A couple, I'll call them Scarlett and Gimp Roberts, lived on property adjoining ours. That property line brought us continual problems, and while Gimp seemed like a nice person, Scarlett was a spitfire.

That's what Grandma told Mother one day when she thought I was someplace else. Spying me, she clammed up. Then said, "Go play, Billie."

Scarlett was very pretty, I thought. Secretly, I wished Mother looked like Gimp's wife, so strapping and healthy looking with her rosy cheeks and reddish brown hair. And her lips always glistened bright red, like after she put on lipstick, she greased her lips with butter, maybe axle-grease.

Grandma said of Mother's slow recovery after my brother came, "Before this baby was born, Dottie worked too hard."

Why should working hard before Jack was born affect Mother? He'd been nowhere in evidence until Uncle Hal brought him in his satchel.

My primary knowledge of baby sources came from Susie Jones' visit home while her parents still lived in our Snow Hill house. For too long that day I waited on Izzie's porch for Mother and Grandma, inside with Susie. Sometimes inside got noisy.

Finally, the door opened, and there stood Izzie, holding a baby, wrapped in a blanket.

"Where'd you get this baby?" I hadn't seen it earlier.

"I went out walking." She gestured toward the road we'd walked up. "This sweet baby girl was tucked into a hollow log, as pretty as you please."

"Near the bridge?" I'd seen a hollow log near there.

"You're exactly right."

"Can I name her?" At Izzie's nod, I said, "This baby's name is Bobby Jean. That's after my number one doll." Later I re-named Cud'n Ted's baby, Peggy Jo. She was my second dolly. I liked naming babies.

Anyway, here was Jack, three weeks old, and still Uncle Hal said Mother should get out of bed only when necessary. With Mother sickly and busy with my new brother, Daddy and Grandma looked after me, although Grandma was anything but swift with her sore knee.

One morning Daddy helped me pull on my clothes and we set off for Arthur's store. Riding down the lane in Daddy's newer Model A, the one from Bayboro, we met Scarlett, walking fast. "Daddy," I asked, "why's Scarlett's face red? I waved and waved and she never waved back."

"No great loss." Daddy shifted gears. "Don't worry your little head over her."

Arriving at the store wiped my mind clear of Scarlett. I saw people I hadn't seen in a while. Some asked me about my new baby brother and how Mommy and Grandma were.

There was the woman with the big stomach, which wasn't big anymore! She must have cut out Pepsi Colas. Mother said that's why her stomach stuck way out.

Look! The woman had a baby! I touched the infant's hand, and like my baby brother's, his fingers curled around mine. "Odell's my little sweetie," his mother said.

That's when Daddy brought me our special, potted meat on sweet crackers. "Yummy!" He always bought me that at Arthur's store.

Returning home, we met Scarlett, heading home. This time I didn't wave. I stared. Scarlett's face flushed as fiery red as her name, and her hair looked like birds built nests in it. But her clothes really caught my eye. Her blue shirt and brown-flowered skirt were torn and hanging.

I said nothing. I was too shocked. Neither did Daddy. He gunned the car's engine and whirled into our yard. He opened the car door and took the front steps three at a time.

I fumbled with the door handle and climbed out. I heard his raised voice before I climbed the steps and walked through the doorway.

There, in our parlor stood Grandma and Mother, both looking as bad off as Scarlett.

Grandma seemed all excited, and like Scarlett, her hair flew all over the place. Mother clutched my baby brother like she'd never turn him loose.

Scarlett must have known Mother wasn't the only female "on the lift" in our household. Everybody else knew.

"What happened, Ma?" Daddy asked.

"Scarlett happened. She stormed in here with nary a word. She certainly didn't knock. She said, 'Nettie, where's Dot?'

"I told her Dottie was with the baby. I said, 'She's with the baby, Scarlett. What's the matter with you?'"

"'I'm here to get our hogs back, Old Woman!'

"She had the audacity to call me 'Old Woman!' I answered her right back. I said, 'Scarlett Roberts, you'll get them hogs just as soon as you and Gimp pay for them turnips they gobbled up.'

"She screamed. Right in my face. She said, 'They're our hogs! We're not payin' for what's ours!' Then, she spied Dottie. Scarlett blared her eyes till I thought they'd pop outta their sockets. That huzzy raved, 'Sneak-thief! Put that baby down. I'll teach you a thing or two!'"

Grandma laughed. "We taught her something, didn't we Dottie? Anyhow, Dot laid the baby on the bed just before that maniac grabbed your wife by the hair of the head and shook her so hard, I plumb heard her teeth rattle. Scarlett flung Dot clear across the room."

Grandma sounded like she enjoyed the fight.

"While Scarlett was shaking Dottie, I ran up behind that 'scarlet' woman. I threw down my stick. I yelled, 'Turn Dot loose, Jezebel!'

"Scarlett was just a'grittin' her teeth, shaking herself like one of her old sows. She squealed, 'Get offa me!'

"By this time Dot was a'squattin' in the corner, but you should'a seen me! I was on that old gal's back, just a-see-sawin' her this way and that. I said, 'I thought old Jezebel was dead and gone. I thought she fell out the window and broke her neck.'

"When one fistful of hair ripped out, I eased my fingers up and grabbed another.

"By now I'd see-sawed that old gal all over the front room and out onto the porch. Her eyes were pourin' tears. She sounded just like one of their old hogs stuck in a fence.

"She begged, 'Let me go Miz Nettie! Let me go! Please!'

"So now, I was Miz Nettie. Not 'that Old Woman.' I decided to oblige. I slid off her back.

"By now Dot had regained her senses. She ran onto the porch and pushed Scarlett down the steps. I won't tell you what your wife called her, but she said, *'Blankety-blank*, go home!' And did that old gal hit the road!"

"Grandma," I said, "why would Scarlett act like that?"

Grandma said, "Honey, most every community has its 'bad apple.' I guess Scarlett's ours."

"She's Gimp's, Ma, not ours," Daddy said, "and if you ask me, that 'bad apple' is rotten to the core!"

That's when my new brother claimed everyone's attention. He yelled to the top of his baby lungs. He'd been ignored long enough.

Daddy still held onto Gimp's hogs. Grandma said, "Son, keepin' them old hogs here is sheer nonsense. You don't want 'em. Who's feedin' 'em?"

"We penned 'em up close to Gimp's line. I told him if he wanted his hogs fed, he could feed 'em. I just want my garden to get a start without pigs nosin' around in it."

A short time later, paper in hand, the sheriff drove into our yard.

"Hey there, Boy," Grandma greeted him. "How's your family?"

"Fine, Miz Nettie. But it's not my family I'm here to talk about."

Grandma asked, "Why did you come, Son?"

"I'm serving Rassie, papers."

Daddy walked around the corner. He said, "What kind of papers?"

"A summons." The sheriff rifled through a file. "You're to appear in court before the end of this week."

Daddy sighed and shook his head. "I was wondering when we'd get to this."

That Thursday morning Mother, carrying Baby Jack, Daddy helping Grandma, since her carbuncle was still trouble, and I, holding onto Daddy's other hand, climbed many steps up the front of Horry County's imposing court house.

Spying a man wearing dark glasses and selling odds and ends behind a counter in the hall, we stopped.

Daddy slapped the man on the back. He said, "Hey there, Andy! How you doing? You take any wooden nickels lately?"

Grandma said, "Rassie, be ashamed of yourself. Pay him no mind, Andy. He's not responsible today. Gimp's takin' him to court."

Andy laughed. "It's his hogs. I heard. Gimp and Scarlett stopped by earlier. They're already inside. Let me know how things turn out."

"Who was that?" I whispered to Daddy.

Grandma heard my question. "That's little Andrew Hamilton. He's younger than your daddy, but he used to come over and spend the night. Tell you about him later."

We went inside, and Daddy spoke with some man who sat down near us. Opposite us sat Gimp and Scarlett. Neither looked our way.

The judge studied papers in front of him and asked Daddy, "Why did you pen up this man's hogs?"

Daddy said, "Because Gimp wouldn't. They'd eaten a whole bunch of my turnips, and I was afraid if they roamed around loose, they'd finish off the rest of the garden."

"Did this man know his hogs were on your property?" the judge asked.

"Yes-sir," Daddy nodded his head. "I went over and told Gimp. I asked him to round 'em up and take 'em home."

"Did he?"

"No-sir."

"Did you pen up your hogs, Mr. Roberts?" asked the judge.

"No-sir. I couldn't get 'em home."

Scarlett nudged Gimp.

"I tried. I tried coaxing. They wouldn't come. Last Saturday, by the time I got somebody to help, Rassie here, he already had 'em penned up, and said I'd have to pay for the turnips they'd eat, if I took 'em home."

The judge said, "Sounds about right to me."

Mother whispered to Daddy, "Aren't you gonna tell the judge how Scarlett came into our home and attacked me and your ma?"

Daddy shook his head. Apparently divulging that tidbit had been unnecessary. The judge fined Gimp for allowing his hogs to roam free, and also charged him court fees. The Roberts were still busy when we left.

Down the hallway Grandma spoke to Andy. "Things went just like they should, Son," she patted his hand. "Tell your Mama Grace to have somebody bring you two to see us."

"I will, Aunt Nettie," said the man called Andy.

In the car home, I asked, "Who is Andy? Why does he wear shades indoors?"

Grandma said, "I'll tell you all about Andy. For now, you just be thankful everything at court turned out right."

Daddy said, "I can't wait for Gimp to take his old hogs home. I hope I never see hide nor hair of 'em again."

Grandma said, "Makes me so sorry for his poor dead mama. She was a sweet, sweet woman."

In the back seat, I stood up and tapped Grandma's shoulder. "Tell me why he wore shades inside."

"Who? Andy? He's blind."

Mother said, "Sit down, Billie Faye."

Grandma's answer created more questions nobody seemed in the mood to answer. We continued home. Jackie-Boy slept. I counted houses the mile between the church and our house.

There were five.

Chapter 17
A Five Year Old's World

After my brother joined our family, he kept Mother occupied. Busier than ever, Grandma told fewer stories. I felt bored, bored, bored. I'd turn five in July. If Mother talked to Mrs. Evelyn Holmes, Bug Swamp Elementary School's first grade teacher, maybe she'd let me go to school this fall. I'd turn six next year.

I pestered Mother. Finally, she spoke to Mrs. Holmes. Mrs. Holmes said, "No."

I walked around the yard kicking up sandy mole trails. I picked flowers and looked at veins in their petals. I watched old bumble bees fly in and out of the nests they'd bored into the soft brick of Grandpa Hamp's ancient chimneys. Grandma came back from the mailbox. She said, "Your Grandpa Hampie sunbaked them brick up there on Snow Hill."

I looked for snakes. One day I bumped my head on a skinny green snake dangling from a crape myrtle branch. Another day I played with some yellow vine that Grandma said, if you pulled off a piece, threw it over your shoulder, and a new growth appeared where you'd thrown it, the person you loved would love you back.

I threw the vine over my shoulder and watched for new growth, although I didn't love any old boy. For pity sake, I was just five.

I did kind-of like Billy Harris. I'd heard tales about his adoption five years ago by Daddy's cousin, Malcolm, and his wife, Janie Sue. Billy had been barely old enough to sit alone when his future parents went to his birth mother's house to bring him home. Janie walked inside and found her precious, new baby boy fishing tid-bits out of a slop bucket, and eating 'em.

Adoption made Billy *not* my true cousin, didn't it?

One night when he, Bertha Mae, and I played hide and seek on Aunt Minnie's stairs, Billy grabbed me and gave me a big old smack on the lips.

That's when Aunt Minnie scared us. She said, "Red Eyes and Bloody Bones'll get you two if you don't trot down them stairs!"

The next day I checked out my yellow vine. It was growing like mad. I still yearned to go to school.

In 'thirty-eight, my Aunt Leatha married Jeff, the fellow who paid me quarters to leave the two of them alone on my grandparents' porch swing. Mama Todd missed her younger daughter; so, for a while we went to see Papa and Mama more often. I loved visiting with them at seven o'clock on week nights. Then we'd listen to Lum and Abner, Amos and Andy, and whatever else exciting popped up on their radio's agenda.

Home again, I felt more "lack" in my life. I wanted a radio.

Papa and Mama Todd always bought the country's latest gadgets: enamel stove, new Chevrolet, an ice chest, a fancy kitchen cabinet, and now, a new radio, long before our family could afford extras.

We took Charleston's *News and Courier,* and Columbia's *State* paper. Those were Sunday papers, and I enjoyed checking out Dagwood and Blondie, Dick Tracy, Popeye the Sailor, and Nancy. Conway's paper, *The Horry Herald,* came Thursdays. I'd hear family and neighbors discuss local events, plus what politician was running for what office. I didn't know a politician from a drummer. The former interested me nary a whit. I wanted a radio.

I loved the times I'd climb into Mother's lap and she'd read me nursery rhymes. I felt sorry Jack Sprat could eat no fat, and his wife could eat no lean; but, I enjoyed having them to care about. I liked rhythms to poems like: *To market to market to buy a fat pig; Home again home again, jiggety-jig.* My Jimmy, Jim Jones, had interested me in fairies so tiny they could hide beneath toadstools, and Mother Goose's book said, "*Here am I, Little Jumping Joan. When I'm not with you, I'm always alone.*" Joan, a little girl like me, stood beside a toadstool on this magic page. The toadstool protruded above her head bare inches. What a wondrous place, the world of books.

Of just as much interest was Papa and Mama Todd's radio, although I wished static on that shiny, glorified box didn't muffle Lum and Abner's funny lines.

Today, anchored in the twenty-first century, we worry about jobs, taxes, house payments. In 1938, Mother and Daddy's main concern was borrowing enough money to live on for the year, and whether earnings from their crops would allow them to break even after tobacco sales. Daddy read to us from *The Horry Herald* the price of a house if we had to buy one. Mother shook her head. She said, "I guess we're pretty lucky we don't have to shell out $3,900.00 for a house."

Grandma was quick to say, "Blessed is more like it, and you can thank God for helping Hampie. He built our house with his own free sweat and cypress wood." She added, "But don't forget. Hampie bought them square-headed nails. Our house wasn't all free."

While our home served us well, we did have to maintain its roof, as well as fix porch boards when they broke loose. I hoped Daddy remembered that. The Great Depression on all minds definitely gave our family pause. While we had plenty to eat from our garden, we still needed staples each week, which we bought on credit. And Grandma. She thought ten cents a gosh-awful amount for Daddy to withdraw from her "waist money-bag" for a gallon of gas, when she knew full well that same dime could have bought her a can of Sweet Society Snuff.

Everything cost more than we could afford. At his Adrian store, Mr. Kelly Tompkins charged nine cents for one loaf of light bread. We preferred Grandma's and Mother's baked biscuits anyway. And a can of Lipton Noodle Soup would have cost us ten cents if Mother hadn't been too stingy to buy stuff she could cook at home. She never lifted a lid off of anything "chicken" simmering in a pot on our old iron cook-stove other than a pullet, a hen, or a rooster hijacked from its coop, before being killed and dressed.

All the while, Grandma said it was her "bounden duty" to help my friends and me know right from wrong, good from bad. Seeing my friend, Joe Hucks, squat before a brick bat and demolish the brick with a hammer, she warned, "Joe! Stop that brick spattering this instant!"

When Joe paid her no mind, she said, "Just you keep doing what you're doing, Boy, and you'll end up just like Andy Hamilton."

So that's how Andy went blind!

I found out later it wasn't.

Andrew Hamilton was Grandpa Hamp's younger brother's son. As a lad, Andy sometimes spent nights with his older cousin, my daddy.

Despite Grandma's protests, Grandpa bought twelve-year-old Daddy a rifle, and a younger Andy wanted to shoot birds with it. Grandma said, "No way. I'm having no boys shoot each-others' eyes out." Aggravated, Andy picked up a brick and clunked it against another. He picked up a handful of sand and fogged it into the air.

Grandma set him down for a talking. She said, "Andy, I want you to think about what you're doin'. Don't spatter brick like that. It could outen your eyes. And don't ever fog sand in the air. Fallin' in your eyes, it could skin your eyeballs. I'm tellin' you this for you to remember. Okay, Andy?"

Andy hung his head. He said, "I'm sorry, Aunt Nettie."

Not long after that episode, a downcast Uncle Boss paid Grandma a visit. He told her, 'Net, I'm bearing bad news. Andy was playing with a gun and got both eyes shot out.'"

Grandma would end that tale by shaking her head. "Chillern, don't ever play with fire arms. None of you! The only thing a gun's good for is to bag game or to shoot a snake. Remember that."

᛫ ✼ ᛫ ✼

Andrew Hamilton never regained sight in either eye. He spent his adult working life in the Conway Courthouse selling odds and ends in a booth set up by Conway's Lion's Club. Lucky for Andy, that year, 1938, this country's first seeing-eye dog was trained and put to use. Before long the Lion's Club provided Andy with his own dog. I liked it when Daddy and I visited Andy's booth. He allowed me brief pats of his short haired, honey-colored, canine friend. I wasn't afraid of him. He liked me.

1938 turned out to be an interesting year. If we had owned a radio, we might have been scared out of our wits, listening to H. G. Welle's "The War of the Worlds." But at Bug Swamp, who knew there was anyone anywhere doing anything worth two cents, except for antics taking place in our own low country community?

That summer, sandwiched between curing tobacco and selling it, I heard my cousins, Frances Marion and Bertha Mae, brag about their new clothes, paper, and pencils their mamas bought them for fall school session. I might be only five, but if they could go to school, why couldn't I? Finally, I prevailed upon Mother to re-visit the teachers at Good Hope Elementary one more time. Mrs. Holmes said, "*Lend* us your daughter. We'll see if she can manage first grade work."

How grownup I felt that fateful day. Mother smoothed my hair as she helped me pull on my navy blue jumper over a white peter-pan collar blouse. Joe, Bertha Mae, Billy Bland, and another kid or two usually walked the two and a half miles to school. As they neared our house, I waved a self-conscious goodbye to Mother.

"You're going to school?" Joe shook his head. An ancient seven, already he was a second-grader. "You'll have to walk fast to keep up with us."

My short legs pumped double time all the way.

About a quarter of a mile from school, I needed a bathroom. Bad. When I couldn't walk one step further without relief, I stepped into some bushes lining the road. Relief dribbled down my legs. It soaked my panties. Maybe no one would notice.

I inched into the class room and found a seat. To my dismay Mrs. Holmes motioned me to her desk. She patted my wet bottom. "Come with me," she said, her mouth as straight a line as Mother could make hers.

Nearby, at the teacher's house, she helped me wash up and lent me a pair of her daughter's panties.

I'd like to say we went back to school. Not so. Mrs. Holmes drove me home and handed me over to Mother. She said, "I'm sorry, Mrs. Hamilton. "Your daughter has a problem."

I cried, for I had to wait another whole year before becoming a grown-up first-grader. However, I didn't have to wait that long before learning to read simple words like the, and, but, of, for I learned those words by following along in my Mother Goose book when someone read to me, "Humpty Dumpty," "Jack Sprat," "Jumping Joan," "The Owl and the Pussy Cat," and other poems.

Our wash house sat open on one side, enclosed by two other walls, single board thick, plus an end wall it shared with our smoke house. The structure housed a huge iron tub, anchored atop a wood-burning, brick furnace. Inside this tub where Mother boiled lye-soapy clothes, a lengthy clothes-punch rested, one end soft and fuzzy from its steamy stirring.

Shelves stretched across the tops of our wash house walls. Odds and ends no one knew what to do with, ended up there.

One day, yearning to be in school and seeking something interesting, I plundered around the wash house. On a top shelf I spied something. That something looked like a thick, green book.

I grabbed the clothes punch and tried to knock down the book. I was too short. Dragging over a straight-back chair, leaning against Grandma's pear tree, I climbed onto the chair, and using Mother's clothes punch, knocked down the heavy tome. *Yeah.* Opening it, I saw mostly big, long, words. How intriguing that book.

About then Mother called, "Billie! Time to eat!"

I hid my new find beneath a discarded guano sack and ran inside. All through supper I told no one of my discovery.

Next day, as soon as Grandma and I finished our chores, I raced outside. I grabbed that book and climbed the mulberry tree towering over the wash house. Holding the book, sitting astride thick-leafed branches tired my arms. Where else could I find privacy?

Under the same roof, actually an extension of the wash shelter, our smoke house consisted of a thickly walled room, about twelve by twelve feet, with firmly packed dirt floor. In the center was a kind of pit, where in the fall, after butchering, Daddy built low fires and smoked our meat. The smoke-house door opened into the washhouse and was elevated by a thick wood block people stepped over before entering the room. That's where I sat to read my book. When our back kitchen-door opened, I'd slip inside the smokehouse and close the door until that person went on his or her way.

Attempting something I equated with first grade, I began to read. I saw the words "the," "of," "that," but was unable to comprehend the book's context. Every day I tackled my book, and gradually, by sounding out words, I learned that it talked about a really big boat. A s-h-i-p. And its name was *The T-i-t-a-n-i-c.*

Day after day of reading, I understood more, although not all. Finally, I reached the place where the boat or ship, hit an ice berg, and the big, unsinkable ship began to do what its builders said never would happen. It sank lower and lower, until lifeboats were de-p-l-o-y-ed. The person in charge said, "Women and children first." Women and children climbed into those lifeboats and were lowered into the water. Sadly they left their husbands, older sons, fathers, and brothers standing on the ship's deck, many of them singing, "Nearer My God to Thee." I knew that hymn! One thing interesting about the men left to sink, some wore suits called tuxedos, and awaiting their fate, some smoked cigarettes.

Reading my first, real book, I felt for every person left on board to go down with the ship, or left floating on an icy sea. With women and children, I watched the Titanic tilt, then sink lower and lower, until finally it slipped beneath the icy ocean's waves. Never, before or since, have I been more affected by a book; plus, I applaud *The Titanic* for teaching me to read.

CHAPTER 18
First Grade, 1939

This year, six years old, I legally entered first grade. Daddy chug-chugged into the school yard with me in the front seat, and Bertha Mae, Joe, and Billy Bland stuffed into the back of Daddy's Model-A Ford, the car he bought from some mechanic near Bayboro.

No wet panties this year. As Mr. Nichols swung the school bell, "Dong, dong, dong," my fellow travelers and I lined up with the rest of the student body before marching up steps onto the porch, on into an echoing space.

How magical, this auditorium, with its oiled floor smells and a huge stage curtain painted with ocean pictures; plus, that curtain could roll up or down like a humongous window shade. Each morning we held chapel there. On Fridays students could perform. I couldn't wait to hop onto the stage and volunteer some ditty Mother taught me. I sang *Fritz Came from School, Pretty Maid, Pretty Maid, She's Dead in the Coach Ahead,* as well as other songs I heard over and over from Mother's lips. Actually *She's Dead in the Coach Ahead* was Grandma's song.

Truly smashing, my first grade teacher was Uncle Bert's wife, Aunt Dalma. In her classroom I enjoyed setting up miniature villages in the sand table. I loved watching Aunt Dalma color, in brilliantly hued chalk, Thanksgiving, Halloween, and Christmas pictures across the blackboard's top. I marveled that words like *laughter* and *daughter*, although spelled with similar letters, were pronounced differently.

Those fall afternoons I couldn't wait to get home. I'd race up our front steps, blue denim book bag un-slung from my shoulder, falling "thud" into a corner of the living room. I'd yell, "Mother!"

Dashing into the living room with arms out-spread, she'd say "You're home!" Dressed like a housewife, not the farm worker she'd been all summer, hands on hips, Mother surveyed her project of the day. Intent on making our old farmhouse homier, she'd buzz around us like a bee searching for nectar. During tobacco season, she'd parked those happy tasks into a "later" mind compartment.

We never knew what would pop up next. One afternoon, stepping onto the porch, I smelled paint. Our previously unpainted kitchen gleamed white. That night we slept with open windows. Another day white muslin, edged in red rick rack, draped from the tops of kitchen counters to the floor. No longer in evidence were containers holding a hundred pounds of flour, a barrel of rice, nor the shiny can filled with glistening white, home-rendered lard. After that, Grandma's iron pots, formerly decorating shelves, played hide and seek with our cooks.

"Where did my griddle go, Dot?" Grandma couldn't find a thing in this, her daughter-in-law's kitchen.

Grandma didn't really approve of Mother's cavorting, but as she told her sister, Aunt Freddie, "Let Dottie have her fun. I just grin and bear it."

Reaching home one afternoon, I sat down on the front steps, took off my shoes, and shook out sand pestering me for the last mile. Inside, I heard Daddy goin' at it. "The last thing I planned to do today was paper a wall," he muttered. "For Pete's sake. How much longer will this take?"

Sock-footed, I walked inside. *What in the world?* Daddy stood on a step ladder, holding at arm's length a strip of cream-colored, flowered wall paper. Mother wielded a wide brush covered in white paste. She alternated between brushing the wall in front of Daddy and the back side of the paper.

I liked Mother's papered walls with their cream background, white cabbage roses, and their tiny, reddish/green leaves. But I wondered, *however will we scald this room?* Between wallpapered walls and those with paint, how would we manage our usual spring cleaning? That consisted of moving every stick of furniture outdoors, and flinging gourds of boiling lye water onto floors, walls, and ceilings.

Grandma asked that same question.

That fall my best surprise was a brand new refrigerator, our first. One afternoon as if by magic, large, square, and white, *it* occupied one corner of our kitchen. Inside a top shelf of the refrigerator sat trays, and in those trays, wonder of wonders, ice. Of course Horry Electric Co-Operative's newly strung wires made that wonder possible.

Whoa. A tray of ice wasn't the best part. Next afternoon I discovered creamy, frozen, ice cream. My brother, Jack, two years old and into everything, would have gobbled it all if I hadn't grabbed my spoon.

I needn't have worried. Mother had made two batches; thus we all enjoyed what was normally a store treat. What excitement, that fall!

We Always Had Enough to Go Around

Several weeks later, at the kitchen table Grandma Nettie smoothed pages of a letter Mr. Proctor delivered. She brought the stationary in close; extended it arms' length; then peered at her mail through bifocals. She clapped her hands. "Guess what, Dottie! Palmer's coming Thanksgiving. That's two weeks from Thursday."

Mother, face pink from cooking, looked up from stirring cake batter. "That's a surprise." With the back of her hand, she pushed damp curls from her forehead. "I didn't expect him till Christmas."

Grandma's face grew serious. "I've been so worried these past months. I can't wait to see my boy."

Neither could I. Always, as soon as Uncle Charles stepped out of his car, he handed me a present.

Lately, we'd all worried about Grandma's baby boy turned Georgian. After graduating from Clemson the year after I was born, Charlie Palmer Hamilton became an agriculture teacher in Waresboro, a wide place in a South Georgia road. We worried, because this past year he'd developed rheumatoid arthritis symptoms; also, he'd recently wed another teacher in the Ware County school system. We'd never met this young woman from Mansfield, Georgia, and she boasted a decidedly, non-Horry County sounding name: Sarah Roquemore.

Fall brought on good hog-killing weather. A cold snap had us all bundled up and shivering. Mother helped Daddy make sausage from pigs

Uncle Dave Holmes came over and shot, since Daddy couldn't kill animals he'd fed and raised. Mother and Mama Todd filled huge cans with lard they'd rendered.

"Don't you lift them heavy cans by yourself," Mama Todd fussed at Mother.

Daddy and David Linen, Daddy's recently hired man from Sandy Isle, hung lots of spiced-up hams and shoulders in the smoke house to cure just right.

Grandma made hog's head cheese. Maybe you know this concoction as souse, or pressed meat. I won't tell you how Grandma arrived at this delicacy; however, by the time she'd boiled and hashed and seasoned her creation with lots of goodies, sage, and such, *she* said it tasted delicious. I never ate the stuff.

The night before Thanksgiving Daddy read some scripture, and kneeling at chairs drawn up before a crackling fire, each of us gave thanks. With my back side burning and my front freezing, I think I said something like, "Thank you, God, for my family, my teachers, and Coca Cola." For a while now I hadn't drunk Pepsis. Mother said they could make my stomach grow big.

Next morning I woke up to the sounds and smells of Thanksgiving. Daddy had bought a turkey from Mr. Ed Stevens, and roasted "Tom" aromas displaced every competing fragrance in our house.

After an endless morning spent sweeping floors with my Billie-size broom, peering through the parlor window for our guests, and fidgeting, finally I spied Uncle Charles wheel his little black, rumble-seated car into our yard. Daddy left the space beneath the cedar tree just for him.

"He's here!" I ran through the house shouting to any and all, and we rushed outside.

Uncle Charles, already out of the car, opened the door for his bride.

Such a bride. While Uncle Charles' shoulders were already slightly bent by arthritis, his new wife made up for any height he'd lost. She stood taller than Daddy. Later I heard Grandma tell Mother, "Dottie, Palmer's got him a six foot tall wife, if she's an inch."

"Meet my better half, folks," Uncle Charles said. "Her name's Sarah, but I call her Rock."

Aunt Rock, I mouthed, as Mother pushed me forward. "Hug your new Aunt Rock, Billie Faye."

I hugged Aunt Rock somewhere around her hips. Meanwhile, she reached for my young brother. "He's a cutter. That's for sure." She pronounced "cutter," "cuttah."

With his adorable, curly, black hair, naturally Jack attracted more attention than I. Which was okay, as long as Uncle Charles hadn't forgotten my present. I hoped he didn't consider that to be Aunt Rock.

Inside, Mother said, "Sit down, Rock. Entertain these men. Charles' ma and I'll finish dinner."

"I know times are hard." Aunt Rock stretched the "a" into several syllables, completely leaving off the "r" in "hard." "I hope y'all didn't put yourselves out for us."

"Hard times or not, Rock," Daddy said, "we always have enough to go around, don't we Bud?" He gave my frail looking uncle's shoulder a cuff.

Grandma appeared in the doorway. "Time to eat."

In a platter on Grandma's best white Damask, Mr. Steven's huge bird "roosted," brown and succulent in his final hours. After Grandma's lengthy blessing, we passed yellow rice, giblet gravy, Kentucky Wonders, pears pink with a tad of red food coloring, hot sweet potatoes, water melon rind pickles I'd helped jar, Grandma's flaky, bite-size biscuits a man with *no* appetite could eat a dozen of, roasted turkey, and Grandma's special dish.

"What's this delicious looking meat?" Aunt Rock looked puzzled.

"Hog's head cheese." Grandma preened a little. "Want my recipe?"

Aunt Rock shook her head ever so slightly as she passed the souse meat to her new husband, who helped himself to an extra-large slab.

After dinner, a lazy bunch of Hamilton's plopped into chairs in our living room until cousins dropped by, Rob and Maude first. Shortly, Elise and Gen came, bringing song books. We gathered around the pump organ and I sang along with the best of 'em. Finally, Uncle Homer and Aunt Sally arrived, bringing my cousin. I was glad, because unlike some, eight-year-old Frances Marian seemed to like playing with six-year-old me.

After everyone left, I remembered. *Where is my present?*

Grandma and I lent our bedroom to the newlyweds. We slept in the room called "behind the partition." I stood nearby, watching my interesting aunt unpack suitcases. From beneath a green sweater, Aunt

Rock pulled out a silvery-wrapped object. First she shook the box, smiled big, then passed it to me.

"Thank you! Thank you!" I ran off to open my gift in private.

Inside the square box nestled a shiny, wheat-colored cup. On one side of the cup, beside a haystack, Little Boy Blue curled up asleep. On the opposite side a cow flew over an orange, crescent moon.

How wonderful! I shook the box. Nothing else fell out.

Running into the bedroom where my aunt had finished unpacking, I said, "Aunt Rock, where's the saucer?"

"Saucer?" she said. "What saucer?"

"The one that goes with the cup."

"I'm sorry, Bill." She'd already nick-named me. "The cup has no saucer."

"No saucer?" By now I felt close to tears. Not only had I embarrassed myself. Probably I had hurt Aunt Rock's feelings. Mother shook her head, her lips their familiar straight line.

Grandma's true blue eyes drew themselves into the triangles they made when she couldn't think what to say. Finally she said, "Little Bushy, be thankful they brought you a cup."

"I am. I love the cup," I hoped to make amends. "I don't need a saucer."

"Then how about a ride? Would you like a jaunt in our rumble seat?" Stooping over, Aunt Rock took my hand, swinging it like she was six.

"Would I?"

As we walked through the parlor out to the car, I knew that this was the best Thanksgiving of my life, and I had the best, the *tallest* new aunt in the whole, wide world.

My new cup would do just fine without a saucer.

Chapter 19
Santa Clausin', 1939

Now-a-days, into our second millennium since the birth of our Savior, goblins, fairies, angels, even presidents spread out through neighborhoods carrying bags, maybe plastic pumpkins, seeking goodies to fill their containers. They ring door bells. They shout, "Trick or treat!" and return home to spread on the floor Silver Bells, miniature Snicker Bars, chewing gum, all manner of delights to rot their teeth. The occasion is All Hallows Eve, or Halloween.

We South Carolina Bug Swampians missed out on the treat-half of this Halloween practice. Minus costumes but hidden by night, we delighted in playing tricks on neighbors and friends. Really I wasn't old enough to take part in such, but I heard Daddy, Leo, Brooke Harris, Uncle Charles, and Rob Hamilton brag about tricks they pulled. Sometimes they hid hay-rakes, ploughs, even mules. They turned over outhouses, hopefully unoccupied ones. Knocking on doors, culprits from the scene of the "crime" dashed away before house occupants could answer the knocks.

Similarly, during Bug Swamp Christmases, many people chose trick-playing on their neighbors. They disguised themselves and paid incognito visits to others' homes. Unlike at Halloween, these tricksters received no treats, unless people visited chose to pass around light refreshments. This Christmas custom we called Santa Clausin'.

In the thirties, people got Thanksgiving out of the way before Christmas began. Then, December turned into one big celebration, for this holiday was a celebration honoring the birth of our Savior, Jesus Christ. I remember feeling intense excitement the year Santa's plane zoomed over our town of Conway, with city hall loud speakers blaring, "You'd better watch out, you'd better not cry; Santa Claus is coming to town!"

Sitting atop the back seat of an open car, old Santa Claus climaxed the parade. Afterwards, inside Barnhill's Five and Dime Store, Mother waited in line with me to greet Santa. She held Jack in her arms. On reaching this awesome gift-giver I said, "Santa Claus, I want a big, big ball for Christmas. One that will bounce really high."

Santa seemed nice enough, although his red suit looked a trifle dingy. He said, "I'll see if I can find you one."

I told Santa, "This boy's my brother. Bring him whatever two-year-olds like." Jack had buried his face on Mother's shoulder.

Each year, about three weeks before Christmas, Daddy cut a cedar or pine, maybe a holly tree, nailed a cross to the bottom for its stand, and dragged the tree into our parlor for our family to decorate. From Mother's trunk we pulled out Christmas tinsel, glass ornaments, icicles, crepe paper ropes of red and green, along with accordion-pleated bells. Grandma would say, "Chillern, you're decorating to a fare thee well!" Mixing flour, salt, and water, Mother made a batter. She'd bring in garlands of cedar or some other greenery, dip woodsy swags into her wet flour mixture. Presto. Snow. She'd hang snowy swags on outside doors, trail snowy swags above windows, and for indoors, she'd poke short green branches along with red holly berries into vases. Meanwhile, we cleaned our house until its old floors and walls creaked, "Stop!"

Our home smelled and looked like Christmas by the time Mother made her pies: lemon, chocolate, coconut, plus her caramel-pear cake. Grandma stirred up wonderful aromas as well, Daddy's favorite, her black walnut cake. She also baked square tea cakes and sour apple tarts.

Daddy's complaint, "Ma, I love your black walnut cake, but I hate picking out these blame walnuts."

Never for a moment did we forget what Christmas represented. Every tree cut, every bauble, every swag hung, pies, rich cakes baked, happy thoughts, all these festive doings would culminate in remembering the night angels hovered over a Bethlehem barn and sang praises to a new-born babe, part human, part God, all Savior.

Prior to Jesus's birthday, Bug Swamp's custom of Santa Clausin' added a special lightness to our holiday. How that tradition began I never knew.

Each evening, two to three weeks before Christmas, Mother and Grandma put early suppers on the table. They bustled around serving meals and washing dishes, for we never knew when pseudo Santas would appear.

"Are you finished with that?" Mother hovered over the person eating slowest, usually me. She wanted the last dish washed and all food stowed before the first knock sounded.

"Rap, rap, rap."

"Get the door." Mother scraped leftover plate contents into the slop bucket, our food waste collection for pigs.

I raced to the door. "Gasp." Several people dressed in outlandish costumes stood outside, much like Halloween's "trick or treaters." Many times they didn't speak. They just stood there looking scary.

Visitors like these might show up each night, or skip several. Usually adult, they might whisper, or speak in fake bass or tenor voices. I thought silent visitors scarier.

I remember one night when two Santas stood at our doorway. A tall person wearing a Santa false-face seemed familiar. The shorter one wore a paper bag over her head with holes for eyes and mouth, cut away. Even a fool could see this was a man with a woman, probably his wife.

I ran to the kitchen. I said, "Two Santas are at the door. Come quick."

"Don't stand there. Let 'em in." Mother dried her hands and patted her hair.

Without a word, our two visitors entered. Grandma, hands on hips, strolled around each. Eyeing one, she said, "Just who are you? I bet you're Lutie." And to the tall person beside the shorter, Grandma said, "You're Worth Abercrombie. Couldn't be anybody else." Lutie and Worth were a married couple, our cousins living nearby. Later Worth became my school principal, also my sixth grade teacher.

That night Grandma nailed our Santa's identities. They unmasked and pulled up chairs around the fire. We reminisced about when Worth came to our area from McCormick, and boarded with Papa and Mama Todd. Actually Daddy introduced Worth to Cousin Lutie. I'd ridden Worth's shoulders over to Aunt Tennessee's and Uncle Fernie's house the Sunday the couple met. Lutie became Worth's second wife, and stepmother to his children, Doyle and Mary Joyce.

Fake Santas didn't necessarily wear Santa masks, nor Santa suits. Some people were so uninventive, like Cousin Lutie, they simply pulled paper bags over their heads with holes cut out for eyes and mouths, little holes lest we get a peek at their faces.

Each Christmas Papa and Mama Todd came Santa Clausin'. Wearing his own red Santa suit, complete with mask and beard, Papa prided himself on a "dummy" reindeer he'd fashioned. Calling it a hobby horse, Papa controlled the dummy's in-tree movements with a thin, extended stick. Mama dolled up in any old thing. We knew her because as soon as she saw me, she'd lean over and say exactly what she always said, "Smell my nose." I always wondered if some of her ancestors were Eskimo.

Occasionally, masquerading children accompanied their parents. I never did, because my family didn't go Santa Clausin'. Staying home and receiving mystery guests provided interesting fodder for conversation. After Grandma Nettie spent the week quizzing Aunt Minnie, Aunt Sally-Will, as well as Aunt Etta, in one direction, and drilling her sister, Aunt Freddie, toward the church, by Sunday, Grandma usually had a fairly accurate idea who'd kept her busy identity-guessing all week.

As you might surmise could happen, thieves spoiled an interesting tradition. A family in the Salem community boasted an extraordinarily beautiful Christmas tree sheltering a wealth of wrapped gifts. A pair of Santas paid these people a visit. Really the intruders were "casing the joint." Later, they returned, pilfering every precious present.

That act took away not only the Salem family's Christmas cheer, it created mistrust of disguised Santas throughout Bug Swamp and the rest of Horry County.

"I'm not letting anyone else I don't know enter my home." Daddy felt "put-out."

"After all these years. It's a cryin' shame thieves can make us doubt our very own neighbors." Grandma's face sagged all the way to the toes of her easy walkers.

This dastardly deed brought about the demise of Bug Swamp Santa Clausin'. Is it any wonder that years later, at Halloween we meet our "trick or treaters" and rarely ask them in?

Chapter 20
Aunt Leatha

In early 1940, three years after my brother, Jack, joined our family, Mother's younger sister, Leatha, gave birth to her baby boy, Randall. Like Jack and me, Randall was born at home, his deliverer, Dr. Paul Sasser. Randall, Leatha, and Jeff, Randall's dad, spent a lot of time at Papa and Mama Todd's home, although Jeff yearned to go further south. He talked about Florida's warm winters, cheap land, and plentiful jobs. Meanwhile his wife had no plans whatever to pick up her little boy and desert Adrian for a hotter, even swampier land.

A couple of years earlier, both Jeff and Mother's brother, Mace, had fattened my piggy bank. Papa's front porch swing was the place for Sunday afternoon courtin', and Sunday afternoons, Mother took me there for visits. Whoever got the swing first, Jeff and Leatha, or Mace and Louise, the fellows paid me countless quarters to disappear, leaving them alone with their girl-friends. In 1938, both couples married. After that, my piggy bank starved.

I always felt that Leatha was as much mine as Jeff's or Randall's. Whatever the situation, my young aunt took a stance in my corner. If Mother called me loudly, Leatha scolded, "Speak softer to that child!" In Leatha's blue eyes I could do no wrong, while Mother had few "mothering" skills. Once I developed a stuffy nose and low grade fever. Leatha insisted Mother take me to the doctor. Mother said, "Leath, we'll put a poultice on her chest. She'll be fine tomorrow."

Leatha turned on her heel. "Take me home, Papa." That morning my determined auntie hired herself out to a neighboring farmer for the afternoon, returned next morning, got me ready, and took me, courtesy of Papa Todd, to the doctor. And she paid the doctor with her earnings.

On marrying, Leatha and Jeff moved into a cabin next door to Jeff's parents. Only a few days passed before I spent the night with the newly-weds, sleeping with them in their bed, Leatha in the middle. Next morning, Jeff set before me my first bowl of cornflakes and milk. Later he introduced me to parched peanuts topped with cane syrup. Delicious. He should have been a gardener or a chef. Maybe both. He grew the first egg-plant any of us had ever seen.

Mother complained to Mama Todd, "Leath is a dunce about my baby." When Leatha became a mother, that nurturing trait magnified. If Baby Randall ran a fever, she sent for both Dr. Paul Sasser and Melton Barnhill, church deacon. On one side of Randall's bed Dr. Sasser plied a stethoscope and tongue depressor. On the other, Mr. Barnhill, one hand on Randall's curls and another pointed toward Heaven, entreated God, "Heal this child." To ward off illnesses, Randall wore around his neck a smelly asaphedita bag. We held our noses until Leatha exchanged Randall's asaphedita for a copper penny necklace.

That sweet baby thrived, but in 1946, six and a half years after his birth, his mother grew tired. Her spleen swelled. Her gums bled. Doctors said, "Leukemia." Luckily she and my dad shared the same rare blood type, AB-RH Negative. Seventeen months of sporadic transfusions followed, accompanied by Duke University Hospital treatments, suffering, and dire family distress. Ultimately, Randall's mommie, my Leath, died. Confused, distraught, addled by too many life-complications, Randall dashed from her death-bed to Mama Todd, sitting in the kitchen. "Mama," he cried, "I want to be your little boy."

In 1948, Leatha's death was my life's most traumatic event. She left eight-year-old Randall disputed over by Mama Todd and his dad. Jeff, suffering from his World War II stint in Burma, his wife's sickness, and his own alcoholism, finally agreed to leave Randall with the Todd's. Jeff sought solace where he'd always wanted to live, Florida. Mama Todd held Randall to her heart.

Billie H. Wilson •

    Most Sunday afternoons found Randall and my brother, Jack, chasing each other around Mama Todd's long porches. The boys made sling shots, shooting and missing birds and squirrels. They played baseball, and some game where they tossed balls to each other over Mama Todd's kitchen wing. They cavorted like most Bug Swamp boys, harking back to when young Waccamaw and Pee Dee braves claimed this, their land.

Chapter 21
A Visit, Plus the Woman and the Bear

This fall, since I was in third grade and every day Bertha Mae walked to school with me, she loosened some restrictions on being my friend. Thank goodness, for many Saturdays when our chores were done and nap-time over, Grandma and I meandered over to visit Aunt Minnie.

"Hey, Minnie," Grandma would say, climbing up the front steps.

"Come in, Net." Aunt Minnie found standing to greet guests unnecessary. "Berth," she'd call out, "Billie Faye's here."

I admired Aunt Minnie. Always her home looked spotless. So did she with her wavy white hair anchored becomingly with the same tortoise shell type combs Grandma used. Come to think of it, all older ladies in our Bug Swamp community used the same kind of comb, although colors varied from transparent, to honey, to brown. These combs must have been sold by some traveling drummer.

Like our house, theirs, originally Grandpa Hamp's family home, sat on high pilings. Older than ours, its underbelly harbored a feathery network of spider-webs, stray frogs, an occasional wasp nest, and like beneath ours, dimpled doodle-bug hills.

In spring and into summer, besides adventuring underneath her house, Bertha Mae and I played in Aunt Minnie's rather large apple orchard.

That's where Grandma picked her green cooking apples for sour apple tarts, as well as June eating apples.

Grandma made sure I knew not to eat green apples till they ripened. "Don't you get no belly ache," she'd warn me.

Across the road, amidst a sprinkle of cypress trees, a pond attracted egrets. I enjoyed sitting on the pond's mossy bank, dreaming of what someday, being "grown-up," would feel like. Even more daring, Bertha Mae and I might venture into her bedroom. Her sisters, Una and Myrt, had married and left her the room they'd shared. Two years older than my six or seven, very pretty with dark hair waving becomingly from her forehead due to a strategically placed cow-lick, Bertha Mae liked admiring her reflection in the wavy mirror, and experimenting with make-up left by her older sisters. That's where I learned how to apply lipstick and mascara. Of course I removed that before Grandma spied me wearing it.

Back home our parlor contained a pump organ, a wicker settee, a couple of arm chairs, a center table housing the family Bible, straight-back chairs easy to pull up to the hearth on cold nights, and Grandma's coral-colored Damask chair. Bertha Mae's parlor boasted plush, soft, heavy furniture I was sure cost a mint. And they enjoyed a console graphaphone. My favorite record on that player was the lilting Spanish ditty, Rosalita. I couldn't get enough of that fast paced tune. I enjoyed setting the needle, winding the graphaphone, guiding the needle to the record, singing along, and swaying to the music.

Another specialty of Aunt Minnie's household was making cane syrup. The entire Hamilton clan took part in that procedure, complete with hauling sugar cane into the yard via their mule, peeling stalks of cane, pulverizing and expressing cane juice, courtesy of that same mule's circular trots around a grinder, and using Aunt Minnie's immense, iron wash pot for boiling fragrant cane juice. Its steamy aroma, wafting over the countryside, smelled better than tobacco curing. Actually, much better.

I loved being a part of that procedure, for Uncle Boss and his host of kids, Uncle Will with his one son, Rob, as well as Aunt Tennessee's children, Lutie and Brooke, all flew toward that annual production. Aunt Tennessee's other son, Malcolm, died during the time I saw the bear, or he would have been a part of the day. "Let me taste!" "I want a taste," echoed over the yard.

As syrup boiled, Uncle Will designated himself official syrup taster. When he determined our coveted ambrosia thick enough, he used a gourd dipper to pour the syrup into two-quart jars. Each family received jars to house in their home pantry. During the year we ladled our syrup onto flitters, maybe hot biscuits. We incorporated it into peanut brittle. When anything called for something sweet besides sugar or honey, we used Great-Grandpa William Hamilton's cane syrup.

"Time to go home, Little Bushy," Grandma sang out.

"Walk home with us," I urged Bertha Mae.

"Can I Mama?"

"Don't stay long, Berth. It'll soon be dark."

We lived about two-thirds of a mile from Aunt Minnie's house. Not as young as she used to be, Grandma liked taking her time walking home. Bertha Mae and I ran around her, playing tag, until tired of that, Grandma said, "What did I do to cause you girls to make me the center of your tags? You're gonna knock me down in this very road."

Slowed down temporarily, we grew restless. "I know, Grandma. Tell us a story, and we'll walk as slow as you please."

"Hmm," she said. "What story?"

"The bear story. The old woman and the bear. You know." I always imagined the woman in the story to be Grandma, and this seemed to be the road where that action took place.

Per usual, Grandma Nettie needed little coaxing to light into a tale. Bertha and I plodded along side-ways on either side of Grandma, looking at her instead of our path.

"Girls," Grandma narrowed her eyes, "this happened a long time ago when swamps here were alive with bears. See these fields?" she gestured toward the ploughed land lining our road. "Instead of open spaces, trees grew right up to what was little more than a path. Both sides of the road were lined with thick bushes, loaded with huckleberries. And everybody knows a huckleberry bush is an open invitation to a bear. I bet there were no more, big ole bruins in a square mile anywhere else in the whole U.S. of A. Well, there was this old woman who went visiting."

Yeah. Grandma Nettie's visits with Aunt Minnie.

"Back then, people lived far apart. A visit to a neighbor meant a pretty good walk.

"The old woman stayed out her stay. She was bent on reaching home before dark, 'cause any number of varmints roamed around at night. Anyway, she started out walkin' pretty fast.

"For some reason, the skin on the back of her neck began to prickle, and kind-of spooked, she stopped and looked behind her. Way down a straight stretch of road, she spied something comin', maybe a calf-size dog.

"Believe me, this old lady didn't like the idea of a dog sneakin' up on her heels; so, she sped up a mite. Ahead, the road curved; then curved again. She completely lost sight of the thing followin' her.

"That freed her to make tracks. She hadn't wanted any dog to see her run, because everybody knows if you try to out-distance a dog, it can, and will, run you down.

"The road curves straightened out. The woman stopped a bit, and bent over to catch her breath, but she had no time to waste. You see, she was almost a mile from home.

"Afraid to, afraid not to, she snuck a glance over her shoulder.

"What was that comin' around the bend? A dog would have been a welcome sight. No. A big old black bear came a-lumberin' down that road, aimin' straight toward the scared old woman. At the rate he was runnin', he'd catch her in no time flat.

"The woman cried out, 'Lord, help me now!' Just her luck. She'd reached an open meadow. No trees anywhere, at least not one close enough for her to climb.

"The bear kept closin' in.

"Rushing to get away from that fearsome thing made the woman hot. Runnin' all the while, she untied her bonnet. It fell out her hand. Certainly she wasn't fool enough to stop for somethin' that trivial, not with a bear on her heels.

"She dared one more look back. The bear had stopped in his tracks, and was pawin' her bonnet, sniffin' it, throwin' it in the air. 'Thank you, Lord,' she prayed.

"By this time our old woman had gasped out her third or fourth wind, but seeing that bear so close gave her heart to run faster, all the while takin' off her high-collared waist. She hated to lose it. It had lace down the front. It was the best she had, but so was her life.

"The bear left off sniffin' her bonnet and made for that pretty waist.

"With the Good Lord's help, the old lady ran on, somehow managing to put one foot in front of the other, all the time, takin' off her clothes. She dropped her skirt; then her petticoats, both of 'em. Last of all, off came her under-drawers.

"Her chest was a'hurtin' something fierce, but at last she could see her house. That old two-by four-cabin never looked so good.

"Stumblin' the last few feet, she flung herself up the steps, slammed the door shut, and dropped the bar across. She was stitch-stark naked, but thanks to the blessed Almighty, she was safe from that old bear!"

Silence.

The tale shouldn't end here. "Grandma," I said, "what happened to the bear?"

Grandma said, "Think a minute, Billie. What would you have done if you'd 'a been that bear?"

"I guess after I'd seen the old woman run in the house, I'd a-pawed and sniffed around it, and when I couldn't get in, I'd a-gone about my business."

"And that's exactly what he did."

Bertha Mae asked, "Aunt Nettie, do you reckon that old woman ever got her clothes back?"

"I speck she got back some of 'em, not in good shape, though."

By now Grandma, Bertha Mae, and I had reached home. Grandma Nettie sank into her easy chair for an earned rest.

I couldn't resist asking, "Grandma, how about telling us what happened to Nan Booth's leg."

"Not today, Billie. You and Berth run along and play." Grandma Nettie was told out.

Chapter 22
A Doggie Story

April was here: "Ooh." My feet felt so good without shoes. Luckily we escaped Bug Swamp School before hot weather bore down in earnest.

In those years, for students to help parents with farm work, school lasted seven months, not nine like today. That meant our 1939/1940 school year began September of thirty-nine, and lasted until April, 1940. Such liberation. Immediately we freed ourselves from shoes causing perpetual back-of-heel blisters. We wriggled our toes in sand and tickly grass blades caressed our feet, except for days we dressed up for town or church.

Finishing second grade my first school year, thanks to *The Titanic,* I looked forward to July when I'd turn seven. I'd been promoted from first grade, to advanced first, then second, and in the fall of 1940, would begin third grade with students previously a year ahead of me. In my estimation, I came up short, and not just in stature. Some claimed boyfriends. I'd never have told a soul if I had liked a boy. He'd never have known. Other girls seemed less anguished over grades. Their hair looked neat and nice. Mine flipped up and out into whatever direction it chose. Some girls' dresses plumped out up front. Really, I didn't care about that, for one girl who came to school last September looking like a mama was talked about something fierce.

My number one problem? The terror I felt on the way to school, walking past Ben Dorman's house. Mr. Dorman's two furry creatures must have had it in for me, for Joe, Bertha Mae, even the Bland kids could priss by those dogs without a halt. My heels, they lit in behind like they craved a bite. Of me.

I liked dogs. I did. They just didn't like me, or they liked me too much.

Well before the blessed advent of my baby brother, Mother would spread a quilt onto the floor, stretch out on it, and I'd crawl over her body, pull her hair, and crow with the sheer joy of babyhood. However, even then I knew I wasn't her earliest off-spring. He was a dog named Topsy.

Before I arrived, Topsy awakened Mother's maternal feelings. In still moments on our quilt, she enchanted me with tales about a pup so tiny he traveled in Mother's pocket. Daddy gave her the miniature, sweet faced animal shortly after they wed. Unwilling to leave Topsy for a moment, she took him everywhere, even to the hog pen. An active little guy, he sailed out of Mother's pocket, landing "smack" into the old sow's trough.

Sad. Mother cried. I cried, every time I thought of Topsy's short life. I yearned for my own Topsy.

One day, visiting Cousin Frances Marion, we met the newest member of her family. My mouth formed a pleasured "Ooh!" as a ball of white fluff with a loud mouth greeted us. He advanced toward me; then, danced away, his toy head bobbing up and down, eyes and shiny black nose flashing.

"Here, puppy," I squatted to his level. Eager to squeeze this luscious, marshmallow dog with both hands, I beckoned to Frances Marion's baby Eskimo Spitz.

"Ouch! Ow! Sob!" The fellow bit me. His incisors pierced my three-year-old skin, bringing blood! Red! Mine!

My soul so fell in love with that dog, and he "done me wrong."

Daddy's cousin, Malcolm, died of consumption, leaving to his sister, Lutie, a white bull dog named Bob. Bob liked me, to bark at and eat up, if ever he got an opportunity. Of that I was certain.

Lutie invited me to a birthday party for her stepdaughter, my friend, Mary Joyce. That day a storage building behind their house served as a roller skating rink for all the girls in the neighborhood: Mary Joyce, Betty Jane, Edna Mae, Bertha Mae, Bobbie, and Billie Faye, yours truly. I'd never skated before, and spent more time on back or belly than on my feet. Sporting skinned knees, I accompanied Lutie to the kitchen where she patched up my boo-boos.

Afterwards, I skipped out through the rear door, rushing back to the party where I knew cupcakes and lemonade awaited. My thoughts failed to include Bob. Suddenly, bone, gristle, and lithe muscle encased in short white hair assailed my heels. The force of his assault threw me onto the sandy pathway, skinning my nose and my dignity. Bob tore at my clothes like I was a bone he felt urged to bury.

Thank goodness, Mary Joyce's dad, Worth, raked leaves nearby. He grabbed old Bob by the scruff of his neck and saved my hide.

Next door to Mama and Papa Todd lived a family named Graham. They owned two huge, "police" dogs, who, with their pointed ears, grey-furred bodies, and alert, yellowish eyes, could have posed for a present day "save the wolf" poster.

While visiting my grandparents, they made certain I never strayed next door. "Them dogs would eat you alive," my young Uncle Mace delighted in saying. A teenager, he said, "Listen here, Billie Faye, if you ever point a finger at Mr. Graham's big old dogs, or smile and show your teeth, they'll chew you up and spit you out!"

After my experiences with "man's best friends," is it any wonder that at six years old, walking to Bug Swamp Elementary, my school career was practically ended by a couple of yapping, yellow dogs?

The night before, I'd suffered nightmares of furry balls nipping my heels, and doggy breath steaming my neck. This morning what could I do or say that would prove my case to my unperturbed mother? Dressed, now desperate, I stamped my foot. "I can't go to school. Ever again! I'm scared to death of Mr. Ben's dogs."

Mother's expressive lips thinned out as she packed my lunch of fried ham and biscuits.

"No mustard," I said, still hoping to stay home and hang out beneath the quilt frame. That day Mrs. Ruby Tompkins, Mama Todd, Mrs. Julie Tompkins, my card class teacher at church, Grandma Nettie, and Mother planned to finish off a crazy quilt in our parlor. I liked nothing better than crawling beneath the quilt frame as needles flashed, punching in line after line of short, straight stitches. Conversation always proved interesting at quilting "bees," but I wasn't destined to eaves-drop that day.

"No staying home for you, my girl," Mother threw on pants and shirt. "I'll walk you past Mr. Dorman's dogs."

That morning and afterwards, Mother got her exercise. She accompanied me over two thirds of the way to school, one and a quarter miles, then returned home each morning. Sometimes Daddy drove the other kids and me in Tin Lizzie. If ever I found myself in the precarious position of passing Mr. Ben's house, parentless, my heart pounded, my breath came in gasps, and my spit dried up; and that was before those yellow-haired stalkers deigned to make an appearance. Thank goodness their owner, Allison, walked home with us after school.

Just wait, I told myself. When I turn seven, I'll be so grown up, I'll never, ever again be scared of Ben Dorman's bad dogs.

July eighth I celebrated my long awaited, seventh birthday. After church our family left for Mama and Papa Todd's at Adrian.

People kept driving into Papa's yard, some bringing platters of food. My vantage point was from the porch bench built by Mama Todd's coffin-maker grandfather, the bench Papa sat on, filing saws for people during his off-farming hours. He spied me. "Billie Faye," he said, "let's go see my tobacco patch."

I didn't particularly care to see an old tobacco patch, but I did like the idea of a jaunt with Papa. We crossed the railroad tracks and picked our path so far around a thick woods we no longer saw Papa's house. He took my hand. "This year we have a pretty good crop if I do say so myself."

"Your field's pretty, Papa. Now let's get back." My stomach rumbled for Mama's dinner.

Nearing the house, food aromas teased our hungry places. A dozen or so relatives gathered around a table loaded with Mama's good vittles. Her brother, Reverend Uncle Bud Williams, soon would ask the blessing. Uncle Bud had left his wife, Aunt Sal, at home, but did bring Mother's best friend and cousin, his daughter, Lottie. Papa Todd's niece, Mary Todd, and her son, Donnie, had arrived while Papa and I traipsed to the tobacco patch. Others as hungry as I waited for our preacher uncle to thank the Lord for his bounty.

The bountiful food featured a huge pot of chicken and rice, two bowls of butter beans, fried corn and okra, potato salad, sweet potatoes, several casseroles, fruit salad, and Mama's flaky, hot biscuits, pies galore, and what else? A cake I knew Mary Todd baked, for that was her specialty, a tall, white coconut cake boasting seven lit candles inviting someone to make a wish.

Papa ushered me to the cake. I felt proud, but uncomfortable, the center of so much attention.

"Happy birthday!" the crowd sang. Blowing out candles, I desperately wished that I'd lose my fear of Mr. Ben Dorman's dogs.

"Please, Daddy," I begged. "Drop me off at the sawdust pile. I need to walk past Mr. Dorman's dogs." That was the only way I could test my seven year-old courage.

Daddy humored me. He parked the car at the sawdust pile located about two hundred feet from the house of my two yellow yappers. Heart pounding, I strode toward the Dorman's yard wearing confidence, like in The Wizard of Oz, The Cowardly Lion wore his badge. Daddy trailed behind.

Almost to the house I spied both dogs, asleep underneath low-growing cedar tree branches. Maybe I could tip-toe past.

They spied me. They barked. They charged.

Alas, on my birthday when I blew out candle flames, my wish must have sailed away with the wind. I screamed, "Daddy!"

As those crazy dogs nipped at my heels, my bravado collapsed, spinning into space like a whooshing, deflating, birthday balloon.

For some people seven might prove a magic number; for me, it offered no quick fix. Thank the Lord for Daddy.

Chapter 27
A Mocking Bird Summer

Before my eighth birthday, my third grade year ended in April, and that's when I remembered: our boxy tenant house on Snow Hill still echoed emptiness. I couldn't believe that My Jimmy and his wife, Izzie, had been gone from us for almost four years. Frank would be twelve by now, and Ben, he could have married. The Joneses had been as much a part of my life as getting up in the morning and going to bed at night.

Then, joy, joy. Five new playmates filled the home plopped within shouting distance of mine. Their ages ranged from two to fifteen years.

Actually seven new people ate and slept in our Snow Hill house. It contained but two rooms, each about fourteen by fourteen feet. Managing, the Faircloth family stashed their excess clothing and furniture into a dilapidated older part of the house connected to the livable, new rooms by a breeze-way.

That year I didn't really gain five playmates. Just like a grownup, James, fifteen and responsible, worked beside his dad. And Verlon. No girl games for him. He pretended he was as big as James. Pearlise, two or three years older than I, thought deep thoughts and kept them to herself. Dularine, brown eyed and honey blonde, captured all of our hearts, but at two years old, she wasn't much of a companion. Mackie, eight years old to my nearly eight, answered the prayer I'd prayed nearly every night the house on Snow Hill sat tenantless: "Dear Lord, please send me a playmate."

With her straight blonde hair cut in "bowl" fashion, Mackie reminded me of "The Little Dutch boy," the one who saved an entire Holland countryside by plugging a hole in a dyke with his finger. Mackie became my closest summer friend.

Our families fought hard to pull free from that mire, The Great Depression. Faircloths and Hamiltons worked long hours. An asset on any farm, children, including Mackie and me, performed multiple chores.

Grandma filled her mornings, occasionally cooking for as many as fifteen tobacco hands. On such days, about 10:30 AM., Mother excused me from barn shelter work to help finish the meal and put it on the table.

One particular morning, already Grandma had filled an over-sized platter with fried chicken piled several layers high, and from the stove removed an iron pot brimming with a combination of field peas and speckled butterbeans. She'd put just the right pinch of sugar and smidgen of vinegar into a large bowl of creamy potato salad. Everything appeared ready to eat except her trademark, tiny melt-in-your-mouth biscuits, which she'd pop into the oven just before serving the meal. Meanwhile, I smelled sweet potatoes roasting.

I decorated potato salad with rings of boiled eggs, while Grandma covered the table with a white cloth. Removing steamy, syrupy yams from the oven, she slid in biscuits, saying, "Little Bushy, put ice in the glasses. No, it might melt. I'm not sure when our hungry folks'll get here."

We proceeded to load the table with food. Our work crew failed to show. Grandma stowed biscuits in the warm oven and covered food on the table with a separate cloth. "Let's take our tea glasses to the 'pizer,' Sugar. It's cooler than this here kitchen."

Fire on the equator would have been cooler than that kitchen.

Grandma's 'pizer' hid behind a lush green vine trained onto a twine trellis. Sitting on the porch, we lolled in the shade.

Grandma settled into her rocker and fanned with her apron. She smiled. "This is nice. I think I'd rather sit right here than eat dinner."

"Me too." Surrounded by all that greenery I could imagine us in Jo Jo, Jocko, and Jerry's African jungle book our math class studied this spring. Birds warbled their hearts out. Early morning rain had fallen, and the air smelled clean and sweet.

Jo Jo. Hmm. Wasn't that the same name Mother gave her brownie she wrote about? The one she left in her dresser? Each time Mother told that story, it sounded so real, I never knew what wasn't.

"What did you say, Grandma?" Grandma's blue eyes twinkled. "Billie Faye, have you ever listened to birds sing? Really listened? After you left this morning, I lay in bed, enjoying. All of a sudden, I knew what they sang. One chirped, 'Lew-is, Lew-is,' plain as day! Another, 'Ed-na, Ed-na, Ed-na.' Still another feathery little throat sang out, 'James, James, James.' One bird from the edge of the swamp called, 'Ver-lon, Ver-lon, Ver-lon,' answered by, 'Pearlise, Pearlise, Pearlise.'

"I know I must have stretched my imagination, but them birds kept on singing until they'd called out every name of the Faircloth family. 'Mackie, Mackie, Mackie.' And the prettiest of them all, 'Du-la-rine, Du-la-rine, Du-la-rine.'

"I don't know how long they sang, 'cause I had to get up and start dinner."

I shook my head. "You're teasing me, Grandma. You really think they sang out all those names?"

"I wouldn't put it past 'em." Grandma's eyes twinkled. "They're mocking birds. Maybe they just repeat what they hear."

I woke up next morning to Grandma's singing birds. One tweeted, "Bil-lie, Bil-lie, Bil-lie." A deeper voice intruded, "Get up!" Of course that was Mother. "Out of bed, Sleepy Head. We need your help unloading dry tobacco."

So much for listening to bird calls, much more pleasant than sand from cured tobacco dribbling down a girl's itchy neck.

I told Mackie about Grandma's mockingbirds' songs, and on lazy summer days, sitting in the cool shade of Snow Hill's hickory tree, we listened to feathery choruses. The birds warbled, bubbled, trilled; they arpeggio-ed every conceivable note since creation. Listening closely, we could make out just about anyone's name in their songs.

Beside Mackie, that summer's work turned into play. We picked up all cast off, too green or trashy tobacco, stringing it onto sticks separate from the rest, and at sales time we got money from our enterprise. I bought a book with a bit of mine, saved some for a treat, and gave Grandma Nettie

God's ten percent to save for me. I don't remember what Mackie did with hers.

Behind the tobacco barn grew a briar-berry patch, just like Br'er Rabbit's. "You and Mackie stay out of that briar patch, Billie," Mother warned. "That place is crawlin' with snakes."

She had little reason to worry. Mackie and I respected the pricklers. We made succulent selections, picking around the edges of the patch. Our purple mouths spoke "briar-berryin'" without words. On days when rain dampened the ground, my friend and I packed deep, clinging sand atop our feet, and carefully slipping out our feet, created frog houses. You'd think the frogs would know we were making them a home. Dularine usually plopped onto them anyway.

When boredom set in, one of us would say, "Let's play house." We'd lay out our walls with tobacco sticks, all the time knowing the other wanted to be Mommie. "It's my turn today." I'd try to speak first.

"Mine." Mackie would poke out her lip.

I'd just as soon be Grandma. With Edna's blessing we called Dularine our baby.

Daddy kept so many tobacco sticks, we could make our play houses as large as we wished. Converting oak tree moss into sofas and beds, we stacked together loose brick for a stove. Jar lids made wonderful pots. Tearing leaves into pieces, collard greens.

The Faircloths lived in our Snow Hill house for one tobacco season before, the story of our lives, they found a farm with a larger home a distance away. Since then I have seen none of my friends. Today, seven years older than Grandma Nettie lived, I pay mind visits to that year of "hard times," "good times" in my memories, and thanks to Grandma's talented mockingbirds, till this day I recall all seven names of that Faircloth family.

I missed Mackie. I had thought we'd walk to school together. However, after my July eighth birthday, followed by an approaching fourth grade school year, Mother prevailed on Cousin Worth Abercrombie to drive me to the school where he was principal. Then, instead of walking two and a half miles to Good Hope Elementary each morning, I'd ride to Eldorado Number One, located in the Shell section of our county. Also I'd have Worth's daughter as a companion. Like me, Mary Joyce was a fourth-grader as well as a step-cousin and good friend.

Chapter 24
An Eldorado Experience and More

One morning I dashed around my house gathering books, paper, pencils. That's when I heard, "Hee haw! Hee haw!"

What in the world? Ears back, tail flying behind, here came a prancing, big, brown mule pulling a wagon. Sitting on the wagon seat? Mary Joyce and her dad, bouncing along and grinning, Mary Joyce's grin a tad wider than her dad's. For what seemed like half a lifetime, we jolted over five or six miles of bumpy, Horry County dirt roads to Eldorado. Soon Cousin Worth's car was back in running condition, and no more did we bounce along in a mule and wagon. Sort of fun while it lasted.

In Mrs. Lillian Watson's fourth grade classroom I discovered Greek and Roman myths. I pored through tattered old Britannica encyclopedias for every such tale, for where else could I meet a man with wings on his heels, or a powerful creature boasting the body of a horse and head and shoulders of a man? Or a sheep-herding giant with only one eye, and that in the middle of his forehead?

That fall of 'forty-one, just months before America joined forces with other Allies fighting for freedom in World War II, our school began its federally funded, hot lunch program. Reciting "twelve times nine equals one hundred and eight," or learning that George Washington crossed the Delaware, we'd smell dry beans boiling and cornbread baking. Unlike at home, I enjoyed school dishwashing duty. With no inside plumbing, we used two, huge zinc tubs, one to wash, the other to rinse dishes for about sixty or seventy students, plus three teachers. To this day, when chlorine stings my nostrils, I recall those disinfecting tubs of plates and spoons set up in the makeshift classroom kitchen at Eldorado Elementary School, plus the fun my friends and I had, missing classes.

My parents decided I should return to Good Hope Elementary for fifth grade. In Mrs. Eugenia Nichols classroom, we students hung our coats and hats on pegs in a room-width cloak room. We placed our lunches on shelves above our coats. Esta Mae Cooper, a pretty brown-eyed blonde girl, shared a double desk with me, and together we battled Mrs. Nichols' dreaded long division.

Sadly, three years later, surfing at Myrtle Beach, Esta Mae fell off of a raft and drowned.

Remember Cousin Worth, Mary Joyce's dad? In our sixth grade year he became Good Hope's principal. Also my teacher. One day Mary Joyce and I were talking when we should have been working. Suddenly, between "You girls want to share your conversation with the class?" and "No Sir," the proverbial hickory stick struck between us, smacking our desks with a loud crack. The blow glanced off my shoulder onto Mary Joyce's.

"Girls, when I say 'Quiet,' I mean 'Quiet!'" Mr. Abercrombie drew himself up to his six feet, two inches height.

Sometimes I embroider a little about the severe beating with "a hickory stick" Mary Joyce and I received that day.

Sixth grade concluded my adventures at Good Hope Elementary. However, let me brag a little about the next year. I rode with another cousin, Maude, to a school near Loris. At this elementary school, designated by Horry County as Eldorado Number Two, I was the smartest girl in the seventh grade. Literally, I was the only girl. Frank Sarvis and I made up the seventh grade portion of the student body. Mrs. Mildred Bedsol taught me everything I needed to know to make decent marks in the eighth grade at good old Conway High, with its nine hundred students.

Back to fourth grade, the year World War II loomed on the horizon, I stored up memories of school. In my mind I can still hear the rattle of paper, the grind of a pencil sharpener. I see my friend up front raise her hand to go to the outside privy. At Bug Swamp and both Eldorados' we raised one finger or two, so the teacher would know time lengths of our personal so-journs. I can smell cloak room lunches, a multitude of breads filled with fried ham, cheese, baloney, raw onion, or peanut butter and jelly, especially Peggy Jo Hardee's mama's bread pudding, all warmed in winter by the class room's tall, pot-bellied stove. In third grade I hear Mrs. Velma Carterette say, "Students, open your books to page sixty-five. Today, let's see if we can all climb to the top of Boy White's hill of health!"

Boy White drank milk, spoke nicely, and acted wholesome in every way. His nemesis, Boy Red, drank coffee, ate sweets, and never, ever managed the climb to the top of our coveted hill. Maybe I should develop a craving for milk.

Chapter 25
Ruby and Lister

"Winter is gonna welcome Jack Frost before I can say 'Jack Robinson.'" Daddy beat the dust out of his hat that balmy, October evening. "We need wood cut, but I need help."

"I'll help." Mother jumped at trying anything new.

"Dottie, you're not strong enough to pull that saw. You might could help if we were working on a level surface, but sawin' down a tree at that angle would plumb break your back."

"Want to bet?" My plucky mother retorted.

Saturday morning at Mother's insistence, she and Daddy piled the cross-cut saw into the wagon and took off for the woods. A couple of hours later they returned. "I hate to admit defeat." Mother pulled off her straw hat, climbed front steps, and plopped into a rocker. "All I could manage was to enjoy the smell of pine. Rassie got us started, but pullin' that saw's jagged teeth through sappy wood, tsk, tsk, too much for me."

Daddy unhitched Old Pet from the wagon and put him in his stall, then joined us on the front porch.

Mother, straw hat parked on her knees, rocked back and forth in a wooden rocker. "I'm so mad at myself. I should be able to help Rass saw down a tree!"

"Never you mind." Grandma looked at me. "Little Bushy, go get him."

"Who? Go get who?" Mother looked pure-in-tee curious.

I jumped up and ran to the back porch, thrilled to be surprising my parents. "Grandma said for you to come around to the front." I woke up the short, stubby man sprawled out asleep, his head on a pillow Grandma sent me for when she saw how tired the stranger was.

That morning, after Mother and Daddy had left to cut trees, I found the scissors I'd bought with my ten cents allowance, and tearing out a page from Grandma's writing tablet, cut out paper dolls strung together. Recently I learned this craft and sought to improve my skill. Grandma's hands were plunged into dish water as hot as she could bear.

"Rap, rap, rap," came from our front porch.

Wiping sudsy hands, Grandma hurried to open the door. I dogged her heels.

In the sandy yard, leaning on the edge of the porch, stood a most unusual looking young fellow. He gazed up at Grandma with eyes made even bluer by their red rims. "I'm L-Lister Hiram." He stumbled over his words. "I n-need work real b-bad." He licked nervous, already wet lips.

Who was this fellow? I knew he couldn't help having big, floppy ears, and his face looked as soft as butter. It wrinkled in funny places.

Maybe he was like a cousin of ours people called "slow-witted."

I eyed Grandma. What would she say to this weird person needing work?

I shouldn't have wondered. Grandma always said, "If a stranger comes to your door, invite him in. He could be an angel. The Bible says so."

"Come in, Son," she said. "Are you hungry?"

Lister Hiram smiled from one side of his pillowy face to the other. "Yes Ma'am," he said.

After eating a biscuit loaded with thinly sliced ham and wolfing down a mug of milk, Lister said, "Umm," more telling than any thank you.

"Son," Grandma asked, "You ever pull a cross-cut saw?"

"Don't think so," said Lister.

"You willin' to learn?"

"Yes Ma'am!" Lister's face split into one, gigantic grin. And that's when he'd wandered out onto the back porch, lay down and cradled his head on his arm. That quickly he closed his eyes and slept.

Hoping to make our visitor more comfortable, Grandma said, "Go get Lister a pillow, Little Bushy."

In the bottom of our wardrobe I found one nobody used. Grandma said, "When I lift his head, you put that pillow under it." She did, and I did. Lister slept through it all.

And that's when Mother and Daddy came home.

Puzzled, when Grandma had said, "Go get him," my parents said, "What? Who!"

On my instructions Lister came around the house from the back, appearing at the end of our front porch. Grandma said, "Folks, meet Lister. This young man is Lister Hiram, and he wants to learn how to cut down trees with a cross-cut saw."

Daddy's face wore a grin as big as Lister's. "You feel like going with me to the woods right now?"

Daddy went out to the barn, brought out Old Pet, and re-hitched him to the wagon. Lister climbed onto the wagon seat beside Daddy. Off to the woods they trotted.

A couple of hours later the two returned, Daddy looking grateful and Lister still smiling.

"We're going back after dinner." Daddy wiped sweat with his handkerchief. "This is my lucky day. Lister, you're one good sawing partner."

Lister couldn't turn off his grin.

The two men and the rest of us sat down to fried chicken, hot biscuits and apple fritters. Between mouthfuls Lister told us, "I guess you know I'm not like most folks. Other boys live with their mamas and daddies. I lived at Shady Oaks all my life till six months ago. That's when they said I'd got too old and was able enough to leave."

Even I had heard of Shady Oaks. It was some kind of institution.

"Don't worry though, Mr. Rassie. I worked on Shady Oak's farm about all my life. I can do most anything you need done, if you'll show me. I've already picked me out a wife, too. As soon as I find a place to live, the school'll find somebody to marry us. Ruby can help you." Lister nodded at Mother. He wiped his greasy chin with a sleeve familiar with grease. "Ruby, that's my girl, she's real good at washing and ironing. You'll like Ruby!" Lister's eyes pleaded, *Let it be.*

The year before, Mother and Daddy had pulled down a corner bedroom of our house and with that cypress wood built a one room cottage on the edge of our back yard, intending it for a handy-man. In the days ahead they fixed it up for Lister and Ruby. Mother and Grandma dragged down an old bed frame from the barn loft, along with a cotton mattress and coil springs Mama Todd found in her attic. Papa and Mama also had a kerosene stove they no longer used. A primitive dining table Grandpa Hamp made many years ago, now stored in a corner of the wash house, plus straight-back chairs, bottoms covered in woven twine by Papa Todd, completed the house's basics. For the two windows Mother sewed blue-checked gingham curtains. Carried away with her decorating, she threw an oval red, white, and blue rag rug beside the bed. From our own linens she and Grandma sheeted the bed, then covered all with a red and yellow flowered jacquard spread, for which never before had Mother found a use.

Finally Robert Gore, a young man Lister had met at Shady Oaks, drove him there to claim his bride.

The day of their arrival I felt like something thrilling was happening. I jumped up and down so, I had my young brother wired. I told him, "Jack, Lister's getting married today. He's coming to live with us. He'll bring his wife."

Lister said she was a teenager. He was only nineteen himself. "Will she be my friend?" I asked Mother.

"Sure she'll be your friend. But not one to pal around with. She'll be a young married woman."

"What's she like?"

"I don't know. I've never met Ruby. Lister thinks she's great and that should be good enough for the rest of us."

All day dark clouds and a chill rain enveloped our house, but not my mood. I couldn't wait to greet the couple. Then, nearly dusk, Robert's blue Plymouth rolled into our yard. Hearing the car, our family turned into a five-person welcoming committee, peering through the doorway.

The car's back door pushed open. Out jumped Lister. He opened the front door, and a girl stepped slowly into our yard. Carrying a cardboard box, Robert walked around the front of the car.

Lightning flashed. Thunder roared, and that's when heaven's floodgates opened. It seemed like a sky giant, holding a monstrous, water-filled bucket, chose that moment to douse Robert, Lister, and Ruby.

Ruby reached the porch first. She carried a rather large beat-up suitcase tied around with a sash. Daddy grabbed her bag. "Come in out of the rain, Ruby. We're glad to see you."

Glued to the front porch, Ruby didn't move. She stared from one of us to another, her huge brown eyes looking as scared as mine must when I've done something wrong and had to go to the principal's office. (That's happened a few times I never told about.) Rain streamed from Ruby's brown hair and ran off the end of her nose.

Robert and Lister climbed the steps, each carrying a cardboard box. "Ruby had more than she could pack in her suitcase, and I had a lot of stuff too." Lister shook rain from the box.

The new husband looked as wet and overwhelmed as his wife, but I was more interested in Ruby. Standing at our front door she looked like "The Little Match Girl" Grandma told me about. Not that Ruby was little. She was a grown woman, if a young one. Maybe I associated her with the Match Girl because her brown eyes looked so pleading. Nice eyes they were, but in a freckled face, ending in a receding chin. Her buck teeth weren't too bad.

I shouldn't stare.

"I thank you, Robert," Lister said. "You were a good best man." Lister turned to Ruby. He put his hand to her back, gently pushing her toward the door. "Everybody, this is Ruby. Ruby's my wife."

"Good to meet you, Ruby. Come on in. You too, Robert. Visit a while. It was good of you to help these two marry today."

"I'd best go home. I promised Uncle Fred I'd have his car back an hour ago."

"Come to see us any old time." Once more Robert braved the rain.

Jack and I hogged the doorway. Grandma pushed around us. She reached for Ruby's hands. "Welcome, Ruby. It's good to have you here. Billie," she turned to me, "go get Ruby and Lister some towels. They need to dry off."

I ran for towels while Mother ushered the newly-weds into the kitchen. They dried themselves as best they could. Lister dried off their two boxes.

Reaching for Ruby's suitcase, still held by Daddy, Lister said, "I guess we'll go to our house now."

Grandma shook her head. "You'll do no such thing. Look at this table a-waitin' you. Sit down and eat. Lister, Ruby, this here's your wedding supper."

Amidst the sound of seven chairs dragged out from the table, we all sat down to eat.

Every time our family made a big deal out of a meal, Jack tried to help. Some days I thought he'd grow up to run a restaurant. He didn't.

I'd peeled potatoes, and I helped Grandma roll out biscuits. Actually I patted one. Mine.

I did keep the water bucket full from the back yard pump. I just couldn't lift a full bucket; so, I let Jack help me with that. Thanks to him, going up the porch steps, we spilled some every time.

Chapter 26
Killing Old Red

My most important job the day before it rained, I could have done without. I helped Grandma kill the old hen now sitting in succulent pieces on Great-Grandma Madora's gold-edged platter.

All along Mother and Grandma knew they'd do something special for the Hirams' wedding supper. They zeroed in on a pitiful old red hen no longer laying eggs.

Mother brought the squawking hen to the back door. She fed and watered chickens, but never could Mother kill one. She left that job to Grandma, who was taking her time changing from house slippers to easy-walkers.

Probably sad to be taking the life of a creature she had coddled since fuzzy chick-hood, Mother cradled the retired egg-layer to her chest. She showed us a trick. Placing the chicken's head underneath its wing, she swung the fated one around and around in circles. Then, she placed it on the ground. I thought the hen would spring up and run away. It lay there, as still as you please.

By now Grandma had on her easy-walkers. She picked up the chicken by its feet, head dangling. Its squawking resumed. Having performed this act countless times, Grandma seemed oblivious that she was set to take a life.

I never got use to my part in this procedure. "Here, Little Bushy, hold its head!" Grandma stretched the chicken's scrawny neck onto the chopping block.

Eyes squinted shut and looking the other way, I stood as far away as possible.

Glancing at the execution stump, then quickly away, I grabbed Old Red's poor old head and waited.

"Whack!" With one, sure hatchet blow, Grandma severed the combed, beaked head from the hen's red, feathered body.

I dropped that head like I would have a rattlesnake. Sickly fascinated, I watched our headless non-egg-layer hop this way and that. Finally, death dance over, our future dinner sank into waiting wood chips.

Time for operation feather removal: Mother placed a foot-tub of hot water, and an iron kettle filled with boiling water under Grandma's pear tree. Holding the hen by a wing, Mother carefully poured boiling water over the bird. Transferring her grip to the other wing, she scalded the rest of the chicken.

Mother glanced at me. "What's wrong with your face, Billie?"

I shivered. "I hate the smell of hot, wet, stinky feathers!"

"If you're ever to be a farmer's wife, you have to get over that!"

"Me? A farmer's wife? Not if I have to scald a chicken. Never ever!" (And I wasn't.)

A corn field spread out between us and the adjoining farm. Lately, about fifty feet directly behind our kitchen, Ruby's and Lister's newly constructed cottage sat in the field's edge. To the left of this corn patch lay Cypress Swamp, ex-home of Grandpa Hamp's nemesis, the seventeen year old gator he'd strung up and skinned on my swing's front yard oak tree. To the right of this corn field grew a pine thicket where Cud'n Bertha Mae and I built play houses from small, fallen pines. Mother took the scalded chicken into the edge of Cypress Swamp, and hidden by trees, pulled the loosened feathers from their moorings and tossed them away. This was our first procedure in cleaning our no longer red hen. Without feathers, a smattering of pin feathers became evident.

Remedying this, Mother set fire to a paper grocery bag, and passing the lit bag over the chicken, she singed off these hairy feathers. To douse the bag she dropped it into the tub. Wielding a heavy butcher knife, made by

Daddy's brother-in-law, Uncle Hartford, Mother scraped off the stubbornmost pin feathers.

Nobody's mother was more meticulous, cleaning chickens than mine. Wielding a wash cloth lathered with sweet soap, she gave the stripped body a good old-fashioned scrubbing, then rinsed it under cool pump water.

"You finished cleaning the chicken?" Grandma called out from the doorway."

"It's ready," Mother answered.

Grandma brought out a large dishpan, and using Mother's butcher knife, gutted the bird and dumped its entrails into the pan. Then, she whacked off the chicken's yellow feet.

"Save me a foot, Grandma," I said.

Time for my job. I ran out to the soft field, and with Daddy's short-handled spade, dug a hole. Wrinkling my nose, with forefinger and thumb, I picked up the hen's poor old head and threw it into the hole. Then I dumped in the rest of the waste before covering it with dirt.

I finished my job before Grandma finished hers. She was cutting out the liver and gizzard, careful to leave the gallbladder intact, because if a little gall were cooked with the chicken, the pot's entire contents would be bitterly inedible.

Next, Grandma split the gizzard and stripped out its lining. This tough organ housed coarse sand, small pebbles, and sometimes bits of glass, even buttons. I considered these odds and ends buried treasure. Shucks. Our old hen had pecked at nothing interesting.

Grandma finished butchering the chicken. After carefully washing each piece, she transferred all into a tall pot. This she placed atop the already hot, iron stove-eye.

I produced the chicken's foot I hadn't buried. "Do you have a wart, Grandma?"

I shifted from foot to foot, waiting for her answer.

Grandma sat down in her corner rocker and pulled out her snuff can. After she'd opened her mouth wide and poured tobacco powder goodness into her back jaw, (She didn't deposit her dip into a bottom lip like most lady-snuff-dippers.) she said, "You might as well have buried that foot with everything else. I don't have a single wart."

I threw the foot into the slop bucket.

Just before Easter Grandma had a wart, on her little finger. I'd heard Aunt Harriet, Aunt Gertie's cook, tell "how to carry away warts." Aunt Harriet hailed from Sandy Isle, where Geechees living there practiced such. We learned a lot from the Geechees. Daddy's helper, David Linen, came from Sandy Isle.

On that Saturday, like this day, Grandma was butchering a chicken. That old hen was quite special. She was Easter dinner. Grandma finished with the hen and passed it to Mother, saying, "I sure do wish I could get rid of this wart. It's worrying me half to death."

I thought, Now's my chance. I said, "Grandma, let me try Aunt Harriet's trick on your wart." She reached out her hand. "Sure, Little Bushy. If that'll make you happy, go ahead."

I took the chopped-off chicken's foot I saved, and rubbed it from top to bottom on Grandma's wart. Afterwards, I ran into the corn patch, dug a hole and buried the magic foot.

Three days later Grandma and I were out collecting eggs, and I remembered what we'd tried. I said, "Grandma, let's see your wart."

She held out her little finger. "Well, I be blessed, Child! My wart's gone!"

"I carried it away with that chicken foot. Remember?"

Smiling, Grandma shook her head. "Don't ever leave God out of anything, Little Bushy."

I still wanted to test Aunt Harriet's remedy on another wart.

Back to the Hiram's wedding supper. Besides stewing, then baking Old Red, Mother had made rice, yellow and fragrant, steamed in that old hen's tasty broth. And for every nice meal, Grandma made potato salad. No one else I knew mashed the potatoes, and I liked my salad creamy. She then finished it off with all of her own tangy stuff. A two quart jar of dry, shelled Kentucky Wonders tasted like "more" to me.

For dessert, Mother baked three tins of yellow cake. Earlier today she'd boiled sweetened pears to the consistency of preserves. This she spread between cake layers. Next, she poured white icing over the whole cake. Cooling, the icing hardened into a shiny surface, over which Mother piped, "Lister and Ruby," in colored, ruby red preserves. Around the cake top's edge she piped more colored preserves, sculpted into flowers. That cake belonged in an art museum.

I tried to be patient, waiting for Daddy to ask God's blessing. Like everyone else at our table, I folded my hands and closed my eyes.

Daddy prayed:

"Dear Lord, we thank you for this day and for this young couple. Bless them as they embark on their sea of matrimony, and all of us, as we partake of thy bounty. May we be worthy of thy goodness. In Jesus' name we pray, Amen."

I ate some of everything except Old Red. I couldn't eat chicken if I were party to its execution.

Soon after supper Grandma said, "Billie," and raised her eyebrows.

That was my cue. I ran to our bedroom and brought out a pint fruit jar full of hardy yellow blooms still hanging on in early November. I loved presenting them to Ruby, for she smiled wide and gave me a hug.

Soon the newly-weds picked up their belongings, and with rain still peppering down, made for their cottage. Lister came back for the second box. Face full of happy creases, he beamed, "Thank you," to us all.

After Lister left, I said, "Mother, I thought brides wore white."

Grandma answered. "I wore blue. What did you wear, Dottie?"

"Yellow. I like yellow."

"Well, like us, I guess Ruby wore what she had." Grandma put on water to boil for her dishpan.

Mother patted Grandma's shoulder. "Why don't you sit down?" She looked at me. "Billie, you're on your first legs. Bring yours and Jack's plates. Empty 'em into the slop bucket."

Until now Daddy had said nothing. He looked serious. "I'm glad Lister came when he did, but we've finished our wood cuttin'. Right now there's not much left to do. I don't want him thinkin' I don't value his work. I do."

Mother stopped rattling silverware. "Maybe he can pick up a job someplace else and still live here, or maybe he can help somebody else cut wood. I'll ask Papa if he knows anybody needing help."

Grandma frowned. "You don't need to worry, Son. What about that land out back lyin' fallow. Somebody needs to sew some rye grass, maybe a legume in that field. You can use Lister for that."

"What about Ruby? What'll she do? Does she have any kin around here?"

"I don't know much about Ruby. Just that Lister loves her."

"Lister said Ruby could help you wash and iron," I told Mother.

"I like to do my own washing. And I like Rass to help me."

"What about ironing?"

Mother smiled. "Ruby's welcome to that job, if she wants it."

From this conversation I wondered why my family invited Lister and Ruby to move in with us if they didn't have enough work to merit it.

Next day was Sunday. Our family got ready for church. Lister and Ruby said they'd wait until the following Sunday to go with us, that today they were unpacking and settling in. At church I heard Grandma ask Mrs. Alta Hardee if she knew anyone needing daily help. Mrs. Alta said she'd ask around.

That Sunday afternoon Lister took Ruby for a walk over the farm. I thought about last night's conversation. I certainly hoped our family could find enough work to keep both of our friends happy.

Monday morning, wash day, Daddy spooned sugar into his breakfast coffee. "Dot, let Ruby help you today. Try her out." He sipped his coffee, then added more sugar. "She's probably a lot better at washing clothes than I am."

"What'll you do?"

"Oh, I'll find something. I'll hitch up the mule and help Lister bust up rows in the old cotton patch across the road. I've been meaning to get that done. And the ditch banks need shrubbin'. You know, I've thought it over. I can find Lister work most days. It's not like I paid him by the hour."

In spite of her aversion to breakfast, Grandma forked in a bite of grits and eggs. "You need to take this couple grocery shopping. I gave them enough for yesterday, but they need vittles for the whole week. You and Lister do that today."

Pushing back her plate, Mother sighed. "I'll put off washing clothes till tomorrow. Take Ruby with you. She needs to learn how to shop. She might need to learn to cook, too."

"No," Daddy shook his head. "She cooked in Shady Oak's kitchen. Hey. Maybe she can get a job as somebody's cook."

"Dottie," Grandma poured herself a second cup of coffee. "You go with 'em. Help Ruby shop."

"When are you gonna stop talking and take me to school? I'll be late." Rain, stopping about an hour ago, peppered down again. I did not want to walk to school in the rain.

That morning Mother, Daddy, Lister, and Ruby went grocery shopping. Grandma and Jack stayed home and messed around.

Darn it, the rain stopped and I had to walk home from school. Oops, I shouldn't have cussed like that.

Tuesday, coming home about three o'clock, I spied Mother in the back yard. She and Ruby were hanging sheets and pillow cases on the line. On the back porch sat a small, square, hand-crank talking machine. A man I'd heard at Papa Todd's Grand Ole Opry Saturday night was singing, "I'll have a mansion, just over the hill top." Mother whistled along.

"Mother, who's that singing? And where'd you get this talking machine?"

"That's mine," said Ruby, pulling a sheet taut and pegging it. "The man singing is Hank Williams. I like his 'mansion' song, but I like 'Lovesick Blues' better."

"Ruby, where did you get this? I want one." Mother had an old talking machine, but it no longer played.

"I won it. A church in Florence sent some people over to Shady Oaks to teach us Bible. I memorized the most verses of anybody in my class. See? 'Jesus wept. God is love.' I know more."

I felt stung to the core of my greedy self. Maybe I should ask for one this Christmas. That didn't mean I'd get it!

"How'd wash day go?" Really, I was curious.

Grandma walked onto the porch. "Hey, Little Bushy. Dottie had some good help today. Ruby is a gem! Heh heh heh. That was good, don't ya think?"

"The best," Mother said.

"Where's Daddy?" I'd have bet my last plug nickel he was happy to give up wash day.

"Rass and Lister are in the Bay Field, clearing more new ground. There's still a corner of the main field that needs some roots dug out."

"Billie Faye," Jack crawled out from underneath the house. "You ready to play hop scotch?"

'Not now. I'm tired. I have to study my multiplication tables."

"Mama," Jack wailed, "make Billie play with me!"

"Come here, Brother Jack." I really loved my booger brother. I just wasn't ready to play hop scotch, not after walking home from school. "I'll read you a story from my reader. All about a wee-wee woman."

"I don't want no wee-wee woman. I want to play hop scotch."

Mother interrupted, "It won't hurt you to play a short game."

"Oh, all right. If I make an F on arithmetic tomorrow, it'll be your fault." I left it to the world to decide whether I meant Jack's or Mother's.

"I'll play hop scotch," Ruby smiled.

Jack stared at the new adult in our midst. "You'll play with me?"

Ruby's teeth, protruding a mite, looked sweet. "I've always wished for a brother. Or a sister."

While Ruby played hop scotch with Jack, I ran inside before she tired and I got drafted.

Ruby proved a willing helper, from holding sugar sacks while Grandma ripped out their seams to playing tag with Jack. She helped Mother wash clothes. She ironed, to Mother's delight. Ruby even swept yards, and that was my job. Some days she went to Grandma's old home and helped Aunt Freddie pull weeds from flower beds.

"Ruby, Ruby, Ruby," Mother said. "She does everything."

Was that a tinge of dissatisfaction I heard in Mother's voice?

Meanwhile Daddy was having trouble keeping Lister busy. He asked Uncle Dave, Grandma's brother, to let Lister help him build, or roof, or patch up things for people.

"I don't have enough for myself to do, Rassie," Uncle Dave told him.

Now that Ruby helped us, I had no yards to sweep Saturday mornings. I could go next door and play with Bertha Mae whenever I chose. Trouble was, Bertha Mae's job, Saturdays, was to sweep her yards and she didn't like being watched by a lazy girl with nothing to do.

Mother liked her ironing done, but she missed Daddy, scrubbing clothes on the wash board, while she stirred white clothes boiling in the wash pot.

"Some days I like a little privacy," I overheard her tell Daddy.

Grandma said, "I'm so glad Lister and Ruby came. That was the best thing that could have happened to them or us."

"It's good you feel that way," Mother said.

Grandma looked at her askance.

Two and a half weeks before Christmas, Lister knocked on the back door.

"Come in," I said, glad it was Saturday and I could stay home.

He looked worried. "Where's Mr. Rassie?"

"On the front porch talking to Leo. I'll get him."

"That's okay. It can wait." Lister shifted from one foot to the other.

Grandma was at the stove, stirring the rice soup Daddy liked. She turned toward Lister. "What's the matter with you, Son? Sit here in this chair. Taste this soup for me."

Lister stood where he was. "I don't want to upset Mr. Rassie."

"What's the matter, Son?" Grandma asked for the second time. She spied me. "Go make up the beds, Little Bushy."

I stopped in the bedroom next to the kitchen door. Plumping pillows and shaking sheets, I heard Lister say, "I hate to tell Mr. Rassie. Ruby and I have to leave. My Uncle Press wants us to go stay with him. He's in bad health, and he and Aunt Mamie need us. I can't turn him down; he's the only kin I've got."

"Blood's thicker than water, Lister," Grandma said, "and if kin needs you, you should help."

"You think so? You people helped me and Ruby. I don't want to leave Mr. Rassie, needin' me. Or you and Miz Dottie. Ruby thinks a whole lot of you both."

"Lister, we'll miss you and Ruby, but Rass and Dottie'll understand. Don't you worry your head a minute. I'll go tell my boy you need to talk."

Grandma brushed past me on the way to the door. She whispered, "You take in all that, Little Bushy?"

"Yes Ma'am," I whispered back.

Aunt Dalma had a niece near Ruby's age. She and Ruby wore about the same size clothes. The day before the Hiram's left, Aunt Dalma brought her a box filled with three or four blouses, skirts, pull-over sweaters, even shoes and socks. Ruby popped open the box and spread out things like Christmas morning. I heard sniffing. Ruby looked up. Tears puddled her nice brown eyes. She said, "I've never had so many pretty things before." Grandma held out her arms. Ruby crept into them and cried like a baby.

Two days later Robert returned with his uncle's Plymouth. He drove around to the back of our house and loaded up Lister's and Ruby's boxes. In the time they'd lived there, their belongings had multiplied. They took with them additional clothes, some pots and pans, even books, paper, and pencils.

Mother helped them load the Plymouth. "Come back and see us."

"Yeah," Grandma said. "Don't be strangers."

Daddy shook hands with the fellow Daddy considered God-sent.

Ruby poked her head out the car's back window. "Jack, can I come play hop scotch with you sometime?" Jack smiled wide. He nodded. "Sure, Ruby. Anytime."

I turned away. That girl with the pretty eyes and nice face shouldn't see me cry.

Later Daddy stirred fireplace ashes. He said, "Every time I put a log on the fire, I'll think of Lister."

Eons later, I still do. Lister and Ruby.

Chapter 27
Summer into Fall, 1941, a Pore Old Man

Besides everlasting demands of tobacco, summer-time at our Bug Swamp farm meant jarring peaches, tomatoes, pickles, field peas, and corn, the "jar star" this day, tomatoes. Mother's zinc wash tub, filled with Grandma's blushing beauties, sat in the middle of the kitchen floor. She poured boiling water over our morning's focus. Sitting on opposite sides of the tub, equipped with separate pans and big spoons, the two of us scooped out huge, red tomatoes, slipping off skins more easily than peeling an over-ripe banana.

Not yet seven o'clock, Grandma and I rushed to fill jars before Daddy got back from town.

"I sure hope that son o' mine finds some dependable tobacco hands." Grandma loaded her enamel pan with peeled tomatoes. "I bet if we still had Ruby and Lister, things'd go easier."

"Didn't Miz Nancy say she'd find Daddy workers?"

"She said she'd try. I know she and her twins, Frances and Nancy will come. And Buddy, although he's not the best help. It's croppers we really need. Maybe Miz Nancy can find some; maybe she can't."

"Have you heard from Ruby lately?"

"Nary a thing. 'Course they say, 'No news is good news.'"

"I don't know about that, Grandma. What're we cooking for dinner today?"

"What do you think? Tomatoes. And we'll have a big pot of butterbeans." She looked at me sharply. "Remember? You went out to the potato bank and dug around for some yesterday. People'll love my sweet potato boats stuffed with crushed pineapple. Add a baked pork shoulder to that."

I said, "If good food could bring us hands, Daddy would have to push people off his running board."

"You know, Little Bushy, vittles can be all important to a working man. If he don't eat, he can't work. Very well, that is. That reminds me:

"Once Upon a time there was this pore old man, a man who went to work for the town's richest citizen."

"What town? What man?"

"Hush up and listen! This here man and his wife were as stingy as they were rich. That's the truth.

"Across the railroad, in a ramshackle house by the creek, there lived a widower. He had no parents, no children, and since his wife flew off to heaven with the angels, he had nary a soul to feed him, to comfort him, nor love him. He was one pitiful old man. Really, he was not so old. He just felt it.

"His pantry grew emptier and emptier. So did his pocket book. When the fellow was down to his last dime, he walked to the nearest general store. His dime would buy him a bit of cheese. He loved cheese.

"Talk around the checker board had it, the town's rich man needed someone to tend his garden.

"'I could use that job,' the widower told himself. Pulling up courage from a rarely used place in his heart, much like pulling on a pair of pants, the man spit on his hand and slicked back his hair. Trudging up to the rich man's mansion, he knocked, timid-like, and tall, double doors swung open. In the doorway stood a fancy man.

"'Yes,' said the fancy man.

"'I heard tell you need a worker. I'll work your fields if you'll hire me.'

"'Beg pardon,' the gussied up fellow said. 'I'm the butler. If you'll come around to the back, I'll fetch Madame.'

"To make a long story short, Madame hired the pore old man on the spot. The butler found a hoe and sent the man to the fields.

"'Chop, chop!' In no time he'd done the work of two men. That's because he was so glad to be earning money.

"Coming home, the rich man looked out the window and saw all the work the poor man finished that day. 'You did well hiring this fellow,' he told his butler.

"Mrs. Rich Man said, 'Summon the worker into the kitchen. Cook, feed him well. Set bowls of clabber and whey before him. All he can eat. Better to feed it to him than the hogs.'

"'Yes, Madame,' said the cook.

"Trembling from working so hard, the man sat down to his supper of clabber and whey. Yuck! He never had liked that end of cow's milk, but he ate. He had to, for he was about starved.

"The next day he returned to his new job. Again, for breakfast the cook set before him clabber and whey, and in the fields, the man's work grew slower and slower. Hanging out the wash, Cook watched the pore old man put down and pick up his hoe. Keeping time with his chopping he chanted, 'Clabber and whey, a'workin' by the day. Clabber and whey, just a'workin' by the day.'

"Cook told the butler, 'That old man's not doin' enough to earn his food.'

"The butler summoned the man. He said, 'Madame says your work's not satisfactory. Don't come back tomorrow.'

"Now it just so happened that the rich man's younger brother's wife was visiting that day. She saw what Cook fed the laborer, and she watched through the window at how slowly he worked. 'Come home with me,' she told the man, now jobless.

"The rich man's younger brother lived in a tiny cottage, for his older brother inherited all their papa's fortune. *Such a difference*, the tired and now hungrier man thought. This couple had no butler, no maid, and no cook; however, they did need help tending their crops.

"'Old Uncle,' the young man said, 'let's chop the cotton behind our house. We'll work together.'

"'Ho! Wait up!' said the pretty wife. 'This man's hungry.' Quickly she scrambled eggs and fried thick slices of ham. Over the plateful she piled yellow cheese, the old fellow's favorite. Smelling the food, his mouth watered.

"In the fields that afternoon, the old man chopped cotton so furiously, his hoe fairly smoked. He far outworked his younger companion. Swinging his hoe like killin' snakes, the hired widower chanted, 'Ham and eggs, look out for your legs! Ham and eggs, look out for your legs!'

"That's the story. What do you say is its moral, Little Bushy?"

"If you feed a man well, he'll work hard for you?"

"Exactly. That's one reason we feed our tobacco hands like we do. If a person eats enough good food, he's able to do better work."

Grandma Nettie had a story ready for almost any situation arising.

By seven that morning Daddy returned from "The Hill" in Conway, bringing Miz Nancy, her children, and three of her neighbors, some crammed into his Model A, others standing on the running board, or clinging to the car's two front bumpers. I wondered how they kept from falling off the car. Daddy drove all of thirty-five miles an hour down a straight road.

Daddy, Grandma, Jack, Mother and I, as well as Miz Nancy and her hands, ate well that day. We didn't say, "Ham and eggs, look out for your legs," but we could have said, "Ham and tomatoes, bring on the potatoes," as we slapped Daddy's crop of green gold onto dozens of tobacco sticks.

I celebrated my birthday in July. Before I could turn around, school resumed in September. The next Saturday found Mother's old White sewing machine whirring away. This time she was making Leatha a dress. Mother had learned to create a Peter Pan style collar by cutting paper into collar pattern, sewing lines of rick-rack onto each other and the paper, then tearing off the paper. She wanted to try out her newest contrivance on Leatha's top.

Days slaving over arithmetic and science, my least favorite subjects, monopolized my mind. Suddenly, leaves, turning myriad fall colors, swamped our roadside.

On this day Mr. Proctor drove up to the house with our mail and tooted his horn. He did this whenever he chose. Grandma, waving a letter she'd read in the parlor, hurried into the kitchen. She said, "Dottie! Charles's coming Thanksgiving. That's gettin' to be a habit with him and Rock."

I couldn't believe we were nearing Thanksgiving.

Jack stuck his head out of the pasteboard box where he'd been playing. "When's Thanksgiving, Mama?"

While I called Mother, "Mother," Grandma, "Grandma," and Mama Todd, "Mama," Jack called all three, "Mama."

"Two weeks from today. That's when!"

Mother's sewing "whirs" paused.

"Did you hear me, Dottie?" Grandma persisted. "Palmer is coming Thanksgiving. In two weeks."

"Does that mean they will or won't come Christmas?"

"Just Thanksgiving. Rock's brother, B. P., and his family are visiting them Christmas."

Uncle Charles and Aunt Rock came Thanksgiving, and we did a lot of eating and visiting. They left for home that Sunday. Never did their visits last long enough.

Chapter 28
"A Day Living in Infamy," Cold Weather, and a New Crop

December 7, 1941, a Sunday, dawned two weeks and four days before Christmas. Like all Sabbath mornings, unless a body was sick, our family members each dressed in our Sunday best and headed for church. Going home, Grandma asked, "Why's everybody so quiet? I thought Preacher Woodle came up with an uncommonly good sermon today, didn't you? That we should all love our neighbors?"

"As ourselves, Grandma."

"That's good, Little Bushy. You make your old grandma proud."

"Is Scarlett our neighbor?" I thought she was.

"Yes she is. She's our neighbor."

I persisted. "Do we love her?"

"Hmm. I'll say this. Do you love Scarlett, Dottie?"

Mother said nary a word.

Grandma thought a moment. "Question I need to answer, myself, is do I love Scarlett? I didn't feel all that much love when she was pulling your hair out, Dottie, and it falling in the baby's face. But that was then. Now's now."

Daddy laughed. "That's not an answer, Ma."

"Well, I reckon I do love the woman. What do they call it in church? Agape love?

"Anyhow, Scarlett's one of God's creatures. He didn't make a soul that couldn't be good.

"The old bad man just comes along and tempts a body, which turns that body into something God never intended. When such happens, there's sadness in heaven. I'll say this. I love the Scarlett God created her to be. I love that Scarlett."

"Humph," Daddy snorted, "I think *that* Scarlett's somewhere besides Bug Swamp."

"Not if she confesses she's sinned and asks God's forgiveness."

Throughout our conversation Mother had been quiet. She sighed. "I don't know why, but today, I feel so blue. Just like something bad is gonna happen."

"Don't think like that, Dot. What could happen on a pretty day like this? Here it is the seventh of December, and the weather's as warm as you please." Daddy rolled down his window.

I was remembering another day Mother said she felt like something bad was gonna happen. Next day Mama and Papa Todd came with bad news. Mama held a handkerchief to her face and cried like a baby. She hugged Mother and said, "Dottie, Mama's dead. One minute she was rockin' in her chair and talkin' like usual. Then, she stopped rockin, and slumped. That quick she left us. She's dead. My mama."

Mama Todd's mother was Mud, Florence Callie Royals Williams, my great-grandmother with the squeaky voice, home-made bonnets, and ankle-length dresses. That Mud. The one with the mother, Emmaline. She died, giving little Callie birth. The Mud whose dad, Daniel Royals, left with a Civil War regiment and never returned. The grandma Mother loved visiting as a child, and although Mother told Mama Todd, "Don't cry Mama. Mud's better off," Mother cried too.

I hoped nobody died this time.

From her front passenger seat Grandma said, "Roll up that glass, Rassie. I'm an old woman and I'm chilly, sun or no sun."

By this time we were home, underneath Grandma's old cedar tree. Jack hopped out of the car saying, "Last one out's a rotten egg."

As soon as dinner was over, Mother went to bed. She said she had a sick headache.

Walking through the church door Sunday night, we heard voices abuzz, all over the congregation. Men stood in clumps around the heater, although the day was too warm for a fire.

Mother led Jack and me to the center section. I liked aisle seats. A stranger, a short man with red, curly hair, walked in with Uncle Oliver who took charge of the service.

"All of you. Take your seats." Uncle Oliver looked serious. "This man has something to tell us." Uncle Oliver added, "I know what he's gonna say, and you'd better listen." He gestured for the man to take the floor.

"My name is Sam. Sam Chestnut. I'm from over next Shell. I'm here to tell you what I heard on the radio today. About four o'clock I had my dial turned to WBT, Charlotte, North Carolina, when I heard a man, I think it was Grady Cole, say Japanese attacked Pearl Harbor. I know many of you have radios, but a lot of times we don't turn ours on, Sundays, except sometimes we listen to *The Lone Ranger*." He grinned.

"I don't even know why I'm here, except Mrs. Rubelle Dorman said I should come tell you what I heard. I visited her and Jesse late this afternoon. Anyhow, I'm here to say: Today, Japanese planes bombed Pearl Harbor."

Over the congregation a few said, "I heard that." "That's right."

We hadn't heard. We had no radio.

Everybody started talking at once. "What happened?" "Was anybody killed?" "Why would Japanese attack us?"

"I don't know much," the man answered. "Just that early this morning, Japanese bombers flew over Pearl Harbor and did a lot of damage. Bombs were still dropping some three hours later."

"One of the older ladies in the amen corner moaned, "Oh, my God. This means war."

Everyone was too dumbstruck to do much but pray and leave.

Back home my parents sat stony-faced. Grandma turned her sadness toward the fireplace. She poked around in the ashes. "What is this old world coming to? I thought we'd had the war to end all wars. That's what they called the last one."

Next morning, from down the road Noah Huggins ran over. He said, "Mr. Rassie, you people be at our house by 12:30. Roosevelt's gonna speak." Noah and Bertie, sharecroppers, had a radio.

At Noah's the adults gathered as close to the radio as they could. Bertie, Noah's wife, pulled up a comfortable chair for Grandma. Jack and I hung back on the front porch, but instead of playing, I listened to the radio man.

"This in from news headquarters," a voice said.

Another said, "We come to you today from a joint session of our Congress. About to speak is the President of the United States, President Franklin Delano Roosevelt. Mr. President:"

Mr. Roosevelt! Everybody I knew said he was one fine man!

Our president spoke softly. (I know exactly what he said. Rather than trust my memory, I researched his speech.) He began, "Yesterday, seven December, 1941, a date which will live in infamy, the United States of America was suddenly and deliberately attacked by naval and air forces of the Empire of Japan."

Infamy. What was that?

He went on to say the U.S.A. had been at peace with Japan, but evidence showed this attack was deliberate. Japan and Pearl Harbor in Honolulu were too far apart for it to be anything else. Those sneak thieves did a lot of damage to our naval and military forces. The president said many lives were lost.

Mother's words: "I feel just like something bad's gonna happen."

The rest of Mr. Roosevelt's speech escaped me. I was lost in my own thoughts. But toward the end he said he was asking Congress to declare war on Japan. Seemed to me, Japan had declared war on us.

War. I'd heard Grandma, Aunt Freddie, and Aunt Laura talk about World War I. Uncle Hal, Grandma's doctor/brother, fought in France during World War I. And in France, Aunt Laura's husband, Uncle Murph, had been gassed. Daddy said my uncle got a check each month for that. He was on "permanent disability." Those were people I knew and loved.

Too much was happening too fast. I wanted Mother and Daddy to get back to worrying over their tobacco crop. Hoeing and suckering and topping, even harvesting sounded so much more manageable.

Before we knew it, Christmas would be upon us. Folks should have things on their minds other than a new war we hadn't asked for. How dare those Japanese pilots fly over a fine harbor named Pearl, and drop bombs onto our navy's finest ships? I heard Daddy say they even bombed ships out in the Pacific Ocean close to our own western coastline.

That night I lay in bed thinking of all those mama's boys and girls aboard the doomed ships going about their business. Some probably never knew what hit 'em. Others probably stared, amazed by those itty-bitty planes buzzing around overhead, raining down bombs like splattering, over-size hen eggs.

I couldn't forget Grandma's glum expression after returning from Noah's and Bertie's the day our president spoke. Rocking in her chair without rockers which she did when upset, she took up her earlier lament. "Oh my, not another World War." She eyed Daddy. "They'll not take my boy. That's not allowed!"

Daddy? The war could take Daddy?

I was glad when Mother announced she needed a tree if we were gonna decorate it this year. That turned our minds toward Christmas. "Chillern," Grandma said, "If we ever concentrated on Jesus' birthday, this is the year."

All while people talked about the war we'd declared on Japan, and the war Germany and Italy declared on us, our family got down to the nitty-gritty of green cedar swags and red holly berries. Mother could work wonders with very little. Still, no matter our intentions for a blessed Christmas, war threw a damper on everything, from the carols sung in church, to the hats, on Christmas Eve we set in our chairs for Santa to fill.

Crawling into bed with Grandma that night, I listened to night noises, just like I did every Christmas Eve. I yearned to hear reindeer paws on our wooden shingles. Wonder if old Hitler had his eye on the North Pole. He seemed set on gobbling up every place else.

As soon as Christmas celebrations ended, Mother enlisted us all in removing holiday decorations and taking down the tree. "I don't want to see anybody in my family face-up in a coffin next year," she declared. "With this war on, I'm taking no chances." Superstition in her family dictated that a Christmas tree left standing on New Year's Day pegged someone in the family to die that year.

Wrapping twinkly ornaments in old newspapers and packing them in shoe boxes, I asked Mother, "Do you think it'll freeze by next Sunday?" Although my newest coat was brown, even I thought its material soft and beautiful. I couldn't wait to wear it to church.

"Sooner's fur's mighty thick this year." Sooner-Dog was my brother's cross between a black lab and some unknown species.

"Hand me those bells and I'll tuck 'em in with these swags." Mother fished out another red and silver glass ball, rolled beneath the couch. "When an animal's hair grows thicker than usual," she smoothed out a wrinkled wise man, "that's supposed to mean we're in for a cold winter."

Usually Jack Frost failed to pay Bug Swamp a serious visit till after Christmas.

Grandma wound crepe paper hangings into circles. "Little Bushy, don't you feel too prideful about your new coat. There's some folks live their whole lives without such a pretty garment."

Grandma knew me well. "I'm just thankful Mother bought my coat, Grandma." Secretly, I couldn't wait to show it off to my friends, even if it was brown.

In my childhood no weatherman behind glass pointed out fronts moving in with temperatures rising or falling. During the night when we least expected Jack Frost, he'd pop in. The first thing I'd hear when waking? Ice breaking in the wash basin, and Daddy saying, "Brr," building up fire in the cook stove and fireplace heater. Outside awaited a winter wonderland of icy sparkle.

And I do mean icy! On such mornings, snuggling in a feather bed with Grandma, I'd listen to Daddy's din, glad I didn't have to brave a freezing kitchen to make my family comfortable. "Clang!" Daddy opened the heater door. He used a poker to rearrange remnants of ash. Soft thuds said he'd thrown in oblong lengths of pine, he and his handy man, Arch Brown or David Lenin or Lister Hiram, earlier that fall, cut and stacked onto the woodpile. Then I'd hear Daddy strike a match to a crumpled newspaper or two, add the kindling to the pine, and roaring fire would lick up the heater's flue.

On this day our heater was cemented into Grandma's huge fireplace chimney, but as a newly-wed, Grandma cooked meals in that fireplace.

With fire chasing away cold, Daddy broke through ice, crusting the water bucket. He'd prime the outside pump if pipes leading to the pump hadn't frozen. When they ice-clogged, Daddy took shavings from lightwood knots, piled them around the pump's base, and lit a fire. That melted the ice, and water flowed out obligingly.

Our kitchen grew warm, though still "airish." Such mornings Jack I took turns dressing in a corner behind the heater.

Neither Jack nor I was fond of breakfast, although Mother never gave up on us. Whether or not we ate, she cooked ham, eggs, grits, plus triangular servings of flour bread smeared with home-jarred jam, the bread cooked in a greased griddle atop our stove.

Before leaving for school, I'd pull on two pairs of socks, swaddle myself in sometimes two pairs of corduroy overalls, plus a sweater, overcoat, warm scarf, mittens, and hat. I'd sling across my shoulder the blue denim book bag Mother made, waddle away from the warmth of home and join Bertha Mae, Joe, Billy Bland, Drunita Bland, and others for the two and a half mile trek to school.

"Wait for me," I'd cry, racing across the yard as fast as my girded body allowed, ankles jarring from feet pounding frozen soil. Jillions of glints sparkled the trees, their evergreen leaves glazed with a coat of ice Mother said I shouldn't sample. Sometimes, feeling guilty, I sucked on a frozen leaf anyway, or, possibly munched on a weird-tasting icicle I broke off the house's eave.

Our walk to school took place in an atmosphere of hushed silence, intruded upon by our breathless chatter, clunky footfalls, the crack of tree limbs, and sudden shards of ice showering onto the wood's carpet of brittle leaves. Our breaths puffed out white steam through chapped lips. Below eyes watering with cold, chilled cheeks rivaled any red in our scarves.

By January, forty-two, our country had braved barely a month of World War II's conflict. Mrs. Eugenia Nichols, wife of our principal, Mr. Harry Nichols, taught me fifth grade. That crispy, cold morning, I marched into school with the rest of the student body. My seat mate, Esta Mae Cooper, already sat in our maple, double desk. The room's pot-bellied heater glowed red. Before roll call, students took turns warming themselves close to the stove.

Leaving home I had slipped my soft brown coat over other warm layers. Thank goodness I ran out of the house before Mother saw me, or she would have made me wear an older, itchy wool.

I looked around the room, wondering if anyone noticed my nice coat. Smells of damp cloth drying filled the room.

Oops! Someone stood too close to the heater. The odor changed from drying out to smoldering. Smoke stung my nose. "Mrs. Nichols," I addressed the teacher who held her pencil and grey roll book, ready to take attendance. "Mrs. Nichols, something's burning!"

"Billie Faye, it's you!" Pauline MacDowell raced toward me, beating at my scorching coat.

As I turned to look, flames broke out and licked up my back. Together, my friend and I stomped my coat onto the floor, putting out the fire.

I dreaded going home and telling Mother.

She surprised me. Though she looked sad, and frowned, Mother took my coat to Bass's Dry Cleaners. They rid it of its smoky smell. Back home Mother cut out portions of hidden coat material and patched the burned spot. Her darn barely showed. My mom could work wonders.

Days, after night visits from Jack Frost, the sun shone brighter. Probably from reflections of all that ice, ice melted away. There went our magic wonderland; but not icy temperatures. They remained for most of January, into February.

Nights, going to bed with Grandma, my feet felt like ten-pronged frozen chunks. One particularly frigid evening we sank into our cool bed of feathers. Attempting to horde body warmth, I drew up my feet. When that position proved uncomfortable, I stretched out full length. Surprise! Mother had heated bricks in the fireplace, wrapped them in thick quilt squares, and placed them between sheets at the foot of our bed. Soon, my feet felt as toasty as if I sank barefoot into warm August sand.

Now, many years later, comfortably ensconced in a home boasting running water, bathrooms, and central heat, I hark back to that winter as well as others, when Mother's heated bricks warmed my feet and my heart.

Thank goodness all winter weather wasn't icy, or Mother and Daddy would have had a hard time preparing their tobacco beds. Like usual, weather permitting, late January or early February found my parents turning tobacco beds into finely sifted seed receptors. War hadn't changed everything.

It changed enough. Several young men in our community already talked about joining the army. Aunt Dalma's young brother, L. D., joined as a second lieutenant. He graduated from Clemson College, and just like Uncle Charlie Palmer, had taken ROTC. I heard Grandma tell Mother, "The only good thing I can think of, coming out of Palmer's rheumatism, he can't go to war. And I don't want Rassie there either."

"He's too old," Mother said. "Just barely, but a miss is as good as a mile." She paused, a worried look etching her forehead. "I can't help but worry about Mace. If Roosevelt and Churchill don't wrap up this war quickly, it could get my brother. That would about kill Mama."

Like always, Papa and Mama Todd, Mace and Louise, Leatha and Jeff, all pitched in to help with our tobacco growing. On such days my parents arose before a whit of sun peeked over our east fields, for Papa Todd's wake-up hour was four a.m. He sought to complete a half day's work before breakfast.

This morning Papa's car was as packed as Daddy's, coming from The Hill with his tobacco hands He drove up and parked beneath the cedar in our driveway, the cedar with two peaks, these days. I still remember the ice storm that broke off Grandma's stately cedar's steeple "pointing directly to God," Grandma's words. That's what she said of most things, tall and stately.

Out of Papa's round-backed Chevrolet piled Mama, Leatha, Jeff, Mace, Louise, Leatha's two-year-old Randall, wrapped in a thick shawl, and, of course, Papa Todd.

Mace and Louise had married late in 'thirty-eight. Like so many in our family, they eloped to Conway Courthouse. No one was invited to attend, for that would have meant no elopement. I still feel I shared their adventure, for I spied Louise leave the church.

On that fateful Sunday, four years earlier, right after Mr. Bud Holmes dismissed the congregation to go to individual Sunday-School rooms, I glimpsed Louise, then Louise Thompkins, venture toward the rear classrooms; but, instead of attending Sunday-School, she scooted down the church's back steps. Strange, I thought, but soon forgot about it with Miz Julie, our teacher, pursing her lips and looking down her nose at each of us entering her domain.

Miz Julie called everyone's name, and instead of saying "Present," we answered with a Bible verse. I usually said, "Jesus wept," or "God is love." We all chose short verses.

Allison Dorman. One day when Miz Julie called his name, he said, "Jesus wept, Moses slept, Peter fell off the back door step." I thought Miz Julie was going to tan Allison's hide right there in church.

Usually at service's end, before anyone else, Louise's family left for home.

This day Mr. Will, Louise's dad, re-entered the sanctuary. "Where's my daughter?" He called out, "Louise! Has anybody seen Louise?"

I pulled at his shirt sleeve. "I saw Louise before Sunday School. She went down the back steps."

Mr. Will's black eyes gleamed blacker.

H.B. Hardee, Grandma's nephew, called out from an aisle over, "During Sunday School I saw Mace Todd, outside with a taxi driver."

Mr. Will's face went from white to red. With nary a word he turned on his heel.

That afternoon Mother, Daddy, Jack, and I went to Papa Todd's house. There, on their front porch swing sat Mace and Louise. Looking sheepish. Mama greeted us with the same words Papa said when Mother wed Daddy. "Them two's as married as a haint!"

While Mace was nineteen, Louise was seventeen. Wonder who signed for them? Even I knew they were too young to marry without permission.

Jeff and Leatha courted on this same porch swing. If I had refused Jeff's "quarter" bribes, they might never have married; but then, neither would they have their precious little boy, Randall.

Three years younger than Jack, Randall dogged his older cousin's heels. They rode tricycles up and down four continuous porches bordering Papa's silver colored house. I thought of his house as a snowball, for its outer walls gleamed silver beneath a bright, aluminum roof. When in any way Randall injured himself, he opened his sweet little boy mouth wide and cried like he wanted the next-door King family to know he hurt.

When I was little, my Aunt Leatha adored me. Although almost nine years old in 'forty-two, I still felt a mite jealous, Leatha showered Randall with so much love. 'Course, I loved him too.

Working with family was always great. Mother would say, "Billie Faye, come back here! You left a pile of weeds around that hill of tobacco." Or, "You're slowing down, Girl. Don't stand there day-dreaming." Every time Mother fussed at me, my Aunt Leatha fussed at her. Leatha still loved me.

Thanks to help from Mother's family, we nurtured our tobacco crop through spring and on into summer's gathering and curing season.

Chapter 29
That Old Time Religion

Every spring Mother sewed me a brand new, church anniversary dress. Not long after I'd burned my brown coat on Miz Nichol's heater, Mother brought home fabric for my new dress. "Not brown, I hope." I was afraid to peek into the bag.

"Billie," Mother moaned.

"Is it brown?"

"Just the background. I'm sorry, Honey." She looked hopeful. "Tiny flowers in it are pink."

I almost felt sorry for her. "Mother," I tried to sound like she did when she spoke to me. "I'll be nine years old this July. I want a dress I like. Make yourself something with the brown-flowered material."

Mother looked truly contrite. She said, "Maybe we can afford more material. Would you like to help me pick it out?"

"Would I!"

Daddy still had his mule and wagon, but somehow he also managed to own first one, then another, Model-A Ford. Jack stayed with Grandma, while Daddy, Mother, and I drove to town for our important shopping. The car sure beat bouncing around in a hard old wagon, and a body could go a lot farther in less time. Daddy parked behind Burroughs's, because he found parking in back easier than the street's diagonal parking.

Burroughs owned the largest department store in Conway. Also Mr. Burroughs owned a mortgage on our farm. Hopefully we could buy our material on credit.

We entered through the rear of the hardware department where metal clinked against metal, and men's voices asking questions about stuff not at all interesting soon would have bored me silly. On through the grocery section I spied a school chum. Peggy Jo Hardee waited with her mother for a wedge of cheese to be weighed. (For school lunch I traded Mother's ham biscuits for Peggy Jo's mother's scrumptious bread pudding.) The grocery's oiled wood floor scent, combined with the aroma of a half dozen or so different fruits, root vegetables, breads, and hoop cheese, smelled interesting.

As Mother and I prepared to pass through these mundane portals to the dry goods department, I held my breath. Here, well-dressed clerks sold suits, dresses, linens, hats, shoes, and fabric. Daddy said, "See you later." He took off for wherever he preferred, probably the stables where he'd bought his mules. Those were also owned by Mr. Burroughs.

A tall, queenly woman wearing gold-rimmed glasses from which dangled a gold chain, pursed her mouth, oh so proper. She asked, "May I help you?"

Mother greeted this royal personage. "How are you, Mrs. Culbreth? We're here to buy dress material for Billie Faye."

Boy. Anything this fine lady sold us had to be perfect.

Bolts and bolts of cloth lined the walls. They filled huge tables. Mrs. Culbreth showed us a pale green, cotton material, nothing I saw myself in. Mother liked a blue, pink, and cream gingham, "Or," she said, "maybe this yellow seersucker."

In spite of the vast selection, I saw nothing I wanted. Suddenly, on a counter across the aisle, I spied *it*, an iridescent, lavender taffeta.

I reached for Mother's hand. "Oh Mother," I breathed, "there it is. That's the material I want."

Mother and Mrs. Culbreth, glancing at my dream material, promptly turned their attention to other cloth.

"Mother," I grabbed her sleeve." I love this fabric. It's the prettiest material I've ever seen!"

"Child, this would be much nicer on you." Mrs. Culbreth held up the flowered gingham.

"I want this!" I actually stamped my foot, and I'd been told what happened to children who acted ugly.

I'm sure I embarrassed Mother. She gave Mrs. Culbreth a helpless look. "I'll take two and a half yards of the thirty-six inch taffeta." Getting into the spirit of the purchase, she bought narrow lavender ribbon for bows.

Before leaving the store, Mother leafed through Simplicity and Butterick pattern books, showing me pictures of pretty dresses. She found one I liked. Producing a piece of paper from her purse, she copied that design.

Success! We were ready to return home so Mother could cut out and sew my dream dress.

Daddy had finished his business with Mr. Jones, the mule store proprietor, and was stomping around the stables.

Cranking up Tin Lizzie, as Daddy called any Model-A he owned, he manipulated the boxy car out of the parking lot and into the street, Mother driving as hard as Daddy. "Rass, don't hit that car! Look! He's backing outta that parking place. Slow down. Turn here."

I wondered why Mother didn't get under the wheel. Of course, Daddy, as well as Papa Todd, knew: women shouldn't drive cars. Driving was a man's job.

"Slow down, Rass. Let's stop at Cherry's."

Daddy had a charge account at Mr. Cherry's store. Mr. Cherry had a hand missing three fingers.

"Bring me a Cherrio, Daddy?"

When Daddy returned, carrying two brown bags of groceries, a frozen, chocolate-covered Cherrio lay atop one of the bags. Beside my ice cream lay silver bells for Jack.

I tore paper off my goody and bit into one scrumptious corner. "Umm!" Mr. and Mrs. Cherry sure did make good Cherrios.

As soon as we reached home, Mother spilled lavender material onto the dining table. In afternoon sunlight, the fabric reflected every color of the rainbow.

"Oh, Mother. It's beautiful!" Never had anyone worn such a dress as this would be.

Taking the brown bags we'd brought home, now emptied of groceries, Mother cut out a pattern, measuring it to my waist, making sure it fit. She did the same with other pieces, putting together a design for a princess-styled dress. I had no patience with the fitting process, but today I'd walk through stinging nettles barefoot, if it meant I got to wear this smashing dress.

Next, Mother cut into the beautiful material. I held my breath. Her shiny, nickel-plated scissors snipped long, smooth strokes, her mouth moving sideways in time with the scissors. I scooped up extra material for making my stand-alone doll, Peggy Jo, a dress.

Too impatient to watch the sewing procedure for long, I visited Grandma in front of the stove. She was stirring ham-bone-rice soup for Daddy.

Grandma was not in a talking mood since she was cooking and watching my three-year-old brother.

What could I do? I could help Grandma with Jack, but I wouldn't unless she came up with the idea. I couldn't go to Bertha Mae's house. Mother might call me for more fittings. I'd read every single story in my newest reader, and I hadn't had it long. Bored, bored. That's how I felt nearly every Saturday, unless I had something new to read.

Grandma said, "What's wrong with you, Little Bushy? You look like somebody ate your candy. How about going after the mail."

I jumped up, bound out the door, skipped across the front yard, and turning left, started down the lane toward the mailbox.

What was my rush? I enjoyed being outdoors. I dragged recently shoe-freed toes through deep sand, all the while looking toward woods on the left for any spying critters, snakes, squirrels, birds, maybe a wildcat or two, anything to make the afternoon exciting.

Something unseen scampered. Gingerly I climbed across the prickly ditch and peered into the woods, listening. Nary a thing. Returning to the road, skipping along, I faced the sky. Buzzards soared, occasionally flapping their wings. I knew they weren't eagles. Grandma said eagles flew way up high with almost no wing wagglin'.

A short distance from our house at a crossroads bisecting a corner of the pine thicket, our mailbox held vigil. The box clung to an ancient board nailed between two old pines. Cousin Brook's mailbox kept company with ours, so that Mr. Clem Proctor, our mailman, might make one stop.

Mr. Proctor was late. I plopped onto a pile of pine needles. A few black ants crawled in and out of their banana-colored mound. And a robin red breast patrolled the area. He thought he owned the place.

Before I could say, "Jack Robinson," Mr. Proctor coasted to a stop, all the while looking through a large handful of mail. He peered at me over his wire-rimmed glasses. "How're you today, young lady?"

"Fine, Mr. Proctor."

"Not much mail. But your grandma got another letter from your Uncle Charles."

"Thanks, Mr. Proctor."

I ran home, waving the letter like a banner. I gave it to Grandma. "Here's a letter. From Uncle Charles." Running hard left me a tad breathless.

Grandma tore into the envelope, half expecting a little money to fall out. But, this news was better than money. "Little Bushy, Palmer's coming the first of August. That's what he thinks, anyway." Grandma's voice lost some of its thrill. August was over three months away.

"Billie Faye. Come here."

Mother had finished basting and wanted me to try on my new dress. I found a wash cloth, went onto the back porch, poured water into Mother's blue speckled basin, then washed my face, hands, arms, and legs before pulling on the sumptuous material wrong-side out. I stood in a chair so Mother could fit me just right. With her mouth full of pins, she nipped in the garment, pinning it from underarm to a little below the waist.

Before I could take off the dress, a knock sounded at the door. "Hello! Anybody home?"

In strode Genevieve and Elise, Grandma's nieces, two of her baby sister, Gertie's children.

"Come in. Come in. Give my old neck a hug. Sit down." Grandma opened her pie safe for tea cakes. She asked, "You girls want milk with these cookies?"

"We've come to practice, Aunt Nettie. Come listen to us."

Grandma piled tea cakes into one of Aunt Gertie's platters. Before Aunt Gertie died a few years back, she had sent some goat barbeque to Grandma in that same platter.

Late in life, Great-Grandma Madora gave birth to twins just months before Grandma Nettie's first child, Aunt Sally, was born. Aunt Gertie had been Uncle Bert's twin.

Like their Mother before them, both Elise and Gen sang in the Bug Swamp Baptist choir, a group singing specials at home and at other area churches. Occasionally we sang at the Conway jail, or the county chain gang, located a couple of miles down our church road. Today, Elise carried a Stamps Baxter gospel song book.

I felt lucky to be born into a family of singers. The Hamiltons, the Holmes, and the Todd family all sang: at home, at church, at work. I considered singing as satisfying as eating lemon meringue, even chocolate meringue pie, and that said a lot.

Somebody, probably Uncle Bert, came up with the idea of a female quartet for this week's Sunday service. That he'd choose me to sing soprano in a quartet with three adults gave me a thrill. Mother, huskier voiced, would sing bass, Elise, alto, and Genevieve, tenor.

We four gathered in our living room, Elise and Gen on the sofa. Mother and I stood behind them. We sang from one book. Of our two song choices, the first was titled, "Over in Glory."

We lit into that one. Grandma said, "Chillern, I love it!"

Next, we tried a harder tune, one where parts split off from each other, each singer, at some point, singing the melody, its title, "I've Got That Old Time Religion in My Heart."

Grandma clapped her hands. "That's the one," she declared.

Finishing some outside chore, Daddy joined us. He said, "I agree with Ma. You won't find anything better than that last one."

Problem solved. We'd sing the "Religion" song on Sunday.

Elise and Gen, pretty sure they had the song down pat, meaning nearly perfect, left, and Mother returned to her sewing.

Friday, Mother finished my dress. She hemmed it and pressed the hem. She beckoned, "Come here Billie Faye. Close your eyes." The dress rustled; slipping over my head, it felt cool. It felt silky. Mother pulled, and tugged, and buttoned. She led me to the wardrobe mirror.

"Open your eyes."

Wow! In my wildest dreams I'd never imagined myself wearing such a happy dress. Its square neck had a tiny bow at each corner. Around the bottom of the dress, two ribbons, inches apart, ran parallel. Short sleeves puffed, and more small ribbons edged sleeve bands. I turned this way and that. With every movement, the dress changed color. Its material fairly shimmered as though pinks, greens, blues, and purples swam through rippling water in bright sunlight.

I liked how I looked in my new dress. Truly, Mother had waved a magic wand. No brown anywhere. I wanted Bertha Mae and Mary Joyce to see this dress.

Waking up Saturday morning, I swallowed. It hurt. "Mother," I wailed, "My throat hurts. What if I can't wear my new dress and sing, Sunday?"

Mother kissed my forehead. "You feel cool. You'll be all right; but, if you are sick, we'll just make the best of it. There are always other Sundays."

"Not like this one." I felt miserable in mind and body.

Daddy said, "Ma, see what you can do for Billie Faye's throat." All his life he'd seen his mother come up with miracle cures.

Grandma busied herself in the kitchen, boiling water and making penny "rile" tea. Meanwhile Mother rubbed my throat and chest with camphor.

"I hate that stuff," I said.

Mother said, "I could get some tallow and mix in asafetidy." She smiled, "If you like that smell."

Jack, jealous, said, "Mama, rub my chest."

I explained to him that he didn't have a beautiful new dress and wasn't supposed to sing in church Sunday, further spoiling his mood. Grandma brought in my tea. "Here, Jackie Boy. Have a taste." It took one sip to convince Jack his sister was not lucky to be sick.

By that afternoon, much of my discomfort had disappeared. Echo Gere, from down the lane, came and rolled my hair. Mother had made rollers like Echo showed her. She cut tin cans into narrow strips and wrapped them around with brown paper. I felt that beauty, like oft-quoted "prosperity," was "just around the corner."

And it should have been if the pain of sleeping on those rollers was an indication.

Sunday morning I sprang out of bed early, allotting myself plenty of time to get ready for church. Thank goodness my throat no longer hurt. However, a new malady set in. Nerves. My heart did flips. How could I sing before all those church people with my knees knocking off-beat time? 'Course, my friends would see me in my Cinderella dress.

While Mother got Jack ready, I bathed, put on my petticoat, black patent leather shoes, and lavender socks. I could hardly wait to slip into my new dress.

Finally, Mother and I stood in front of the mirror. Mother maneuvered the taffeta over my head and adjusted it atop my lace-trimmed petticoat. One by one she removed tightly fastened curlers, brushing my blonde hair until static electricity crackled. Except for a few peculiar bends and odd square curls due to the flat rollers, I thought my hair perfect. A fairy godmother couldn't have accomplished more. I was Cinderella, dressed for the ball.

Good Hope Baptist welcomed its church members, sheltering them with wide, cavernous hospitality, its beaded cathedral ceiling, arched floor-to-ceiling windows, and shiny, dark mahogany pews a home away from home. Two ante-rooms lining either side of the foyer greeted members. Teachers taught Sunday school classes in these twin rooms. Directly beyond the foyer and behind the center row of heavy pews hung a rope leading up to a belfry. A loud ringing of this bell peeled, "Time for church! Time for church!" Also those peels alerted the community of emergencies.

Sad to say, when adults weren't looking, naughty children, Billie included, grabbed the thick rope and swung up and down. Bell tolls cut this play time short.

Three sections of pews formed two aisles and a semi-circle before the front altar. Mother, Gen, Elise, and I sat in one of the two front amen corners, ours to the left of the pulpit.

Service began with a congregational song, after which Uncle Oliver Hardee, Aunt Gertie's widowed husband as well as Sunday-School superintendent, led the congregation in responsive reading. Nervous, I reached for Mother's hand and caught her eye. Her face appeared calm. My heart settled down from flying leaps, to mere somersaults.

After the reading, our quartet arose to sing. Standing on a stool, I held our song book, while Mother, Gen, and Elise gathered behind and on either side. My eyes met Grandma's in the opposite amen corner. She smiled. In a center front pew with Jack, Daddy smiled. Jackie-Boy grinned.

Mother hummed the pitch. "I'm glad Jesus came; Glory to his name; oh what a friend is he." Then we launched into the spirit of the song, "I've got that old time religion in my heart," answered by the three harmonizer's "I've got that," until we swooped through three verses and three stanzas.

I felt a pleasant buzz in my forehead with the blending and melding of our voices. Possibly my young voice harmonized with adults because we sang with little vibrato. Our singing flowed out in even tones, much like that of South Sea Islanders I'd heard at the Carolina Theater.

"You sang well today, Billie." "Pretty song, pretty song." I was happy to receive compliments; but, wearing my pretty dress meant more to me than any compliments.

After church, Bertha Mae held a piece of my skirt between thumb and forefinger. Her brown eyes held yearning. "That's the prettiest dress," she said.

"Thank you, Bertha Mae. I'll let you wear it sometime." I tried not to smile too broadly. I knew my dress would be short on her.

Back home Mother and Grandma bustled about the kitchen putting Sunday dinner on the table. Very carefully I took off my lavender dress and hung it in the wardrobe. Still hugged by a warm glow, I pulled on old clothes, picked up the longest of our home-made straw brooms, and swept away all recent accumulation of sand from the porch.

Chapter 30
I'll Have a Bite of That

Summer of forty-two, when Daddy complained, "Day after day, all I do is sweat my life away in a tobacco field," his lament must have leapt at him from some muddy ditch he'd slogged through after a pouring rain, or from the aggravation of a broken swingle-tree on "barnin' day." Maybe he complained because most Bug Swamp men his age were off fighting Adolf Hitler, Benito Mussolini, or Hideki Tojo, while Daddy, safe on his tobacco farm, battled plain old weeds and weather.

When man and God cooperated, Daddy relished his allotted struggles. What Daddy abhorred was the lowly worm: blood, earth, inch, meal, even caterpillar. He detested the plump, beautifully emerald, horned tobacco worm, clinging to a sticky leaf with back legs, its head with rhinoceros-like protuberance waving the air, seeking an ever fresh patch of gummy green on which to engorge itself. "Away! Get away!" Daddy would shriek, if someone chased him with a worm. Any kind.

"Daddy, if you're so scared of an itsy bitsy worm, why aren't you afraid of snakes?"

"A snake's larger. It's not soft and gooey when it's stepped on." Daddy wrinkled his curvy upper lip. "And a snake won't bother you if you don't bother it."

Famous last words!

Daddy worked hard to sustain our family, and Mother worked beside him. Grandma Nettie busied herself around the house. She mended clothes; she cooked, making the most of sugar, lard, coffee, and meat rationing. World War II's apportioning impacted our diets less than those of urban dwellers.

I worked, although, according to Mother, never enough. Mother's protest pendulum, that I read too much, swung from encyclopedias, comic books, young adult novels, to true detective and romance magazines left at our barn by some indiscriminate reader.

My brother, Jack, too young to farm, ate. And played. He'd stick a finger into one of Grandma's biscuits, fill the well with syrup, and nibble all around the hole. He'd eat the syrupy part last. He liked playing underneath our house. He'd push "brick" trucks through dusty, fine-grained silt surfaces. That was okay, but I hated seeing him fly live horse flies, sometimes mosquito hawks, tied to twine like poor old miniature kites. In preparation for his future in engineering, he constructed tractors out of spools, sticks, and rubber bands.

Mother sought to keep us in line. Extending a lower lip and puffing at a dark curl clinging to her sweat-wet forehead, she'd say to Daddy, "Where are our young'uns now?"

Daddy would laugh. "On the roof?" Sometimes we were.

Through the heat of the day our family napped. In that respect we Bug Swampians resembled our "South of the Border" neighbors. Conversely, accounts of our plain old afternoon snoozes failed miserably, compared to visions conjured up by the Spanish word, "siesta." In a library-truck book, I'd seen pictures of handsome, sleeping senors, sombreros shielding their eyes from the sun. Nearby, on shaded verandas, dark-eyed senoritas dreamed of those same senors. Closing my eyes I could envision their naptime lulled by softly strummed guitar music.

In my young mind, while Mexico's siesta symbolized peace, Bug Swamp nap-time meant, "Let's put a halt to everything interesting we could be doing this very minute."

One afternoon, a day or two into curing a barn full of what should soon turn into several hundred pounds of Horry County's brightest, Bug Swamp smelled like it did back in Great-Grandpa Bill Hamilton's molasses days. All day Daddy had done this and that, continually returning to the barn, making sure his latest cropping cured at proper temperature.

I swept off sand from our tenant house's porch, waiting for Mother to begin grading and tying. With no one living in the house, we used it to store our "yellow gold." Mother pulled out sticks of tobacco, and she and I commenced our job, preparing tobacco leaves for the soon-to-open market. Mother loved the feel of dry tobacco in her hands. It made my skin crawl.

"I'm going to the house, Dot," Daddy called to Mother from the nearby barn. "It's time to feed up."

Enough daylight remained for Mother to sort gold from trash. She told Daddy, "I'll be home shortly."

Staying with Mother, I gathered leaves into a beautiful ochre cluster. Lately I'd practiced until I could fold a satiny, mellow leaf, soft parts just covering the stem, and wind this wrapper around stems of a fistful of tobacco, tying up the hand as beautifully as Papa Todd ever dared.

That's when we heard our dinner bell. "Clang! Clang! Clang!"

Our bell rang only for midday meals.

Mother cut her eyes at me. Mine widened. We jumped up, spilling whatever was in our laps. In no time we'd cleared the quarter mile distance from Snow Hill, home.

Daddy sat on the third front porch step, Grandma and Jack bent over him. Grandma had pulled off her calico apron and ripped off a sash. This she was tying around Daddy's right arm just above the wrist.

"What's the matter? What's the matter?" Mother cried.

Grandma looked up from her task. She worked deliberately like she approached everything, but I saw fright in the tilt of her brows. "A snake bit Rassie." She spoke sharply. "Run, Dottie. Get Leo."

We had no telephone, and Leo lived almost a mile away. Thank goodness he was home and not in Normandy, or Burma. Partially deaf, Leo, like Daddy, was exempt from the draft.

Mother tore off running through sand so thick it made walking difficult. Jack and I closed in on Daddy and Grandma, both of us scared, but curious to see a snake-bit finger.

"What kind was it, Daddy?" My voice shook.

"A rattle-snake pilot, I think." Daddy smiled at Jack and me.

I let out the breath I hadn't known I held.

"As soon as I stuck my hand into that corn crib, fire shot into my finger. I knew I was snake-bit. I stirred around in them corn kernels, but that was one sneaky snake. He bit and run."

Grandma said, "Don't talk so much, Son!"

"That rascal snake took a look at my finger. He said, 'I'll have a bite of that!'"

From the tip of Daddy's right hand forefinger, twin, ruby red drops oozed.

Daddy and Grandma seemed too calm. I tried not to cry. Meanwhile, my heart felt like a trip-hammer breaking up concrete. Didn't they know? Snake bites killed people!

Finally, Leo drove up, Mother in the front seat of his dusty old Ford. She got out and Daddy got in. Mother climbed in back.

Doctor's hours had passed. Although Uncle Hal kept his office door unlocked, he wasn't there, and Grandma's younger brother did all of our doctorin'. However, across the hall, Dr. Archie Sasser just happened to be working late. Daddy ran inside his office.

"What's this?" The doctor yanked Grandma's apron string off Daddy's wrist. "You want to lose this arm? A tourniquet can cut off circulation and do worse harm than a snake bite!"

Later, when Daddy commented that the doctor seemed aggravated, Grandma reasoned, "That there doctor wanted to go home to supper. Then, here comes this snake-bit man, and Rassie not even Dr. Sasser's patient! I'd've been aggravated too!"

Now comes the part I can't remember for sure. I think Dr. Sasser split Daddy's finger and drew off some poison, but I wouldn't swear to that, even if Grandma hadn't taught me not to swear. Anyway, he doctored Daddy's arm and sent him home, minus Grandma's apron string.

(That sounds familiar.)

Waiting at home beside the road down which we'd seen Daddy disappear, not knowing whether he'd live or die, Grandma, Jack, and I paced. We worried. A neighbor, I'll call this man Curt Bailey, drove by in his truck and spotted us. I guess he saw trouble in our faces. Anyway, Curt stopped and backed up.

"Somethin' wrong, folks?" he asked.

Six year-old Jack answered first. "My daddy got snake bit. But he'll be aw'wight. I pwayed for him!"

Curt's immediate response, "Good God! He'll die!"

Hearing a grown-up vocalize his fears, Jack broke down. He sobbed into Grandma's apron. She comforted, "There, there, Son. Don't cry."

His crying ceased. Eyes shooting venom, Jack turned to Curt. "My daddy won't die, Mr. Bailey. I pwayed for him!"

And Daddy didn't die, until over forty-five years later from something entirely different.

Dr. Sasser instructed Daddy to immerse hand and arm in a pan of water, to place the pan on the stove, gradually heating it hotter and hotter until the water almost simmered, or until he could no longer take the heat. For several weeks Daddy repeated this procedure at least once each day.

His snake-bit hand and arm swelled up like a blown-up glove at the end of an expanded, oblong balloon. For a few weeks the swollen appendage, black and purple and blue, retained its bruises.

In the beginning Daddy suffered high fevers. He endured a lot of pain because of that elusive, corn-loving snake. Dr. Sasser said he thought its fangs glanced off Daddy's finger, that if the snake had let loose its full dose of venom, Daddy's problems would have been greater.

One day Leo came over, and like usual, we sat around palaverin' about this and that. The subject got around to Daddy's arm. "You know your blood has a million little snakes runnin' around in it, don't you, Rassie?" Leo liked to tease.

"Snakes!" Jack's imagination twirled cartwheels. "Little bitty snakes? Little enough to swim in Daddy's blood?"

"Yep," said Leo, "You can't see 'em, but your daddy'll carry 'em around the rest of his life."

Jack turned to Daddy. "Yeah?"

"Maybe," Daddy said. I couldn't detect if he was serious.

The summer the snake bit Daddy brought our family excitement we didn't want, or need; however, it gifted Daddy with a vacation from tobacco gathering. Papa and Mama Todd came from Adrian to Bug Swamp and helped in Daddy's place.

At the end of one trying day, when in the morning Old Pet's trace chain broke, and in the afternoon a million yellow jackets stung one of the croppers all over his head, Papa Todd said, "Rassie, today I think I'd 'a been willin' to trade places with you."

Daddy said, "No sir, you wouldn't."

Daddy's arm returned to normal just in time to market the last of his season's crop in Smithfield, North Carolina. He and Rob hauled off the tobacco and spent the night.

Chapter 31
A Year Later, Our Radio

Grandma, Jack, Mother, and I lolled around the house one scorching August afternoon. We had harvested our tobacco, placed it into the barn, cured, graded, and tied our precious commodity. Finally, we loaded it onto Daddy's old piece of a Ford truck for our blessed endeavors to be hauled off to market. Then yesterday Daddy and his cousin, Rob, carried their double load of tobacco to Tabor City, a favorite North Carolina market.

Tomorrow our family would commence work all over again; but right now we couldn't wait to learn how much money Daddy would bring home from his sale. Not that we'd keep that money long. Mother declared, and many times her word spelled law: "Pay Burroughs first. What's left is ours."

Ours? Really? Our preacher said that ten percent of all we had belonged to God.

Squinting at Roman numerals on our old mantel clock, Grandma leaned forward in her easy chair. Her eyes turned into frowning triangles. "Dottie! Rass should be home by now." A few seconds later, "Oh, I pray Rassie didn't have a wreck."

Familiar knots gathered in my stomach. While Mother was usually the worrier, this time she chided Grandma. "Don't worry so, Ma." Mother had put the last few stitches in the hem of Grandma's newest calico apron. She knotted the thread and bit off its end. "Rass should be home around two. It's just one-thirty."

In agreement Great-Grandpa Bill's clock chimed one "boi-oing."

"Did I say I was worried, Dottie?" Grandma held her head just so. "I said I was praying. Didn't I?"

My knots relaxed a trifle.

Grandma looked chastened. She said, "I know I shouldn't worry, and I don't want to. It's just that ever since that boy of mine fell out of his hospital bed and split open his belly, I've been over-anxious about him."

"Daddy's not a boy, Grandma. He's a daddy."

"And Daddy's here!" Jack leaped up from pushing his "buddin' buddin," as he called his spool toy. He bounced up and down like a kangaroo from "down under."

Before our dad could open the door of his old pick-up Uncle Bert literally sold him for a song, Jack and I reached him.

Mother yelled, "Rass, how did the tobacco sell?"

"Seventy-five cents a pound!"

Grandma said, "I told you not to worry, Dottie. I knew my boy'd bring home good money."

Meantime, while Daddy lifted something heavy from the car, Jack and I searched his pockets. Jack searched the left. I searched the right.

"Can't you kids give me a minute?" Daddy shook his head. But he smiled and his eyes twinkled.

I found my Silver Bell kisses before Jackie-Boy pulled out his.

Slamming-to the truck door with his foot, Daddy proceeded up the almost porch-long steps, my brother and I close at hand.

Curious, Mother and Grandma peered from the porch.

"Move," Daddy said, "I don't want to drop this thing."

"Whatcha got there, Rassie?" Grandma asked.

A grin wore Daddy. "You'll see." He pushed his way through the front door. "Careful now."

"Can I help?" Mother had her hands on Jack's shoulders making sure my brother didn't levitate.

"Hold this." Daddy handed her a two-by-two-and-a-half foot box, stripped of its wrappings and shiny brown. Mother's arms sagged.

Grandma frowned, watching Daddy lift our family Bible from its usual perch atop the parlor's center table. "Son! Where you goin' with God's Good Book?"

He handed Grandma the heavy tome. "Put it wherever you want, Ma."

"Well I want it where it's been, nigh on to the last forty-five years!"

Daddy scratched his pompadour. He shook his head. "Dot, you got something else this radio can set on?" He added, "It's battery-powered."

Mother set the radio labeled ZENITH on the wicker couch and relieved Grandma of her heavy book. "We don't have another table, Ma, but we'll find someplace special to keep this Bible." And despite Grandma's protest, Mother took Grandma's Good Book to the kitchen, placing it atop one of our most treasured possessions, our electric refrigerator.

To appease Grandma, Daddy brought out a wallet thick with cash, waving it underneath her nose. "Here, Ma. Put this in your money bag."

She grabbed those bills and scooted for the bedroom. Grandma's money bag was tied around her waist and she had to lift up her dress tail to reach it.

"Don't put that money away till we count it," Mother called out. Later, we'd make that a family production.

For nearly an hour Daddy dashed from inside to out, outside to in, driving down a metal stake beside the chimney, snaking wire in through the window, stringing wire from the stake to the radio. He clicked on the radio. A rectangular window glowed yellow, revealing numbers. Daddy twirled a knob. Nothing came out of that fool box but a growling mess of static.

I went from excited to disappointed, then grew tired of waiting for voices to escape that glorified chest. I wasn't surprised the radio didn't work. After all, it belonged to us.

Nothing we owned, in my eyes, was as good as our neighbors'. We lived in what I considered the gosh-awful-ugliest house in Bug Swamp Community. For nearly fifty years it hunkered right where Grandpa Hamp plopped it, in the midst of a grove of mossy oaks so ancient they sheltered early Indians. Grandpa picked a home site about two hundred yards from a gator hole, and in his heyday had to corral the yard to hem out the sneaky critters.

At least Grandpa didn't have far to drag cypress trees he hewed into planks. Going against his independent grain, Grandma said he bought square-headed nails from Adrian and hammered everything together. At first he shuttered the windows. Then, like Pa in *Little House on The Prairie,* he installed real glass window panes. Grandma said, "Chillern, when I first looked through them panes and saw the trees and the sky, I felt ever so proud!"

I would be "ever so proud" to live in a white house. Or yellow. Even blue. Grandma's home we lived in had never known a smidgen of paint. And that's how she liked it. Grandma said, "It'd be a plumb sin to smear paint over natural cypress planks!"

A season or two ago Mother painted the kitchen and papered our parlor. Grandma said little, then. Just as my mind reached our old iron cook stove in my list of basic complaints, the radio popped on, and voices, actual voices jumped out of Daddy's radio!

"How'd you get it to work, Daddy?"

"I put up an aerial."

That night we listened to a line-up of shows that would entertain us for months and years to come.

Daddy twirled the knob. He flipped past a conglomeration of babble so quickly I couldn't understand a word said. Then, following some haunting music, a man introduced, "... Peter Lorre, in *I Love A Mystery*!"

I later learned that Peter Lorre was one of many talented German entertainers driven from Berlin by Chancellor Adolph Hitler, because Mr. Lorre was born Jewish.

Hitler's loss was my gain. That first night, listening to our new radio, Peter Lorre and his African Adventurers mesmerized me. I shadowed them through a sweltering jungle, an exotic land where headhunters prowled. I stalked Peter's crew up and down spooky paths where glowing eyes studded edges of darkly wooded paths. Wading through a flowing stream, we narrowly escaped the jaws of an over-sized triple-scaled crocodile! That's when we entered the headhunters' compound. Did headhunters really hunt heads? Huts, opened to the clearing, looked deserted. Where were those inhabitants? While they seemed invisible, in the center of the square, three pots boiled, emitting an aroma none of Peter's crew, nor I, had a clue as to their contents. What could be cooking? I felt afraid to guess. At that moment eerie music intruded. "Join us tomorrow night in the steamy jungles of Belgium Congo, same time, same station."

What? I'd have to wait till tomorrow night to learn the contents of those pots?

Other programs followed. I remained enthralled by Peter Lorre's drama. While the rest of my family listened to Amos and Andy, Lum and Abner, followed by Jack Smith, a warbling singer who murdered melody, I brushed my teeth, stewing. Glory! If I put on a radio show like Peter Lorre's, I'd broadcast a whole show in one sitting!

Daddy interrupted my reverie. "Time for bed, Billie."

"Do I have to?"

"Tomorrow's a big day. It's our last tobacco barnin' this year."

Two years ago Mother would have gone around the house whooshing out kerosene lamps. Not tonight, for these days we were the proud possessors of lights so bright, Grandma said, "They could outen our eyes to look at 'em." Daddy turned to a news program. Boring. Never mind. I could hardly keep my eyes open anyway. Still drifting through the jungle with Peter Lorre and his African Adventurers, I became faintly aware of a man speaking. His was the nicest voice:

Men and women of America, there's good news tonight. Most of us feel safe, sending our kids to school with a full lunch box, picking up pay-checks we had no means of earning a few years ago. We're so busy climbing out of The Great Depression we give little thought to that ex-wallpaper hanger, Schicklgruber, who is busy taking over our world. (While these are not Gabrielle Heatter's exact words, this is the gist of his message.)

Schicklgruber? Who was that? I thought Hitler wanted the world!

Great Britain knows all about it, and we're learning faster than any of us care to. We at home owe it to our troops abroad, as well as to ourselves, to do everything we can to help the cause. Save your grease. Round up any iron, or other metal you can spare or find lying around. Do your part to help our boys win this war. And buy Kreml Hair Tonic. You'll be glad you did.

Peter Lorre and I will save America, I thought, drifting off to sleep.

CHAPTER 32
A Tobacco Barn Birthday Party

By now World War II had stirred up our universe for almost three years. No day passed without a succession of airplanes flying overhead. Myrtle Beach Air Force Base saw to that. Earlier our government took over a wide stretch of land near the ocean for a bombing range. At Bug Swamp, hearing distant bomb blasts became common place. Not long ago, if a body heard even a plane's drone, he ran outside, anxious to see the oddity. War changed everything. So did time. Turn around, and mid-summer, 1944, I felt like the grown-up lady of eleven I was.

In my young school life I had dashed hither and yon: Good Hope Elementary, two years, Eldorado one, Good Hope, fifth and sixth grades, and this fall my brother and I anticipated riding with Cousin Rob's wife, Maude, to still another school, this one, Eldorado Number II, near Loris, South Carolina.

Really, Maude wasn't a trained teacher; but, with the war raging overseas and our support for it at home, authorities stretched points in numerous places. A person could apply at county level, cram in a few training sessions, and teach at any state elementary school. Maude would teach Jack. This year he'd enter second grade.

On August twenty-second, Daddy would have lived thirty-nine years. All of his life he'd heard, "Hamilton's die young. They fall dead." In 1889, Great-Grandpa Bill Hamilton died at nearly fifty-four. On June twenty-first, 1920, Grandpa Hamp died at forty-nine. Now here was Daddy, in 1944, turning thirty-nine. Daddy figured his time on earth could end at any minute.

In the Bug Swamp community, like elsewhere, we honored our mothers in May, and our fathers in June. On this warm, late August evening in 'forty-four, while war raged on and across both oceans, our family paid an August tribute to my dad. And he never saw it coming.

Thursday morning Daddy got up before daybreak. He ran from field, to barn, to town for tobacco workers, back home to the fields.

"You'll work yourself into bed, if you keep this up," Grandma fussed, when Daddy stopped for a drink of water.

After tobacco hung from every tier in his barn, Daddy drove Buddy, his mama, Miz Nancy, and the others home. Then, he fed livestock and did other chores. He had no time to remember his birth.

But Mother remembered. Several days before, she'd captured and penned up one of her guinea hens, and before work this morning, she and I filled a dishpan with young cee-wee beans from the garden. As we bent over bushes, picking fistfuls of dewy pods, Mother said, "Billie, I hope you know just how hard your daddy works to keep a roof over our heads."

After hearing about The Great Depression all my life, I took that statement literally.

Mother stopped her picking. "Guess what. We're surprising him tonight."

So. While Daddy raced around like a madman trying to catch up on all his work, Mother, Grandma, Jack, and I whispered secrets. Daddy never noticed.

Late that afternoon, Mother posted me in a patch of tall corn, along with pots of hot food she and Grandma cooked on the sly. I plopped down in the corn row, waiting. And waiting. That field grew lonelier and lonelier, the ground ever harder. A patch of sky overhead changed color: blue, red, purple. Then disappeared.

Night. I'd never liked being alone in the dark, not even in bed beside Grandma. Fire flies dotted the dark. A light breeze drifting through stirred dry corn blades. Were those angels, rustling their wings? Glory! That would be so much better than island zombies soldiering through. (I'd seen a serial like that recently at the Carolina Theater.) A grasshopper, rubbing his legs together, kept better and faster time than Uncle Bert, directing church songs. And what Grandma said was true! Bull frogs in the swamp did croak "Who stole? Who stole?" While spring frogs, who didn't know it was August, answered in tinny voices, "Tobacco! Tobacco!"

The packed mound beneath my bottom turned into what felt like a pile of rough rocks. I shifted to a crouch. How could Mother take so-o long! Good food smells seeping from beneath closed pot lids teased my stomach. And my heart pounded. At any minute I fully expected to hear the unearthly cry of an old "painter" cat whose screech, Grandma claimed, pierced the air like some last century ghost girl's eerie cry; worse still, an icy death hand might reach through corn stalks and seize me. Drag me to his grave. Maybe mine!

Nearby came, "Swish!"

Thank goodness Mother's face emerged, although it did shine with a creepy glow above her flashlight. She carried the cake.

"Hurry," she prompted.

It took us three trips to carry all the food from field to barn.

Mother shook out a snowy cloth and spread it over benches holding green tobacco leaves scant hours ago. On top of this, she placed a pot, brimming with rice so yellow and fragrant, my mouth watered. Nestled in a deep platter, the guinea hen swam in its stock. Grandma had shelled the cee-wee beans Mother and I picked. She'd cooked the speckled beans tender, along with a small, cured ham hock. Oh, and she'd sugared the sweet potatoes. They glistened with goodness in the light of that swinging lantern. I couldn't wait to eat.

Grandma thought no one else could stir up Daddy's cake, layers tender, yellow, made with home-churned butter, sugar, eggs from Mother's hens, and flour moistened thoroughly with buttermilk. The icing gleamed, shiny dark chocolate, ready to crack when sliced.

Mother said, "They'll be here soon!" We bustled around, anxious that Daddy's dinner look perfect. Just as we clinked the last shard of ice into tall bubble glasses, and tea inside them glowed amber, up chugged Daddy, Grandma Nettie, and Jack in Uncle Bert's rattling old pick-up. It bounced to a halt in the sandy road.

Spying Jack's grin, I laughed. All day he must have about burst, keeping our secret.

Daddy climbed out of the truck and just stood there. A smile erased his tiredness. "So," he boomed. "We eat out tonight!"

I hugged his waist. "Happy birthday, Daddy!"

Jack ushered Daddy to the table.

As our birthday honoree doffed his sweat-soaked hat, his eyes looked suspiciously shiny. He bowed his head. As nearly as I can remember, this is what he prayed. "Thank you, Lord for this great looking food and the hands that prepared it. Bless us that we will be worthy of thy bounty, and Lord, bless me that I can be deserving of my family's love. Amen.

"Let's eat!"

Grandma Nettie took off her spectacles, and dabbed at her eyes.

I marveled. In the light of the lantern swaying in the breeze, Grandma's glasses reflected everything twice.

I hugged my thirty-nine year-old daddy. "You'll live to be a hundred," I whispered in his ear.

After a few more weeks of work, Daddy sold this season's last tobacco leaf. He came home from sales smelling like town. "What did you bring me, Daddy?" I asked him.

"Why do you think I'd bring you something, Little Chu?"

The twinkle in Daddy's eyes exactly matched his mama's faded huckleberry blues. He lifted out a girl's red bicycle hid beneath a croaker sack in the back of the truck. "Billie Faye, you'll have to share this with your brother."

Mother frowned. "Rass, how much did you pay for that bike?"

Glory! Why couldn't Mother just be glad for me instead of worrying about every plug nickel?

"I paid fifteen dollars for this beauty. Look how heavy it is." Daddy picked up the bike, setting it on hard packed sand. "See those rubber tires? Jack can ride it when Billie out-grows it."

I liked that my new bike was made for girls.

With tobacco season, 1944, behind us, a bate of work still called out to our family. Like on many fall days our kitchen steamed with a conglomeration of simmering fragrances, those of tomatoes, beans, and field peas. On Saturdays, home from school, I helped Grandma. I ran any errands necessary, since, these days, arthritis made it hard for her to move around. Also I helped Grandma shell peas and beans and slip skins off of tomatoes she'd poured boiling water over. And I brought in water when her pail ran low.

I enjoyed kneeling before a tub of tomatoes, looking across at Grandma. She'd start in on a tale, and I'd never know I was busy. Grandma's stories of possums and gators and snakes and bears were more entrancing that even Peter Lorre's "I Love a Mystery."

Pity. Since Daddy brought home the radio last fall, Grandma didn't tell nearly as many tales. But we listened to enough news. Overseas fighting was going on full blast, while we fought to make a living here in good old Bug Swamp. Thank goodness my daddy had been declared 4-F, due to that ruptured appendix he suffered as a boy. It kept revisiting him in the form of hernias. Cousin Leo was also 4-F. He couldn't hear well enough to fight a war.

Every fall mimicked the one before. Grandma and I prepared beans, Kentucky Wonders, tomatoes; we packed them in jars; placed them into a boiling water bath atop the hot stove; waited for jars to cool; lined them up on pantry shelves. Then we admired our handiwork.

Saturday afternoon I said, "Grandma, you do everything so well. Like usual, your jars sparkle like jewels."

Grandma beamed. Then her expression clouded. "You know, Little Bushy, sometimes I feel guilty living my life like usual with the whole world overseas going crazy." Seeing my frown, she pinched my cheek. "Don't you let old Grandma dampen your spirits. The same Good Lord's watching over us and them."

Friday morning after feeding hogs, Daddy started moving things around, looking. He lifted newspapers. He checked under the pile of laundry Mother folded and stacked on the dresser top. "Where'd you put my Progressive Farmers?" During tobacco season, Daddy took little time to leaf through magazines. "You hid 'em somewhere, Dot. I know you did."

He remembered how Mother hid my books when she said I should be working.

Finding his magazines between their bed and mattress, Daddy poured through his farm journals. Then he read every page of the new seed catalog Uncle Bert brought over. I wondered how Daddy's face could look so blissful, dreaming of something that next year would work him half to death. Glory! I never could understand either of my parents.

Many days life at home seemed so normal, I could almost forget about foreign soldiers killing and maiming so many of our boys overseas. Thank goodness my daddy wasn't one of them. Jeff, Leatha's husband and Randall's dad, he was. He'd shipped off to Burma. Uncle Mace, Mother's brother, after training at Fort McClellan, Alabama, recently sailed overseas, probably to France. Mace's baby son, Roger Dale, slipped into the world just in time to greet his soldier dad with a "wah" of a hello, and a goodbye cry. Roger was born August first. His dad left for overseas three days later.

Fall school's opening ended our frantic work season. Our family still worked, just not at such a tilt. Jack and I did our chores. Mother sewed, if possible twice as furiously. Daddy said it was to forget Mace had just left for War. Grandma milked the cow. She and I churned butter by shaking two-quart jars filled with Petunia's cream. Daddy always found jobs to fill his day.

Mother remained trim regardless of how hard or not so hard she worked. Grandma called her own year-round weight, a hundred and eleven pounds, that of a dog's, and she felt at ease saying about Mother's relatives, "That Todd family eats so much, it makes 'em plumb pore to tote it!"

Daddy needed two wardrobes, one for winter and light work seasons when he relaxed more and gained weight, and a skinny wardrobe for the months he worked off all he ate. Alas, I took after Daddy's winter weight, and Jack stayed slim like Mother.

No matter how lazy we grew in off-season, we always knew spring and summer lurked around the corner, and come tobacco season the following year, we'd all work like we were killin' snakes. I hoped no sneaky serpent would turn the tables on us.

Speaking of snakes, even after bitten by one a couple of years earlier, Daddy preferred the sneaky serpent to the lowly worm. His dander never rose higher than when sneaky old Leo pulled an inch worm from his chest and placed it on Daddy's shoulder. "Don't get so riled up, Rassie," Leo grinned, watching Daddy rip off buttons in haste to shed his "wormy" shirt. "That inch worm's just a'measurin' you material for a new shirt!"

"I'll measure you," Daddy growled.

A decade later Grandma Nettie's arthritis claimed her life. Fifteen years after that, Mother suffered Multiple Myeloma, and in 1968, at age fifty-five, she died. In 1978, ten years alone, in poor health, Daddy moved his most precious belongings to Savannah, living there with Jack and his family. Several months of each year, Daddy visited my family in Athens, Georgia. Since growing tobacco, corn, and beans, was no longer possible, he helped us grow his grandchildren.

One day he said to my sons, Jimmy and Bryan, "Boys, guess what your old grandpa has playin' tag all through his blood stream."

"Daddy," I scolded. "Don't tell him that!"

"Snakes," he told my impressionable young sons. "Little bitty snakes swimmin' all around."

I remembered my horror, listening to Leo's teasing. Jimmy and Bryan looked captivated.

Daddy lived to be four score and three years-old. A squamous cell skin cancer metastasized to his liver, and six months from the time of discovery, during a stay with me, he died. Wonder, like Leo said, if after the snake bite, for the rest of Daddy's life his blood did contain "a million little snakes, swimmin' all around." Anti-venom?

Chapter 33
Fishing at the Waccamaw

One fall afternoon Daddy and Mother visited Papa and Mama Todd at Adrian. Back home, Mother announced, "Bright and early tomorrow morning, we're all going fishing!"

"Fishing," I moaned. "Let's go to the beach. I want to go to the beach!"

I left my elders to talk fishing. I lay down on the front porch with legs crossed, staring at the cypress ceiling nailed there by my long-dead Grandpa Hamp. Maybe Mother and Daddy would decide we'd go to Spivy's Beach instead of the Waccamaw River. Maybe Aunt Minnie would let Bertha Mae come along. I swatted at a gnat. The weather might have turned too cool for a swim, but I loved walking in the sand. And at the beach Bertha Mae and I wouldn't need to whisper our secrets.

My brother, Jack, was getting too big for his britches. Lately that booger hid under the bed. He crouched outside the car, the porch, anywhere, to eavesdrop on me and my friends. Last week I tattled on him to Mother. She just grinned, pretending to frown. She said in what I thought was too nice a voice, "Boy, leave your sister alone!"

After raising a couple of boys and a girl, I realize now that Jack had no playmates and just wanted to be a part of my world. I feel a trifle guilty that I didn't spend more time playing with my little brother.

Saturday morning Mother got us out of bed much more easily than on barnin' days. While she packed up to go fishing, I lay on our smooth porch floor, pretending I was at the beach. I closed my eyes, imagining surf crashing onto the strand. It swooshed back to sea, ebbing and flowing; roaring; I could taste the salty air. Three gulls quarreled over a washed-up star fish. I counted them.

I sat up, sick of a dream that would probably be just that. The ocean always filled me with such longing, I never knew for what. Maybe to know how the sea got to be the sea. Whose feet had the water, frothing around my feet, touched before? Had it strained through sand on some shore, faraway? Had a girl my age with skin as lemon yellow as first grade tobacco leaves felt the same sea foam swirl about her ankles? A girl whose eyes tilted like moon crescents curved aslant?

I loved walking over wet sand, looking for shells splashed in multi-colors. At that moment, while I lay on my front porch at Bug Swamp, curvy shells awaited me, Billie Faye Hamilton, to amble along the strand and claim them for my basket. More than anything I'd enjoy sitting on a blanket, hugging my knees. I'd gaze out to where the sky met the sea. Beyond a shadow of a doubt, our earth truly curved. I had seen that!

Jumping up, I ran to the kitchen. "Grandma," I begged, "tell Mother and Daddy to go to the beach. Please! I don't want to go to the river!"

"I'm sorry, Billie. Your mama and daddy are looking forward to this trip. Rassie bought our poles new lead and bobbers."

Daddy fastened cane poles to our car's side, and off we went. To the Waccamaw River. No way would I see any ocean today.

A short while later, here I sat on an old river bank. Thick, scary trees draped shade everywhere but the middle of the river, and in some narrows, tree-tops met. No Bertha Mae. Just me. I shivered watching snakes drop from mossy limbs and swim across coffee colored water.

"Take this, Honeybunch." Daddy handed me a cane pole with a line, hook and sinker, and a bobber.

"Where's the bait?" I asked.

"In that can yonder."

"Bait it for me?" I tried to talk sweet.

"You fish, you bait your hook!"

Turning his mind to more important things, Daddy left me to ponder the possibility of picking up a slithery, slimy creature, only to poke a hook through its gooey body and watch it squirm. Yuck! I don't know how

Daddy managed to bait his hook. He certainly had a "thing" about worms. Maybe earthworms were an exception.

Wearing waterproof leggings, Daddy picked his footing around cypress knees, searching for a deep, dark hole where big bream lived. He whistled a song we heard on the radio this morning: "Gone fishin', there's a sign upon my door…"

First Papa, then, Mama Todd, Grandma, Mother, Daddy, everyone I came with but Jack, sauntered by, noting that I sat on the riverbank, reading a book. Jack didn't care what I did. Mother just shook her head. Grandma had brought a chair from home and pulled it up next to me. She talked so much, I had to read everything twice.

Louise and Roger Dale didn't come with us. Certainly Mace wasn't along, although he loved fishing. Mace was across the briny fighting Germans.

Jeff was overseas and Leatha stayed home with Randall. He'd gotten an ear ache, or something similar.

Nearby, Mama Todd cast in her pole. The tired old worm on her hook wriggled a bit, but had no real means of protesting. Then a fish stole Mama's worm. Opposite Grandma, Mama Todd sank onto the mossy river bank beside me. "Why aren't you fishing, Billie Faye? You'd enjoy it. Catch a fish for Papa to fry!"

Never, if I had to poke a hook through a worm.

"I bet you'd fish if Mace was here. He'd have a boat on the river, I know."

"Why didn't Louise come?" I asked Mama.

"Little Roger's too young. Louise took him to her mama's."

I'd be glad to fish if it would bring my uncle home.

On these trips, Papa Todd considered himself our chef. I put away my book long enough to help Jack gather Papa some sticks. He propped our sticks against each other into a circular pile, and striking a match on his shoe sole, lit a campfire. Several of our fishing party watched, as Papa pulled a cast iron spider from what appeared to be his bag of tricks. He filled the spider about a third full of bacon drippings brought in a Mason jar, and set the three-legged iron pan over the fire. Papa never dipped fish in batter, nor rolled them in corn meal or flour. Instead, one by one he dropped naked, salted fish, swimming a bare hour ago, into blistering grease. They "pop, pop, popped," spattering anyone nearby. The fish's revenge.

When the platter of fried fish threatened a "fish slide," Papa revisited his bag of tricks. He pulled out a pot of grits, filled the pot with salted water to boil, then set out sweet potatoes, already sliced. He fried those in leftover fish drippings.

"Umm! Everything tastes so good, Papa," Mother rubbed her full tummy. "I wish Mace was here to enjoy this." She gazed across the river at a young man near her brother's age. "Mace loves this river."

"I wish Mace was here too, Mother." I gave her a hug.

I nibbled a potato round or two and munched on a small hush puppy. How could I eat a fish I'd seen tricked into biting a worm, then deprived of his scales and sizzled in grease? Instead I munched on one of Grandma's tea cakes.

Every night that fall Mother and Daddy huddled around the radio and listened to news. "I wonder if Mace was a part of that." Mother had just heard that ships landed on the coast of France about the time Mace would have crossed the Atlantic.

The week after our fishing trip, Mother pitched headlong into making clothes for me, Grandma, and herself. I'd grown about an inch this summer, and Mother was cutting out my new, bib overalls.

After I had lectured Mother eye to eye, then pleaded with her concerning my color preferences, she bought me brown corduroy. I just shook my head, took a deep breath, and rolled my eyes.

Chapter 34
The Day of Liberation

When World War II began, I was an eight-year-old fourth-grader. Desperate to do everything toward the war effort President Roosevelt asked of us, my friends and I ploughed through woods and swamps looking for metal. Filling my red wagon, we piled heaps underneath Daddy's barn shelter until the scrap man came.

The war wore on. Early summer, 1944, certainly we knew Grandma gave up all of her bacon grease, for none of her vegetables were as tasty, and at school bond rallies Daddy and Mother bought as many war bonds as Grandma's money bag allowed. Since he was classified Four-F, Daddy felt doubly responsible for helping boys overseas, piling out of boats and wading onto dangerous strands where Hitler's troops' aim was to kill every last Allied soldier.

Early that year Mace had joined the army. A foot soldier, for a time he trained at Ft. McClellan, Alabama. Meanwhile his young wife, Louise, had been expecting Baby Roger.

No one dared mention to young me that Louise was pregnant. That word wasn't used in my presence. I knew nothing about sex except what I'd learned at school, and those ideas were definitely skewed. I remember reading a story in a True Confessions magazine I hid from Mother. In the story a boy danced a girl out onto the terrace. He kissed her. Looking soulfully into his eyes, she told him, "I'm pregnant."

Then and there I decided a boy would never kiss me if that would make me pregnant.

One sunny afternoon, late spring of 'forty-four, Mama, Papa, and Louise had visited us. I'd never seen Louise so pretty. Her dark eyes sparkled, her cheeks were pink, and her feet wore tobacco green sandals. I did noticed that her swollen feet desperately needed to burst out through their straps.

"I like your shoes," I said, "but don't your feet hurt?"

Mother said, "I'll get you a stool. You can prop up your feet."

"I'm all right. I'll lie down when I get home."

"At least take off your shoes."

"I might not get 'em back on."

"Girl, at a time like this you need to take care of yourself. I don't want Mace coming home and saying his mama failed to do right by his little woman." That, from Mama Todd.

I was beginning to smell a fish. "Mother," I said, "What's the matter with Louise? Is she gonna have a baby?"

Eyeing me over her bifocals, Grandma's eyes twinkled at the same time she drew down her mouth's corners. Mother looked at Mama Todd. "We might as well tell her," Mama said.

"Yes, Billie Faye, Louise is expecting a baby. In about a month."

"That's when Mace comes home on furlough."

"Just before he goes overseas." Louise's dark eyes darkened even more.

Mace came home in July, and in August, three days before he left for France, that's when Louise had given birth to their baby boy, Roger Dale Todd.

Mace did get to see his new son, and he did get to hold him, just barely. Our soldier boarded a ship and sailed off for Europe. We heard from him less and less. The few letters we received had many words cut out, Mace's actual whereabouts and such.

Mother kept remembering Aunt Dalma's brother, L. D. Suggs. He'd sailed off to sea, his ship was bombed by enemy planes, and he died. Each night when we read our Bible and prayed, we asked God's protection for Mace, and for Jeff on the eastern front. We felt for every mama's boy fighting the enemy. But especially for Mace and Jeff.

Spring, 1945, found us going about our Bug Swamp business, this Sunday caught up with dressing for our church's annual singing convention.

"Proud! That's what all of you are! You're everyone as vain as a flock of pouter pigeons!" Grandma drew her lips into a drawstring and shook her head from side to side. Like usual she had dressed early and now waited for the rest of us. We'd soon jump into our car and head for church. Today, a fifth Sunday afternoon, spring, 1945, our Good Hope Baptist would host the dozen or so other churches in our area's Waccamaw Baptist Association.

Mother had made me a dress of blue batiste, laced up the back with tiny ribbons. I peered as best I could into the wavy mirror hanging above a chest of drawers housing Grandma's and my clothes. Hoping no one was looking, I checked the tad of rouge on my cheeks. Almost twelve years old, I was too young to wear makeup, but hopefully people would think my cheeks looked pinker than usual due to excitement.

That was true enough.

"Brush your hair, Billie Faye," Mother said.

Did she think I wouldn't?

I'd heard her cry last night, after she thought we were asleep. This morning, hoping to help her feelings, I said, "You look pretty, Mother."

Mother worried constantly about her baby brother. Early this year after The Battle of the Bulge, he'd been reported missing in action. Military men drove up in a car and told Louise that German soldiers had captured Mace. Today, something about Mother looked untouchable, like you could see her outside, but not the real person.

People said she was a pretty woman. I always thought they were being nice. A child of the roaring twenties, Mother's slim figure looked perfect for those loose, straight dresses. Suddenly, I could see her on a dance floor doing the Charleston. Not that she did. Her parents thought dancing a sin. Today Mother's skin glowed like pale porcelain, and her deep-set eyes were the color of clear emeralds. While my unruly hair was corn colored, Mother's was brown, nearly black, with a sheen like Mary Joyce's plus Betty Jane's curl.

Today she'd painted her top lip into a coral, twin-peaked version of Clara Bow's "vee," and always she dusted her face with Pond's powder. That was after moisturizing it with Hinds Honey and Almond Cream, the same lotion she'd slathered on me since birth.

World War II hit a lot of families. Hard. Last Sunday, Good Hope Baptist joined in prayer for Jason Andrews, a marine captured by Japanese in the South Pacific. I'd heard that Japanese prisoners sometimes had their fingernails pulled out by the roots.

Uncle Mace's capture hit closest home. At nineteen he'd eloped with seventeen year-old Louise. And running around and around our house's perimeter, Mace held onto my bike's fender while I pedaled, and I learned to ride, despite the number of times I crashed into Grandma's blue hydrangeas. On Sunday afternoons Mace sat on Papa's front porch, strumming his guitar, sometimes singing "The Great Speckled Bird," or "My Little Mohee." That precious member of my family, held in the clutches of enemies. When would this awful war end?

In spite of the war and Mother's grief, she had bought dress material in honor of the up-coming singing convention. She sewed herself a garden of a dress, pink rosebuds standing out against midnight black crepe.

Daddy dressed in his "Sunday-go-to-meeting" best, starched white shirt, navy tie, gray suit and vest, as well as black leather shoes I'd buffed to a high gloss. He paced the porch. "Hurry up in there," he yelled. "Don't make us late!"

Still waiting, looking every inch a town lady, Grandma lolled in her Damask chair. "What is it the Bible says? 'Pride goeth before a fall?' I'd be mighty careful if I was you I didn't get myself too puffed up. Somebody might just come along today holdin' a pin," she said to any and all.

"What? You too, Jackie-Boy?" My eight year old brother grinned as he crept up to Grandma. Mother had decked him out in patriotic navy blue pants, white shirt, and red bow tie. Grandma gave Jack a quick squeeze.

Daddy stuck his head inside. "Let's go now or we'll be late."

At the last minute Grandma took a compact from her purse and dusted Ponds Powder over her face. She adjusted her navy crepe dress over her girdle, centered her Peter Pan style, white lace collar, and tugged at cotton stockings, relaxed above easy-walkers. Silk and nylon stockings were impossible to come by with the war on, but Grandma Nettie had worn cotton stockings most of her life anyway. "Sugar," she said. "Can you straighten my seams? My arthritis."

I knelt and straightened Grandma's stocking seams. I couldn't resist urging, "Wear a little lipstick, Grandma. You'd look great with your lips colored a mite."

"I'll do no such thing," she said. "I've told you before and I'll say it again. I didn't wear lipstick for your Grandpa Hamp, and I'm not about to start now." She tilted a finely woven, black straw hat at just the right angle, its brim turned down in front, and up in back, settling above her tight grey bun.

"You never colored your lips?" I asked.

"Well, when I was young," Grandma confessed, "I'd wet a little red crepe paper and rub it on my mouth."

"Load up!" This time Daddy meant it.

Our family climbed into the car. Grandma needed a little boost onto the running board.

At the singing convention every church brought out its best singers and prettiest songs. A strong sense of competition swept through the crowd, each group hoping they sang best. Not that they were rated other than by praise and compliments of their peers.

We considered our Bug Swamp choir more talented than most. Mother sang alto, she and two or three other women. The soprano section rang out strong and true. I was a part of that, and Daddy sang bass. Our bass and tenor sections were certainly adequate. The only group which threatened Bug Swamp's choral supremacy was the ensemble singing now, The Johnson Quartet from Mt. Herman Baptist. Their alto was the only singer in the conference Mother ever bowed to. Donzelle Lundy's voice, while not exactly mellow, poured out in a lyrical twang. Hers blended with the other three voices like raw silk a-lace with shiny satin threads.

The words to their song went, "It won't, it won't be long, not long, till I reach my mansion in the sky." Bug Swamp members leaned forward in their seats, entranced with the singers, their message, harmony, the music. In a final dramatic sweep, the joyfully strident quartet proclaimed, "For the day of liberation is nigh!"

In light of my uncle's capture, the word, "liberation" held significance for our family. Drafted into the army, Mace had been sent somewhere in the eighty-five miles stretch from Belgium to Luxembourg, where he joined General "Blood and Guts" Patton's troops. Only recently had we learned anything other than the message the uniformed man brought Louise, Papa, and Mama on a Sunday morning two months earlier. He had said, "I'm sorry," as he handed Louise a yellow envelope every spouse dreaded receiving since, in 'forty-one, President Roosevelt declared we'd joined the war. The telegram read, "We regret to inform you," and ended with "Missing in action."

We had returned home from church that Sunday to find Papa and Mama Todd's black Chevrolet in the driveway, Mama and Papa in the car's front seat, Louise in back, clutching six-month-old Roger Dale.

We got out of our car. "What a nice surprise," Mother said.

That's when we'd learned of Louise's uniformed visitors' news.

"What happened, Mrs. Todd?" Holding my crying mother, Daddy looked helpless.

"Mace is missing in action. Army men told us this morning."

"What else did they say?"

"Nothing. Whatever they know they didn't say. Missing could mean AWOL, lost from his unit, it could mean…"

My brain answered, *dead*.

From that day on our family lived with "The Sword of Damocles" hovering over our heads, although every night, even the news commentator, Gabriel Heatter's somber voice brightened, as he conjured up visions of more and more Allied victories. People celebrated because soon, the war might end. Not the Todd's. Nor the Hamilton's. We were afraid the end would fail to come soon enough for Mace.

And then exactly four weeks later, our family returned home from church by eleven thirty, because later that Sunday morning, Preacher Woodle was to preach at New Home Baptist. Just as we finished dinner and were clearing the table, we heard a car horn blowing, and blowing, and blowing.

Mother jumped to attention: "That's Papa's car horn!"

All of us ran outside. Papa and Mama wheeled into the yard. Still inside the car, Papa said, "Don't get your hopes up, Dottie. We don't know much, but we do know Mace is not dead. He's been captured by the Germans."

We laughed. We cried. Mace was alive, maybe. At least now we had hope. With the Allies inside Germany, Americans had to reach Mace soon, and on that day, he, as well as all of the people who loved him, would be liberated.

And that's why Mt. Herman's Johnson Quartet's song hit the right note with the Hamilton's at the singing convention.

That day, sitting with the choir, I waited with others while Uncle Bert beckoned. We lined up in five rows. Shortest, I stood in center front. Uncle Bert pinged his tuning fork against a mahogany pew, do-re-mied, and we Bug Swamp musicians belted out our prettiest gospel song, "Over in Glory." It pleased the congregation, but even I knew: our choir had been bested by The Johnson Quartet. And that was okay. If Good Hope singers always sang best, for what more could we strive? At least after church that's what Uncle Bert said.

The most important result of the morning service was Mother's mood. She seemed happy for the first time since the news of Mace's capture.

On the way home we discussed the convention. "I'd never have believed anybody could drag out a song on and on like that woman from Baker's Chapel," I said to any and all. "It must have had a hundred verses."

"Seven," Grandma said, hastening to add, "but you mustn't say anything unkind about that poor soul. I say she was mighty brave. She did the best she could."

"Ha!" Daddy laughed. "You must have been awful tired of listening, Ma, if you counted verses."

Mother broke her silence. "It was a sign. I know it was."

"What was a sign?" I asked.

"The song the Johnsons sang. *The Day of Liberation*. Maybe it is 'nigh.' Maybe Mace will be freed soon from wherever he is."

"Could he be in a place like our prisoner-of-war camp?" I had an inkling about prisoners-of-war.

"Could be." Daddy turned in under our cedar tree.

After the war dragged on, and our soldiers captured enemy soldiers, some of them were shipped to South Carolina. That's when Horry County turned its chain gang camp, located a mile or two down our church road, into a war camp. Fastened to their ankles, German prisoners dragged around heavy balls and chains, and many times they worked on the road in front of our house. Curious, I sat on our front steps, listening to prisoners, as they conversed in their strange, abrupt language. The men seemed peaceful enough. They'd work a while, take a break; leaning on shovels, they smoked cigarettes.

One day my cousin, Bobby Hamilton, and I sat on the porch talking about the teenage club we were too young to join. Suddenly a truck loaded with German POW's stopped in front of our house. The prisoners began cleaning road ditch-banks. Bobbie said, "I dare you to take them some water."

"Double dare," I said. "I will if you will."

These enemies looked like regular people. We filled a pitcher with water and grabbed a glass. First, I offered water to the guards. Actually, Bobby's dad, Rob, was a guard. With his permission we offered the prisoners water. One man, a tall, blonde fellow, all of thirty, pulled out a snapshot of a tow-headed boy no older than Jack. He said something sounding like, "My son." All the Germans seemed friendly. One jabbered… I had no idea what. Another man with closely cropped, sandy hair, smiled. He said, "Thank you." In English!

Afterwards, I almost felt like I'd been to Germany, in better times. "They don't seem any different from anybody else, do they Bobbie?" I told my cousin. "I can't believe we're at war with these fellows. That one man has a little boy. And the others, they have parents back home who worry about them just like we do Uncle Mace." Bobbie also had an uncle in the war, Uncle Lauris. Like Leatha's Jeff, Lauris fought the war in Burma.

"Bobbie," I said. "Wonder if the Japanese are more like us than we think? They have families too."

We reached a conclusion. What was wrong with this world wasn't people; it was war. If folks like these men working our Church Road held my uncle captive, he should be treated fairly.

Immediately the picture of Mace, wearing a ball and chain, shoveling debris from a German road and guarded by men with guns, came into focus. Not good, but better than dying. Trouble was, from talk I'd heard, German captives didn't fare as well as these prisoners. I told Grandma my thoughts. She said, "Little Bushy, the same God made these Germans that made us, and he loves them just as much. He created us all. The Japanese too." She closed her eyes and took a deep breath. "Billie, it takes just a few bad men to sour a whole world."

A lot happened that April. Often I listened with my parents to the evening news. While I'd rather have spent my time reading *Anne Rutherford and the Key to Nightmare Hall,* or *The Yellow Book of Fairy Tales,* after my uncle's capture I couldn't help taking an interest in the day's happenings. One night I heard that American and Russian troops had joined forces ready to march together into Berlin.

Way last year, General Eisenhower had crossed the Siegfried Line, whatever that was. And a journalist, Ernie Pyle, said, that as he wrote, he sat astraddle that line, watching our brave soldiers cross over into Germany. I imagined the line to be a giant fence with a seat on top, or maybe a picturesque stone wall where the writer sat safely out of harm's way. I later heard that Ernie Pyle moved his news to the eastern front and died there.

What a terrible place to be now, Germany, with Allied ground troops advancing, firing on anything that looked armed, and airplanes dropping bombs on buildings built many years before I was born. Uncle Mace could be killed by our country's very own bombs.

Occasionally Jack and I spent our Saturday afternoons at the Carolina movie theater. Just before the Spider Woman serial, newsreels showed German men and women pushing baby carriages, or wheelbarrows overflowing with possessions, or people with nothing but the clothes on their backs, riding bicycles, running, scurrying this way and that in their efforts to escape rubble piling up from buildings demolished by bombs dropped from the sky, and where was that, that paper hanger with the weird mustache who started all this? Could he be buried under brick and stone from the fall of some of those official looking buildings?

In April after Italy was freed, I heard of awful happenings there. Mussolini, and some woman for whom he'd left his wife, they were killed, left to swing upside down in the street. Thank the good Lord up above, I lived in the U.S. of A. I just wished Mace was home and out of all that horrible mess going on in Germany.

Amidst this news, good and bad hammering home, our church bell rang, its tones hollow and sad. "Go, Rass. Quick!" Mother urged.

At home we waited on pins and needles.

Shortly, Daddy returned. Shoulders drooping, he said, "Our president died. At Augusta in the Little White House."

The President of the United States, the man who, in his "fireside chats," told us what we could do to help win the war, he died; just when it seemed the Allies were headed toward victory.

Vice-President Truman became our new president.

That night Grandma slung dinner plates onto the table, so hard they danced and rang. "What does Harry Truman know about this war? He's just a haberdasher."

What was a haberdasher?

"Not in a million years can he hope to take the place of our president." Grandma's voice broke. "Why, oh why did this have to happen now?"

"Ma," Daddy chided, "it's not like you to look on the dark side. Give the man a chance. He's not Roosevelt; but, he knows what he needs to. That's the way our government works."

May seventh rolled around like any other spring morning; but, after that, what a difference. Germany surrendered! Hitler was no more. He'd burned to a crisp, the newsman said, outside his underground bunker. The only thing left for American soldiers to do in Germany was to mop up and move out. No one seemed to know how long that would take, but our neighbor, Mr. Sam Bland, inventive farmer and school teacher who always knew everything worth knowing, told Daddy, "I don't think our boys have so much to do over there that most of them can't be home in a good three months-time."

Trouble was, no one seemed to know what had happened to Uncle Mace. Then, in mid-July, about ten o'clock on a Wednesday morning, two months after the war in Europe ended, Mother and Daddy were taking a break from tobacco curing. Jack sat at the table eating one of Grandma's tea cakes I was trying to avoid because Joe Hucks said I was getting fat. The day before, I had gotten my hands on *Little Women,* and now lay stretched out on the bed finding my "place." Just when it looked like Jo and Laurie might finally get together, a car horn blew, again and again, one time after another, non-stop.

We all jumped up and ran to the front door. Papa and Mama Todd sprang out of their car. Clutching eleven-month-old Roger Dale, Louise scrambled out of the back seat.

"He's liberated! Mace is free!"

"How? What happened? Is he all right? When's he coming home?"

Finally Papa got in a word. "Around Christmas time, during *The Battle of The Bulge*, some Germans captured him. And finally, just days ago, Americans reached where he was bivouacked."

"Bivouacked?" I questioned.

"The Germans who captured Mace and his buddies knew the war was over. They stayed just in front of the Allies. But when Americans overtook them, those Krauts surrendered without a shot being fired, themselves and their prisoners. Mace's been taken to London or Paris for debriefing."

"Thank the Lord," Mother sighed. And then she burst into great tearing sobs like her heart might break.

Why was she crying? "Mother, what's wrong with you? Remember the Johnson's song? Mace is liberated. He's free!"

"I know that," Mother blubbered. "I'm just so happy!" And she cried even louder.

Grownups. Never could I understand them.

For our family the war ended in May. For Rob's wife and Leatha, war in the East continued.

"Don't they know when to stop?" Grandma asked me since no one else was within earshot. "They see how we've bested Hitler and his crooks. Can't they see they haven't a Chinaman's chance against us? There's Hitler as dead as a door nail. So, what about Hirohito and Tojo? When will they cry 'Uncle?'"

"Yeah. When will they cry 'Uncle Sam?'" I thought I'd said something smart.

Chapter 35
Questions and Answers

About an hour later Mother and Daddy returned from Aunt Sally's. For a while now Grandma's oldest daughter had been ill, something to do with her kidneys and diabetes.

Grandma's forehead turned into anxious lines. "Dottie, how's Sally? Did that new Dr. Medlin help her any?"

"I'm not sure, Ma. Sally's not in pain. That's good."

"She always was one to have kidney problems, the gravel, we called it. And now, that old sugar diabetes. You know, when Sally was a little girl, I had to fight to keep her out of the brown sugar jar. She'd scoop out handfuls of the sweet stuff. Oh me oh my. I wish I could keep my family well."

"Is that a tinge of worry I'm hearing?" Mother asked. "Don't you go and set me a bad example."

"You're right. I've asked the Lord to look after Sally, over and over."

"What did you girls do while we were gone?"

"We made quilt squares. Me and my granddaughter kept ourselves busy."

"I wish that was all anybody had to worry about. Thank the Lord some problems are out of the way."

Grandma said, "Like Hitler and Mussolini."

"Right now I'm thinking of those poor people in Japan."

"Dottie, are you feelin' sorry for the people who got us into this mess?"

"Think about it. Most people don't want war, just certain higher-ups, a few who crave being King of the World, or some such. Those people in Nagasaki and Hiroshima, they were little different from us, plain, ordinary people. Yet, our planes rained down fire and brimstone on 'em. Makes me think of Bible end times. I heard somebody say those weird bombs carry radiation, like in x-rays, and they keep on killin' and killin'."

"I don't understand any of that." Grandma folded the quilt square lying on the arm of her rocker. "When do you think Mace'll come home?"

"I don't know. He's in Paris, or London, somewhere. He'll come home when they're ready to send him."

"I know Miz Todd and Louise will be glad when he gets here. You'd think they'd send him home before another war blows up over there."

"I'm just glad to know Uncle Sam's taking good care of Mace before bringin' him home."

"Look out the window at what Jack's up to. Again. Billie Faye, go tell that boy to get off the barn roof. The aluminum over the porch is about ready to fall through."

I raised the kitchen window. Stuck out my head. "Jack! Get off that roof! Mother says so!"

"What are we gonna talk about, now that the war's over?"

"Plain old ordinary talk. 'How's the weather today? You been stuck with any wooden nickels lately?'"

"Ha! Grandma," I said.

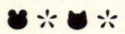

🐱 ✳ 🐱 ✳

"I've thought about this day. I've prayed for this day. I can't believe it's here." Beside Grandma, Mother bent over the kitchen table, stacking twenties on twenties, tens on tens and even a few hundreds on hundreds. "Have you ever seen so much money in your life? And it's all ours. Well, not really ours. We're lent it just long enough to count it and give it away."

"Just think," I said. "If we could spend this money anyway we wanted, I'd paint our house white, or blue." I looked pointedly at Mother. "Maybe even a pale brown."

She said, "This is money we owe Burroughs. All of it, or practically all." Mother sighed. "If we give the man everything, we just have to borrow more. Like we've been doing these past nine years."

• Bug Swamp's Gold

"I wish money was all we had to worry about." I knew Grandma was thinking about Aunt Sally. Grandma brightened, then sniffed. "Thank the Lord a lot of problems are out of the way."

Was that a tear she dabbed at?

"The Lord has truly blessed us. Can you imagine where we'd be if Burroughs had foreclosed on us? We'd be somewhere sharecropping. That's the truth."

I couldn't help saying, "Is that why ten percent of it belongs to The Lord?"

Grandma drew herself up straight. She looked at Mother, then at me. "Don't think I forgot that for one minute, Little Bushy. Ten percent of anything we end up with will go straight to Him. It's not ours to start with."

The back door swung open after Daddy stepped "Pop" on the loose porch board. "Oh yeah," I said. "If I had money, I'd patch that board."

Daddy said, "Little Chu, I don't need extra money for that. I just haven't gotten around to fixin' it."

"It is past time you do." That, from Mother.

Daddy stopped short. He eyed the stack we'd placed on the table. "What are you folks doing with Burroughs's money? Don't lose a one of them hundred dollar bills." He wrinkled his straight nose, shook his head right in Mother's face, and grinned. That was one way he showed Mother, love.

"Well, when's the blessed day? Tomorrow?" Grandma shifted around in her rocker. "Whenever, I plan to celebrate."

Next morning our family woke up with the chickens and dressed in our Sunday best. "Just think," Grandma said, settling into the car's front passenger seat. "We have enough money here and now to buy us a brand new car."

"And then some," Mother said. "Don't you feel rich, carrying around all this treasure?"

In town we parked behind Burroughs's store, just like we weren't rich. Entering through the back grocery section, I saw the black-eyed little fellow that recently greeted us. I heard somebody call him Larue. "Come in!" Larue's dark eyes plumb sparkled. "Glad to see ya!"

Leaving that area we proceeded into the dry goods division. Here, dangling her jeweled spectacles like gems around her neck, Mrs. Culbreth gazed at me down her long, regal nose. She smiled. I smiled back. "May I help you?" she pursed her lips just so.

Mother shook her head. "Not today. We have business with Mr. Burroughs." Raising her eyebrows, Mrs. Culbreth stepped aside.

Daddy led us almost to the front, took a right-angled left; and there we were, inside the heart of this massive store. From here, money spoke volumes throughout Bug Swamp, Conway, and all of Horry County, possibly all of South Carolina. Maybe the world!

"I'd like to speak to Mr. Burroughs, please," Daddy told a lady, greeting him from inside a large, wire cage.

I heard Jack's in-drawn breath. Mother grabbed his hand.

"I'm sorry. Mr. Burroughs is out for the day."

"Oh," said Daddy. "He's the one I wanted to see."

"Will I do?" A tall, skinny man whose bald, shiny head domed above crinkly blue eyes, smiled the width of his face. He reached for Grandma's hands. "Nettie," he said. "How good to see you."

Was Grandma blushing, or was that a reflection off the man's red tie?

Yeah. I'd heard of this fellow. He'd been Grandma's beau before Grandpa Hamp, and his wife had been dead almost as long as Grandpa.

"Let me find you a seat." The man led Grandma through a gate and placed her before a large desk, behind which, he took a seat.

"How are you, Lexipher?" Grandma said.

Lexipher? What kind of name was that?

Daddy followed, leaving Mother, Jack, and me cooling our heels outside the large cubicle.

"Lex, we really need to see Mr. Burroughs," Grandma began.

"I can take care of anything he can," Mr. Lexipher assured Grandma.

"Well, all right." Grandma looked at Daddy. "Is it okay with you, Rassie?"

"I guess so," Daddy said. "A debt paid is a debt paid."

"The only thing is," Grandma looked around the wire cubicle, "I'll need some privacy."

"Privacy?" Mr. Lexipher looked puzzled.

"Do you have an office I can use?"

Eyes twinkling, Burroughs's glorified bookkeeper led the way to a small, side room. He held open the door for Grandma, then started to follow her inside.

Grandma raised a finger. "Privacy, Lex."

Shortly Grandma returned, carrying her stuffed-to-the-gills drawstring bag. Partially loosening the string to her calico bank, using both hands, she let fall its entirety onto the top of Mr. Lexipher's desk.

Grandma's friend shook his head. "What's this?"

"Your money. We're paying off the debt you helped us get, years ago."

Business-like now, Mr. Lex counted out the money, much like Mother, Grandma, and I did at our kitchen table. Stacked, the pile looked smaller than I remembered. Leaving Grandma for a moment, Mr. Lex went over and spoke to the woman greeter, who shortly produced a paper.

"Hmm," Mr. Lex pursed his lips. "You don't owe all of this." He divided the money, his pile larger than the one he shoved in front of Grandma. He beckoned toward Daddy. "Rassie, sign right here and we're in business."

As Daddy bent over and signed his name, he said, "I thought business was what we've been into these past years."

"Quite right," said Mr. Lex.

Was this all there was to owing a debt? Borrowing and borrowing, then paying off everything in "one fell swoop?" Was that regret I saw in Daddy's eyes, as Mr. Lexipher placed all money paid into a nearby till?

Mother shook her head. Grandma grabbed the pile left to her and shoved it into her pocket book. Daddy shook Mr. Lex's hand, thanking him.

The trek back to the parking lot decidedly lacked the momentum propelling us into the office. Climbing into our car, nobody spoke, and before we knew it, we were pointed toward home.

"Wait," Grandma said. "We haven't celebrated. It's not every day one gets to pay off a mortgage. Turn around this car. Let's go to Donzelle's."

For a while now this restaurant had been our favorite place to eat out, for Donzelle's prepared cakes and goodies, as well as mid-day meals.

Grandma's kitchen never smelled better than Donzelle's restaurant.

Donzelle! She was the alto who sang with the group from Mount Herman Baptist Church. The singer whose voice sounded like rough silk a-lace with satin threads. That's how Mother described it.

A waitress brought us menus with specials of the day.

"I'll have pork chop with rice and gravy and green beans," Grandma ordered.

"Bring me chicken-fried steak and round fries," Daddy said. "Add to that a big dish of banana puddin'."

Mother sighed. "I've never seen so many good things I didn't cook. I think I want the vegetable plate. Make that green beans, turnip greens, butter beans, sliced tomatoes, cucumber pickles and half a sweet potato. If I don't eat everything, may I get a 'to-go' box?"

"Certainly," said the waitress.

Jack and I ordered hamburgers. I said, "All the way; hold the raw onions."

Jack said, "I want onions."

Mother inquired, "Is Donzelle in?"

Shortly, Donzelle Lundy came from the kitchen. Instead of dressed in her Sunday best, like the day she sang, Donzelle wore a wrap-around apron, and one cheek wore a smudge of flour.

Grandma smacked her lips. "Donzelle, I want to tell you. This food is the best in town. I've never sunk my teeth into a better pork chop."

Donzelle's smile rid her of her tired look. She said, "Thanks for the compliment, Miz Hamilton. When people choose our kitchen, I want them to enjoy their food."

"It's not just your food we enjoy," Mother gave three small hand claps, "although it's delicious. I want to tell you how much I love your singing. That song you sang at our church a while ago, 'The Day of Liberation?' That was the prettiest thing in song form I've heard in a long time. Your quartet gave us faith the war would soon be over."

Grandma nodded. "That's the truth."

"Your choir sang pretty too. 'Over In Glory' is a song our quartet sings."

Mother said, "Nothing beats Stamps Baxter gospel songs."

"Speaking of good things," Grandma looked sheepish, "give me half a dozen of your square tea cakes. I want to compare 'em to mine."

Before the waitress brought out the cookies, Daddy pushed back his chair and helped Grandma up from hers. He whispered into her ear, "No way will Donzelle's tea cakes beat yours."

Daddy paid the bill. Before leaving, he called out to the establishment's singer-baker, hurrying toward her kitchen, "Mrs. Lundy, next time we eat out, it'll be right here."

Donzelle clapped her hands.

Going to the car, Grandma said, "Son, I had one good old time. I hope we don't have to pay off another debt before doin' it again."

"If Dot has her way, we will." Daddy helped Grandma into her usual front passenger seat.

At home, before settling down Daddy called us together. He said, "Listen you all, it's time." He headed for the front porch.

Mother and Grandma plopped into porch chairs. Jack and I sat on steps, and in the yard before us, Daddy took his proud stance. In one hand he held a paper, in the other a match. "Observe this." Daddy waved the dreaded mortgage through the air. With a thumb nail he broke off the end of the match head which flared as though ready to burn up the world. Holding fire to paper, Daddy lit the legal document. It smoldered, turning ever darker. Then, in a whoosh and a crackle, the bane of our family's last nine years vanished. All left of our nemesis was a small corner burning Daddy's fingers, and as soon as he let fly that bit of torture, it turned to ash.

Rubbing hands together, Daddy danced a jig. "That reminds me. We need us a new car."

I threw in, "A red one. With a rumble seat."

Nine-year-old Jack got in his jab. "A car? Buy us an airplane!"

Grandma failed to appreciate our humor. "I wish we could conquer all our problems this easy."

"You call getting rid of that mortgage easy?" Mother looked pointedly at Daddy. "That's the first and last paper I plan to put on this place. Agreed?"

Daddy settled down with the adults. "I hope that's the last note we need. But Dot, you'll have to admit, that mortgage saved our hide."

Rocking rhythmically, Grandma stared into space. "We're lucky we have a friend in Burroughs and Company."

"Grandma," I said, "we're lucky Mr. Lexipher is your friend. Daddy says he's the one who told Mr. Burroughs to give us credit, year in, year out."

"Wonder how Pa would like knowing Ma has such a friend," Daddy waggled his eyebrows at his mama.

"Lex was Hampie's friend too."

Mother took the heat off Grandma. "We can thank our lucky stars we didn't end up like the Smiths." They'd forfeited their farm to our obliging Mr. Burroughs.

"Lucky stars my eye. We can thank our Maker. God. That's who helped us, and I'm gonna thank him right now. I'll pray my prayer, you pray yours." A minute or so later, Grandma declared, "Amen." She always found a way to bring us back to the Lord.

Chapter 36
Bug Swamp Teeters into Balance

After VE Day, before and after Victory in Japan, knowing Uncle Mace had been liberated, that Hitler, along with his mistress, Eva Braun, were but charcoals in a bunker, and misguided Germans no longer dogged the heels of their lunatic leader, I'd wake up in the morning, agog. My uncle and scores like him were free to return to their lives in America.

Battles in the Pacific raged months after war ceased in Germany. However, thanks to our country's "haberdasher" and his use of a bomb so powerful it must have been a weapon from God's arsenal, on August fourteenth, Japanese hierarchy formally surrendered. Unable to face dishonor, Tojo unsuccessfully attempted honorable Hari-Kari. Emperor Hirohito bequeathed his title to a relative.

Later, we learned that in remote areas, weeks passed before certain enemy forces acknowledged Japan's surrender. We heard that in Burma, a stray squadron of Japanese soldiers held several Americans captive. When approached by a convoy of U.S. soldiers, the Japanese presented their guns to their captives. Bowing and smiling, the ex-captors said, "We your prisoners now."

In spite of awful destruction caused by Mr. Truman's atomic bomb, I still liked our president. I thought he had kind eyes, and he was a good dad. He worshiped his daughter, Margaret. Walter Winchell said so; although he didn't think Margaret was such a good singer. She'd have been an asset to our Bug Swamp choir.

How must she feel with a president for a dad?

Glory! I'd rather have my own dad any day of the week, especially when on Saturdays he took us to Horry Drug Store and bought us chocolate-pineapple-nut sundaes.

Used to dealing with the scourge of war, I didn't know how to handle peace, except to feel grateful for it. Some mornings I'd wake up and wonder how many of our boys were killed while we slept. Then, I'd remember. None, due to war!

After being liberated in early July, Uncle Mace made it home in late September. For the fourth and last episode of our scary POW affair, here came Papa Todd's car, barreling down our country lane, his horn blowing for all it was worth.

The whole Todd family piled out of the car, Mace first. Mother attacked her baby brother, hugging him until Daddy said, "Dot, you're not gonna share your brother with a soul?"

I felt bashful until Mace chucked me under the chin. He gave Jack and me tiny American flags. Then he handed us unfamiliar candy bars. Their wrappers read "Bit O' Honey." They reminded me a little of Mary Jane candy.

Mace backed up and looked at Jack and me. He said, "I don't know these kids. Did Billie Faye and Jack take off with the gypsies? You two have grown tall!"

That was the nicest compliment I'd had for a while. I sidled up to Mace. "Do I get to call you 'Uncle Mace' now?"

He said, "Girl, not on your life. I'm still plain old 'Mace.'"

I hugged his neck. "You do look handsome."

He did. I'd never seen him so filled out and rested-looking. His black hair, the color of Mother's, dipped across his forehead in neatly combed lines. His skin was almost as darkly tan as his brown shirt. I smiled at Louise. She couldn't keep her eyes off of her "hunky" husband.

"You should have seen me before Paris," Mace laughed. "I was as scrawny as a gnawed-over dog bone. The army fed me good. I've put on some thirty pounds since July."

"My Boy," Mama Todd said, and silent tears made circular paths around soft, high cheek bones before landing on her "Dottie-made," rick-rack collar.

Mace reached for his boy. Thirteen months-old, Roger pulled away, distrustful of a new man in his life. "Boy, this won't do," Mace said. "The two of us need to get together."

"Wait!" Mother said. Where's Leatha? Has Leath seen you yet?"

"We'll see Leath, Jeff, and Randall on the way home."

They were having a family get-together at Jeff's dad's house. Jeff recently returned home from Burma.

Daddy ushered us inside. We found seats in the parlor. I sat on the floor where I could stare up at my long, lost uncle, no longer lost.

"What was it like, being a prisoner of war?" Mother asked.

At first I thought Mace wouldn't answer. Memories darkened his eyes. Papa Todd said, "Dottie, he doesn't want to talk about it."

"That's okay, Papa. I'm home now." Mace turned to Mother, but he was telling us all.

"Dottie, it got pretty bad. We trekked through ice and snow all across Germany. We walked till the day was done, and then we slept under whatever shelter we could find. Sometimes we robbed hen houses, although those poor Germans had little of anything left. Local farmers supplied us with potatoes, so we mostly ate potato soup. Then potatoes got scarce. Where at first we picked out beetles floating in our soup, we soon got hungry enough we gobbled up every bug in sight."

Yuck! I'd remember this later when I complained to Mother about leftovers.

"Didn't you get tired, walking?" I asked.

"It wouldn't have been as bad if a German hadn't demanded my boots. I wore his, too small for my feet."

Jack said, "Were the Germans mean?"

"Not really. They ate what we ate, did what we did. They knew it was just a matter of time before Allied troops caught up with us. Actually, when the Red Cross dropped us supplies, we shared cigarettes and candy bars with our captors."

Bobbie and I were right. The average person hadn't wanted war. Americans and Germans, well, most of them, make that a lot of them, desired the same things in life we did, enough to eat, places to live and worship, good health, peace, contentment.

On this day our world felt like a teeter-totter with props placed under both ends. No longer would World War II knock our family off-balance.

Mace didn't tell us that day, but later he told us how he was captured. In France last winter, during The Battle of the Bulge, he, some fellow soldiers, and their lieutenant got lost in the woods. Returning, the group discovered that Germans had massacred every last member of their unit. Mace and the other soldiers holed up in a vacant house, but were soon shelled by enemy fire. A grenade flew through a window. It fizzled out on the floor, but not before that thing had them trying to shinny up sheer walls. They were clawing at floor boards when the door burst open. Nazi soldiers, pointing rifles, filled the doorway. That was how Mace and his fellow-soldiers became POW's, and how they were sent on what newsmen termed *A Death March*.

About the time American soldiers freed my Uncle Mace, I turned twelve, and that fall I became an eighth grader. Now, instead of being the lone girl like in last year's seventh grade, my eighth grade encompassed over a hundred students. And no longer did I walk to school or ride with a relative. Like a monstrous yellow bug ploughing through a Bug Swamp maze, every day the bus I rode wove in and out, down dirt, as well as black-topped roads. Over and over Mr. Booth, our bus driver, braked the bus, swung open the creaky door, and waited for kids to dart from home to bus, climb its steps, and drop into a seat. Stop after stop, students packed our bus the twelve or so miles we traveled to and from school.

Of course we stopped at Bertha Mae's residence, and Joe's, and at Betty Jane's house. Mary Joyce met us at Betty Jane's. Making a sharp left turn onto a road off my own, we picked up Billy and Henry Bland, and their sister, Drunita. From there we took another sharp left. Skirting through tree-lined, narrow roadways, we stopped at a house with no front walls. Really, except for supporting elements, the parlor and kitchen of a girl I'll call Doretha, opened entirely to the road.

Poor Doretha. Head down, she sped to the bus. I saw shame in the tilt of her head. Meanwhile I watched her mother pull out a pan of biscuits from their oven. Yummy aromas drifted all the way out to my nose.

Of course I bore my own shame. Every fall, cold weather brought on Daddy's hog-killing day. That morning before leaving for school I begged, I pleaded, "Please, Mother, don't cook hog guts today. I can't bear coming home to their clammy, stinky, yucky odor."

That afternoon Mr. Booth stopped the bus all of fifty or sixty feet from my front door. I sniffed the air. "Close the door, Mr. Booth," I said, "I'm going to Bertha Mae's."

I spent the night with her too. When I didn't get off the bus, Mother knew where to find me. She came over and brought me some clothes for next day's school. Even they smelled like hog guts. I hung them outside to air.

Each day our round-about trip from home to Conway High School took a whole hour. Reaching school, arms wrapped around a stack of books and notebook, I stumbled toward the front. From his driver's seat, sometimes Mr. Booth mumbled, "Have a good day, Billie Faye." I didn't hear him say anything that nice to another soul. At church his wife told Grandma Nettie, "Mack says Billie Faye Hamilton is the only good kid ridin' his bus."

I wasn't good. I just didn't sass our driver like some did. And I knew "bad" could get back to my family more easily than "good." Knowing Mr. Booth thought me better than some, did help in my effort to walk Grandma's "straight and narrow." Not that I always kept to that path.

Years later I heard a softer Mr. Booth say, "I guess students ridin' my bus thought I was awful. That was the only way I had to keep order." He did that.

Chapter 37
1946, A New Beginning

The year following World War II's end brought about shocking changes in the lives of our family. We moved from Bug Swamp to Homewood community, located ten miles away and about two miles from Conway proper. It started like this:

A family living in one of Uncle Bert's tenant houses expressed an interest in farming with Daddy. Daddy told Mr. Lane, "My Snow Hill house is too small for your family." The Lanes consisted of Mr. and Mrs. Lane, Ruth, a daughter my age, and a son, Bobby. Also, Miz Edna was expecting a baby. Ruth told me.

Out of the blue Mother said, "Rass, you said you'd like a holiday from farming. This is it."

A few days later Aunt Dalma came. Mother looked at Aunt Dalma out of the corner of her eye. "You don't happen to have a house we could rent, do you?"

"You? Move? Who would work your farm?"

Oh-oh. The Lanes' were Uncle Bert's tenants. This could get sticky.

Mother sat down opposite my great-auntie. "Dalma, tell me. How would you feel about Fred Lane moving into our house here and runnin' this farm? If we could rent one of your houses at Homewood, Rass could try for a job at Dargan's Lumber Company. You think that's a good idea?"

"I'd like to rent you a house, but I don't know about Bert. He might want to keep the Lanes. They're good people. Have you talked to him?"

"No. I haven't even mentioned it to Rassie's ma. She's the one we deal with."

That could turn into an uphill battle. First Daddy sought Grandma's sympathy. "Ma," he said, "I'm tired to death of farming. Mack Norris, over at Maple Swamp says he can help me get a job at Dargan's Mill."

"A lumber company? Why would you want that job? People there work nights. Can you imagine?"

Grandma was forgetting that we got up in the middle of nights to coddle tobacco. "Better than the sizzling sun." My two cents worth.

"Ma, just think about it. I'd get half of what's made on this farm, plus my salary. And Dot could get a job too. You'd be cramming so much money into your bag, it'd plumb break your back to tote it."

"Hm." Grandma studied air in front of her nose. "Hm. How long would we be gone from here? Never would I stay away long."

"Two years. Maybe. Could you live somewhere else for two years?"

Grandma kept on air-studying, but I did see a slight shift in her expression. She liked the idea of a weighty money bag.

Little by little my parents wore her down, and before anyone could say "Jumping Jehoshaphat," we were loading up Uncle Homer's truck, and following Uncle Bert's also loaded, blue pickup down the road. Our Bug Swamp house looked lonely without us.

Turning in her seat, Grandma eyed her empty home, then looked ahead. "Chillern, this makes me think I'm following a hearse. What would Hampie say?"

"He'd say, 'Can I come too?'" Mother told Grandma.

Daddy joked. "I already told him to come along, and any other spirits that want to."

"Don't you go telling ghosts to follow us, Rassie Hamilton." Mother meant what she said.

Grandma chimed in. "I'm not worried about ghosts. I'm worried about my hydrangea bushes. And my shade vine. Rassie, you tell them Lanes they're to leave everything growin' around my house just like it is. You hear me?"

Funny they should talk about ghosts. Shortly we were to encounter certain, shall I say, mysteries in our new home of choice.

I hadn't seen the house where we'd live, but I was told it sat on a side road just beyond the beautiful, brick near-mansion Uncle Bert and Aunt Dalma recently built. His and Grandma's mother, Great-Grandma Madora, died the year after I was born, and their ancient house needed too much repair. Uncle Bert said he hated to move away from his farm and church, but he visited our community every Sunday anyway, most times eating dinner with us. Now where would he hang his week-end hat?

I said, "Mother, where will Uncle Bert and Aunt Dalma eat Sunday dinners, now that we're moving?"

Mother said, "That's their problem."

I thought, *that's not nice,* but I kept my mouth shut.

Moving to Homewood, we passed Good Hope Church, turned right, and drove about two and a half miles before reaching the railroad track with Mr. Kelly and Mr. Purley Thompkins' Adrian store beside it. Further down the road, on the Conway/Loris highway, we turned left, and headed toward Conway. About seven miles further, from a recessed, right side of the road, Uncle Bert's house greeted us. Why my own uncle's home put everyone else's I knew to shame.

His truck slowed down. "Uncle Bert's turning." We turned too. At the right corner of this road sat a ramshackle house. Two children played in the front yard. Old tires burning in back sent up thick, black smoke.

A few hundred feet further Uncle Bert made an abrupt turn across a deep ditch, halting in a side driveway.

I opened the car door, stood, and gazed. My home.

So many times I'd complained about our old unpainted cypress farmhouse. Why couldn't my home be cream colored like Uncle Oliver's? Or silver like Papa Todd's? Why couldn't our yards boast grass instead of sand?

Someone had painted this house. White! And green grass carpeted every inch of our new yard. Why this house even had two stories. How lucky could a girl get? And I hadn't even seen inside.

Uncle Bert produced a key and gave it to Daddy. He unlocked the door. Entering the living room, I could see through French doors into a dining room, and beyond that, the kitchen. To the right of the living room, a door opened to a bedroom. Grandma said, "That's where we'll sleep, Little Bushy." Steps hugging the wall beside our room led upstairs.

Bug Swamp's Gold

I'd have preferred sleeping upstairs, but I knew Grandma couldn't climb up easily. I'd rather sleep anywhere with Grandma than alone.

Almost nine, Jack took stair steps two at a time, Mother and Daddy at his heels. "Mine's on the side toward the road," he yelled down at me. "It's big, too."

"Lucky you." I meant that.

Two young men appeared at our door. "Mrs. Dalma sent us to help unload." The bigger one looked like he could lift the truck plus our belongings.

Soon mine and Grandma's bed, dresser, and wardrobe filled the space of our new room. Our family's maple china cabinet, table, and chairs sat in the new dining room, and our wicker sofa, two arm chairs, two straight backed chairs, the square center table, and Grandma's peach Damask chair sat... it should sit beside a fireplace. No fireplace. How would we keep warm?

"There's a wood heater in the kitchen," Uncle Bert said. "And Dalma says she's got an electric heater you can use in here."

"What about upstairs?"

"We'll figure that out. Let's just get you situated."

"Knock, knock."

"Somebody's at the door. Let 'em in, Little Bushy."

I opened the door. Why did the old woman standing there look familiar?

"Miz Miller," Grandma said. "How did you find us?"

"We live next door. See that house yonder?" She pointed to a square, one-story bungalow a hop and a skip from ours.

Miz Miller looked much the same as the old woman I'd known not quite ten years ago, maybe a trifle droopier.

"Lucy!" Mother ran and hugged a youngish woman following Miz Miller. "It's been years! How are you doing, you and James?"

"Fine. We've got us a boy now. His name's Jesse." Lucy pointed at Jack. "'Bout your age."

I remembered. Old Miz Miller dipped snuff with Grandma. I said, "You fed me possum gravy and biscuit! Where's Irene?"

"Irene married a young fellow from over next Ketchup Town. She comes to visit, once in a blue moon."

"I'd like to see her." I'd thought Irene such a pretty girl, and I did remember more about the family than that they'd let me sop a biscuit in possum gravy.

That night, the first in our new home, Grandma got ready for bed. Since it was a mite chilly, she wore her long, flannel gown and bedroom slippers Uncle Hal gave her last Christmas. She pulled her Damask chair so that it faced the dining room where Mother and Daddy sat. Mother asked Daddy, "Are you going to Dargan's in the morning, or tomorrow afternoon?"

He said, "Neither. I don't start work till Monday. I thought I'd help you women straighten out things here."

Grandma said, "First things first. Rassie, find the Bible. Turn to Luke 17:6."

Daddy said, "Dot, where's the Bible?"

Mother ran up the stairs. A thud said she'd dropped something.

"It was in my old hat box. What book?"

"Luke."

"Chapter and verse?"

"Seventeenth chapter: sixth verse. Read it, Rass."

Mother found the verse and handed Daddy the Bible. He read:

"If you have faith as small as a mustard seed, you can say to this mulberry tree, 'Be uprooted and planted in the sea.' And it will obey you."

Grandma said, "Did you hear what you read? I've been sittin' here, thinkin'. I've prayed long and hard about this move. Rassie, I just hope it's God you're leaning on, uprootin' your family and bringin' us here. And Dottie, you've got just as big a stake in this move. We all need faith. Think of that Bible verse. If we had no more faith than the size of a wee mustard seed, we could speak to our mulberry tree, at home growin' right beside our wash house. That's where Hampie planted it. We could say, 'Old Tree, shake the Bug Swamp dirt offa them roots of yours. Fly off to Myrtle Beach. Jump in the ocean and poke your roots into that briny.

"If we believe the tree'll mind us, it'll move. It'll thrive in that ocean; but only, if with every fiber of our being, we believe it will. And that's what we need to decide for ourselves about this move. We have to have faith that right here, in this place, in this time, we're going to spread our branches and thrive in Homewood's soil."

• Bug Swamp's Gold

Grandma worried about Mother and Daddy, because they'd never publicly professed their faith in Christ. Mother said she sinned every day, and didn't want to be a hypocrite like some of Good Hope's church members. Daddy said nary a word. Grandma said, "If you let a hypocrite stand between you and God, the hypocrite's closer than you."

I didn't worry about my parents. I knew they loved the Lord. (Spring, a few years later, both professed their faith at Good Hope's Revival service.)

That night my tired mother stretched and yawned. "Ma, I don't know about your mulberry tree, but I have faith that as soon as I lay my head on my pillow, I'll fall asleep."

I said, "Goodnight, Mother," then brushed my teeth. Funny. The water here had a different taste from that at home. Oops, I reminded myself. I am home.

We were all tired from moving. Eight-thirty found us each in bed. Snuggled in familiar feathers beside Grandma, I heard Daddy's snoring from all the way upstairs.

I hoped Grandma could stay awake a little longer. I whispered, "Grandma?"

She whispered back, "Yes, Little Bushy?"

"Do you think we'll like it here?"

Grandma said, "I have faith we will, don't you?"

"I plan to love living here."

"Billie, you have snagged a'hold of faith! I'm with you, Girl. Put it there!" We joined pinkies.

"One more thing, Grandma. Well, two more. What about church? Uncle Bert and Aunt Dalma stayed with us most Sundays. Who'll we stay with?"

"I'll probably end up at Sally's part of the time, and you'll probably spend Sunday afternoons with Mr. and Mrs. Todd."

"The other thing. You know, I never understood exactly what Daddy meant, talking about Bug Swamp's gold. Is any real gold buried there? Where is it?"

"Billie, gold's here at Homewood, too. You could say it's all around us. It's everything good, God puts before us. It's the food we eat, our shelter, the bird songs wakin' us in the mornin'. It's the people we love. For your daddy, when he talks about gold, that's probably his tobacco. He works at it, day in and day out. Even the brand he plants is called Gold Leaf. And, good old Bug Swamp soil nourishes that tobacco."

"I'll tell you what my Bug Swamp gold is, Grandma."

"What?"

"You and your stories. I love your tales."

"Little Bushy, you haven't heard the last of 'em yet." Grandma yawned. "Now say your prayers. Go to sleep. We've got us a brand new day tomorrow."

Continued in: Bug Swamp Palaverings